SCENES FROM THE PAST

DELPH

SADDLEWORTH AND GREENFIELD
TO
OLDHAM

INCLUDING LEES MOTIVE POWER DEPOT, MOTOR TRAINS AND THE OA&GB TO ASHTON

Oldham Clegg Street, c.1952. This fine picture by Jim Davenport encapsulates the four main ingredients of this boo, namely the Delph Branch, the Oldham Branch to Greenfield, the push-pull coaches, and the locomotives of Lees Motive Power Depot. On the left of the picture, Class C13 4-4-2T No **67438** has just arrived from Guide Bridge, while on the right, Lees-based Class 3 2-6-2T No **40056** waits to set off along the Oldham Branch and Delph with the 'Delph Donkey'. Both trains operated on the push-pull principle wherebye the loco hauled the train in one direction and pushed it in the other using specialy fitted carriages. The leading carriage on the Delph train was converted to push-pull operation in 1951. To the extreme right of the picture is Oldham central station, serving trains between Manchester, Royton and Rochdale. This route is covered in *Scenes From the Past 42; The Oldham Loop (Part One)*. Central's Booking Office and covered footbridge are visible above the Delph train. This footbridge was removed c.1953. The sleeper built fence above the embankment was a favourite spot from which to view the comings and goings through the two stations. *Jim Davenport*

WRITTEN BY
LARRY GODDARD & JEFFREY WELLS
COMPLILED BY LARRY GODDARD

PRINTED BY
THE AMADEUS PRESS
CLECKHEATON, WEST YORKSHIRE

PUBLISHED BY
FOXLINE (PUBLICATIONS) LIMITED
P O BOX 84 BREDBURY SK6 3YD

THIS BOOK IS DEDICATED TO
OLDHAM
RAILWAY PHOTOGRAPHER
JIM DAVENPORT

AND RAILWAY DEVOTEES

MAJOR IVAN HURST
ERIC CHRISTOPHER

CONTENTS

(Below) For countless generations of train watchers, this view from the low sleeper-built fence overlooking Oldham Clegg Street and Central stations was their first view of the railways of Oldham. BR Standard Class 2 No **84010** awaits departure with the 'Delph Donkey' from its usual place in Clegg Street station on a chill autumn day in 1954. Firemen often took the opportunity to clear any unwanted material from the grate while laying over on the Delph service, hence the piles of clinker between the running lines. The OA&GB lines to Ashton (Oldham Road) can be seen behind the train while the former L&YR Manchester to Rochdale lines through Central station are in the foreground. Clegg Street goods yard fills the background, coal wagons prevailing. *Jim Davenport, courtesy B K B Green*

Typical of the cavalcade of main line trains through Greenfield, unrebuilt Royal Scot Class 7P No **46156** *The South Wales Borderer* makes the valley sides echo as it passes between the platforms of Moorgate Halt with the 9am Liverpool Lime Street to Newcastle express c.1950. The loco is in lined black livery with the full BRITISH RAILWAYS insignia on the tender. Apart from the leading LMS coach, the composition of the train appears to be a collection of ex-North Eastern, Great Central and Great Northern stock, none of which has been repainted from varnished teak to BR carmine and cream livery. Only the Delph branch trains stopped at this station.
Jim Davenport

INTRODUCTION - AUTHORS NOTES (1)

The Second World War was raging when I joined the human race in Cheshire in 1942. I was born in Newton, Hyde, but we shortly moved to Gee Cross, so my earliest recollections of life are of blackout curtains decorated on the inside with brightly-coloured ribbons, the steady drone of aircraft, and journeys by Stockport tram down to Hyde market. Mother was from over the border in Lancashire and so I looked forward to visiting relations in Oldham as the journey served to feed an embryonic interest in trains and buses. Her father had been a footplate man at Newton Heath loco depot until his death in 1940, so his railway colleagues must have presumed "young Lawrence" had more than a passing interest in trains on the occasions when they lifted me onto the engine at Royton. It is hard to remember if I viewed these footplate experiences with exhilaration or terror; nevertheless, some things did stick in my mind such as maroon carriages and the initials 'LMS'. Although I did not know it at the time, seeds sown so early in life would eventually blossom into a lifetime interest and even put bread on the table for much of my working life. Granddad Goddard spent most of his working life at Daniel Adamson's in Dukinfield after serving his apprenticeship on steam boilers at Beyer Peacock in Manchester, so some railway DNA also came from his direction!

I was very happy in Hyde living surrounded by my aunties and uncles and grandparents of the Goddard family, but it became

clear that my mother was never really settled in Hyde. The inevitable move to Oldham in 1947 was a choice over which I had no control. Compared with Hyde, this smoky cotton town seemed very oppressive, although it was probably no more so than any other heavily industrialised town, but our lifestyle and location among rows and rows of old terraced houses did not help. Traipsing off to the gas works with other children with bogies and old prams and queueing in drizzling ran for sacks of coke probably sounds quite draconian in the 21st Century, however, Oldham had some compensations. A bewildering variety of buses ran through the town on chassis from AEC, Bristol, Crossley, Daimler, Guy and Leyland, and if this was not enough for the transport enthusiast, there was a bustling railway system within easy reach of our home on the Coppice. Train watching from the sleeper-built fence that overlooked Oldham Central and Oldham Clegg Street stations was a regular pastime by 1950. The abundance of trains and shunting movements around the extensive sidings that stretched from Clegg Street to Mumps Bridge kept me absorbed for hours on end while, in the foreground, my attention was drawn always to a two-coach train that was often part of the fixtures and fittings of Clegg Street station.

One day I decided there was nothing for it but to buy a penny platform ticket and take a closer look at this train. From there, it was but a short step to riding in the distinctive carriages with their with their deeply recessed doors and so it was that I came to know the train known as the 'Delph Donkey'. It regularly took my friends and I to Lees where, from a field below Carrhouse Farm, we would watch the comings and goings at Lees locomotive depot, or to Greenfield and Delph to explore the surrounding hills with our girl friends from school. When the girls were not with us, the call of the busy mainline over Standedge was stronger than any longings we had for hill climbing! Greenfield station, on a warm sunny day, was the perfect place from which to watch the seemingly endless cavalcade of passenger and goods trains working between Stalybridge and Huddersfield, or just bask in the heat that radiated from the front end of a Fowler 2-6-2T waiting in the bay to return to Oldham. At the end of the day, the 'Delph Donkey' would wheel our weary bodies back home to a well-needed meal and pleasant dreams of our next trip to Greenfield.

It was necessary to move to a new out-of-town housing estate at Holts during the winter of 1954/5, a distraction that severed friendships for a while. Nevertheless, like the Railway Children in Edith Nesbit's famous novel, I soon remembered the railway again. The little train was in its customary platform when I arrived at Clegg Street and occasional trips to Greenfield continued much as they had done before but in the company of new friends. I knew nothing of British Railways plans for the line so my heart sank a few weeks later when a picture of the final passenger train to Delph appeared in the Oldham Chronicle. It was a valuable lesson in life that nothing lasts forever.

The LMS was not the only railway company in town, nor was the Delph train the only push-pull service. Locomotives of the London & North Eastern Railway (LNER) were to be seen plying between Oldham Glodwick Road station and Clegg Street Station on their way to Ashton and Guide Bridge. This push pull service was worked by some unusual coaches of Great Central Railway origin. The Driving Trailers remained in LNER brown livery after Nationalization. Scrubbed and revarnished, they were a familiar sight well into the 1950s, but to my everlasting regret, I never rode on these trains.

The Delph branch was a little over a mile long, but the trains went further than this and travelled along the busy London & North Western Railway (LNWR) Manchester to Huddersfield main line as far as Greenfield before diverging onto the Oldham Branch. The development of the Delph branch was well documented in The Delph Donkey (published by Michael and Peter Fox, 1984), though very little was written about the line from Greenfield to Oldham. For many years, the Oldham-Greenfield-Delph service was something of a byword until the LNWR intro-

(Above) This field below Carrhouse Farm provided a good vantage point from which to watch the activities at Oldham Lees Shed. A young Lawrie Goddard was a Passed Cleaner here when this view was captured on film on 22 June 1960. Coal wagons stand on the elevated track between the coaling stage and the water tower extreme left, while a 16-ton mineral wagon stands beside the ashpit. LYR 0-6-0 No **52322** is having its sandboxes filled and Austerity 2-8-0 No **90306** is awaiting its next call of duty. The ex-LNWR Toplight corridor coach beside the shed served as the breakdown train. In the foreground note the typical L&NWR style close boarded boundary fence of sawn-down second-hand sleepers. However, it is unclear why the boundary line to the right is marked by timber post and rail fencing. **G Whitehead**

(Right) Fowler Class 3P 2-6-2T No **40012** stands on shed at Lees in front of the original wooden roof in the early 1950s. The replacement roof of 1955 can be seen in the picture above. A Fairburn 2-6-4Ts takes on water on the disposal road. **J Davenport**

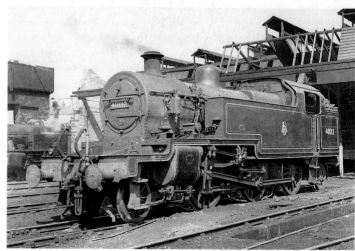

ways unique rolling stock that worked the line has a chapter of its own. Several photographs in this book have appeared in other works but they are necessary to present readers with a broad based history of the line on this, the 50th anniversary of the end of passenger services between Oldham and Delph. Memories and experiences from my childhood have benefited from present day research, which has provided me with an insight that I never achieved in the 1950s. No mention of the Oldham Branch would be complete without reference to Lees Motive Power Depot, a local shed largely unheard of outside Lancashire, but whose men boasted a surprisingly wide orbit.

On 30th April 1955, the 'Delph Donkey' ran for the last time amid choruses of Auld Lang Syne, signed autographs and a few teary eyes. So, what was the Delph Donkey? Well, for a start, it was not a racehorse as everyone who rode it can swear. Yet, it is a phrase that for many people brings to mind memories of a vanished way of life; an institution that was part of the fabric of local life in rural Saddleworth.

The 'Delph Donkey' was in fact a passenger train linking a small community in the hills of Saddleworth with the more important railways of Lancashire and Yorkshire. Like many branch trains of the period, it carried an unofficial title but the origins of the equine connotation are difficult to pin down. According to history, horses might have hauled trains on the branch in the early days although there is no mention of a specially prepared track bed. Furthermore, the directors of the LNWR would have been horror-struck at the thought of horses plodding along their busy mainline to Greenfield with the ever-present risks to animals and trains. What is in no doubt is that the inhabitants of Delph learned to accept the many inadequacies of their new railway with amused tolerance. Add to this the unwavering stubbornness of the LNWR to listen to protest or put into action any improvements, and it is likely the 'donkey' part of the title was simply a nickname, an epithet not be taken too literally.

Larry Goddard, Abergele, July 2005

End of the line, not just for the train but also for the service, for this was Saturday 30th April 1955. BR Class 2 No **84015** stands at Delph prior to returning to Oldham Clegg Street on the last day of the passenger service. This, the 12.6pm to Clegg Street was a Saturdays Only working, the only Oldham-bound train of the day to include Measurements Halt in its schedule, at least according to the BR timetable of the period; From Mondays to Fridays, it would be the turn of the 5.33(SX) ex-Delph to serve Measurements. Intriguingly, three minutes were allowed for Down trains covering the half-mile between Measurements and Delph, yet only two minutes were deemed necessary for Up trains (to Oldham). For those interested in station *minutiae,* the photograph provides good examples of L&NWR 'standard' furniture and fittings. As well as the 2-wheel sack truck, so commonplace throughout the railway system, there is the station seat, usually with station name in a recess on the back rest. The stone built station building, not entirely of a design associated with the company, seems perfectly compatible with the large cast iron angular nameboards above entrances to the appropriate rooms/offices. The nameboards required securing to the station wall as well as underslung rodding from the canopy. The wall mounted poster/timetable board still carries the letters 'LMS'. Note also the buffer stops, hiding the fact that there was as much rail beneath the ground than on view. Last day photographers form a cluster at the far end of the platform, whilst the 'young man' has his attention on something nearer. Are the 'badges' on his coat the sign of a new generation of 'trainspotters'? **R J Buckley/J Wells**

I was born in January of the same year as the attack on Pearl Harbor, and became a resident of Chadderton, a few miles as the crow flies from Oldham town centre. My earliest recollections of Oldham were not of its grimy railway stations so much as the run-down town centre shops, and Tommyfield Market, which, in the late 40s and early 50s, had a host of market traders selling a plethora of commodities: linoleum, green vegetables, toys, muffins and cakes, to name but a few. The fact that three railway stations existed in the town (four if you count Werneth) never came to my notice. I accompanied my

parents by bus to Oldham on their weekly buy-in, and found the Corporation bus fleet of more direct interest, noting that in contrast to Manchester's buses, the local services were indicated by letters of the alphabet! Thus it was that we travelled by the 'D' bus from Mough Lane, Chadderton, to the Star Inn, Oldham, whence we trudged up George Street to the town centre, and the market.

My interest in all things related to railways, like my later interest in the opposite sex, sprang from, well, who knows where? No one in the wider family worked for the railways, with the sole

exception of Uncle Jack who fired locomotives at the Trafford Park Depot. I hardly saw him during my childhood. Yet I became an enthusiastic train-spotter from an early age and embarked on years of misspent youth watching trains go by at different locations between Middleton Junction and Newton Heath Motive Power Depot. I have to confess that it never occurred to me to venture on the 'D' bus to Oldham to see what was going on at Mumps, Clegg Street, and Central Stations, or at the large area of sidings opposite the gas works.

During a one-off cycle trip to Greenfield

This view of Clegg Street goods yard shows how the all-pervading soot and smoke of the district had blackened the buildings and given them the appearance of having been there for years when in fact they had only been there some thirty years when this picture was taken in the mid 1880s. Railway company-branded wagons are in the minority with representatives from the Great Northern Railway and the Great Western, but the majority belong to private owners. Rocher Colliery Company Ltd of Park Bridge is well represented together with Halliwell & Buckley of Oldham, Robert Mercer of Oldham, Bickershaw Colliery, Clay Cross, Silkstone, Bibbington, Lords Field Colliery of Ashton-u-Lyne, and Duckingfield Colliery. Just visible in the cutting behind the yard is the eastern portal of Central Tunnel with Wellington Mill above it. The original Clegg Street station with its overall roof is on the right with the LYR Central station booking office visible across the street. The cotton industry was still expanding and the railways were responsible for transporting almost all that was required, from building materials to coal and raw cotton.
E M Johnson collection

The Lancashire & Yorkshire was the first railway to reach Oldham in November 1847. BR Class 4MT 2-6-4T No **80093** climbs away from Oldham Central with a Manchester-Rochdale train in 1957. Allocated to Newton Heath early in 1956 after a year long spell at Bury, 80093 remained until November 1957 before being transferred to Blackpool (24E). Perth beckoned in 1960 and for the next six years until withdrawal, the engine spent the final years of a comparitively short life with modest duties including the Killin branch and the Aberdeen stopping trains *(re RCTS; BR Standard Steam Locomotives: Volume 3).*   *J Davenport*

with a friend in the early 1950s, I rested and peered at the station over a wall. Not a single main line train came into sight as I looked down at the intact station for several minutes, let alone the push-pull service running between Delph and Oldham. I remember only the summer sunshine and the deep shadows in the station tucked away at the foot of a precipitous slope. In my ignorance, I didn't even know where the railway ran to in either direction! This was my brief encounter with Greenfield Station – we were soon on our way back to our homes in Chadderton.

During my early teenage years, I occasionally glimpsed bouts of shunting at Hollinwood, and saw trains chuffing heartily along the lofty embankment from there to Werneth Station, or coasting down from the shadow of Platt Brothers' works before stopping at Hollinwood Station. At the time, I considered the local trains running to and from Oldham were

relatively nondescript and, sad to say, had scant regard for them. So, it might be asked, why am I involved in researching and writing a book about local railways I had no first-hand experience of, and apparently holding so little interest? The answer is quite simple. I like the rigour of research into railway history, and feel a sense of achievement on unearthing a nugget of information hitherto unseen or forgotten. I am intrigued with the erstwhile Oldham Branch, its stations, engine shed, and its tunnel. So too with the line between Oldham and Ashton, the OAGB line as it was known. In equal measure to Larry Goddard's interest in rolling stock and modelling, I have a penchant for infrastructure (bridges, stations, signal boxes, good sheds, and retaining walls), and in the human aspect of the railways under study (contractors, navvies, railway employees, and the travelling public). For me, the Delph to Oldham, Oldham to Ashton line possessed

all these items of interest as they obviously did for Jim Davenport and other photographers. We have them to thank for recording so much on film before the rot set in. I have to acknowledge the enthusiasm of two gentlemen (now deceased) who spoke to me of their acquaintance with the Delph Branch and the Oldham Branch in their younger days. A posthumous thank you is due to Major Ivan Hirst who knew the lines well, and to Eric Christopher who worked for a short period at Clegg Street Station. It is to them that this book is dedicated.

Larry and I hope that his book contains much for the reader to enjoy. Our dual aim to entertain and inform will be successful if what used to be radiates from every page. It is hard to believe it was all part of the everyday scene two generations ago.

Jeffrey Wells, Greenfield, 2005

HISTORICAL OVERVIEW

In 1926 The County Borough of Oldham (pop.150, 000), together with its satellites, the urban districts of Chadderton (pop; 30,000), Royton (pop;17,500), Crompton (pop;17,000) and Lees (pop;4,500) in Lancashire; and Springhead (pop; 5000) and Saddleworth (in Yorkshire) pop; 13,000); comprised the greatest cotton-spinning district in the world. Situated in this area were 247 firms operating some $17^{1}/_2$ million spindles. Needless to say, the railways played a prominent part in building up this commercial prominence.

Oldham was exceedingly badly placed from a transport point of view and was not an easy place for railways to reach. To give some idea of the climb the railways had before them, an average grade of 1 in 76 was entailed between Manchester Victoria and Hartford Sidings (Oldham), while the OA&GB line climbed all the way from Ashton, with a slight dip at Park Bridge, then continued to rise at an average of around 1 in 71.

The Manchester & Leeds Railway (later Lancashire & Yorkshire Railway) was the first comer to the town on 31st March 1842. This branch curved off the M&L main line at Middleton Junction and ended at Werneth at the top of a mostly 1 in 27 incline. Werneth remained the terminus of the line for five years until the line was extended to Oldham in November 1847. The final stretch to Rochdale opened in 1863. During the 1863-80 period, Oldham had been growing amazingly, particularly in a south-westerly direction, following the line of the Manchester to Oldham turnpike. This factor coupled with rapidly increasing traffic caused directors to decide on acompletely new route for Oldham traffic; consequently, on 17th May 1880, the deviation from Thorpes Bridge Junction via Hollinwood to Werneth, 4 miles 6 chains in length opened. As may be expected, a large amount of raw cotton came into the area and large warehouses were erected at Hollinwood, Middleton Junction, Werneth, Mumps and Royton Junction. Large mineral yards were also provided at all the above points.

The next railway to enter the town was the Oldham Branch of the London & North Western Railway in 1855. It left the main line at Greenfield in the West Riding of Yorkshire, climbed to Lydgate tunnel, entered Lancashire, and ran due west through Grotton and Lees to its original terminus at Oldham Mumps, then later Glodwick Road. In 1851, a single line branch had opened from Greenfield and curved off the main line in a north-westerly direction to the small manufacturing village of Delph, situated amid romantic and almost mountainous surroundings.

Next came the line that brought the Manchester, Sheffield and Lincolnshire Railway (MS&LR) into Oldham, namely the Oldham, Ashton and Guide Bridge Junction Railway (OA&GB), opened in 1861. The following year it was leased to the L&NWR and MS&LR to be worked as a joint line although the shuttle service was always worked by engines and coaches provided by the MS&LR (later GCR, then LNER, and BR Eastern Region. The OA&GB was a tenant at Oldham Glodwick Road station with its own bay platform, but was owner of Oldham Clegg Street Station. Just before entering Guide Bridge a line went off to the right at Crowthorn Junction and joined the Droylsden - Denton - Stockport line of the L&NWR. By means of this spur, a service of trains was operated between Oldham and Stockport, some of which had through coaches between Rochdale/Oldham and London (Euston). They were attached to Manchester-Euston trains at Stockport......

EARLY DEVELOPMENTS

It was on 18 April 1844 that an inaugural meeting took place at the George Hotel, Huddersfield, to discuss the surveys that had been carried out for a railway between Cooper Bridge (north of Huddersfield), and Stalybridge. Two surveys were under scrutiny, one by Joseph Locke and another, more extensive one by Locke's pupil and assistant, Alfred Stanistreet Jee. On 1 December 1844, a Notice of Intent was forwarded to solicitors outlining details of the proposed railway. This read: *We beg to inform you that Application is intended to be made to Parliament in the ensuing Session for an Act for making a Railway from the Sheffield, Ashton-under-Lyne & Manchester Railway at Stalybridge to the Manchester and Leeds Railway (M&L) at Kirkheaton, near Cooper Bridge, to be called the Huddersfield & Manchester Railway (H&M), together with a Branch from such intended Railway to Delph".*

The H&M Company was re-incorporated (from a Canal company) on 21 July 1845. The proposal was supported for several reasons by local tradesmen and merchants. The existing route to Huddersfield from Ashton (along the Manchester & Leeds main line) involved a circuitous journey of $47^{1}/_2$ miles, the final 3 to 4 miles between Cooper Bridge and the town being made by omnibus. It was envisaged that by the H&M this distance (between Ashton and Huddersfield) would be reduced to $19^{1}/_2$ miles, a considerable saving on distance and time. When completed the line would also form part of a trunk route linking Liverpool with Leeds, and because it traversed cotton and woollen industrial districts, containing high populations, it was expected to be highly profitable. The commercial interests in Huddersfield alone backed the scheme, the intention being to bring to an end the town's isolation from the railway networks.

At the first meeting of the H&M it was reported that construction of the line as to be in the hands of Alfred Jee. Jee's reputation as an engineer had been enhanced by the completion of the Woodhead tunnel – no mean achievement. Nevertheless, there were opponents of the H&M scheme especially from the Manchester & Leeds Railway, which saw its monopoly of the railway business between Lancashire and Yorkshire under threat. It was contended by the M&L's chief engineer, John Hawkshaw, probably in a fit of pique, that the single line Standedge Tunnel would be dangerous to work.

A duration of three years was to elapse before the H&M line was expected to be completed, *"Consistent with permanence and economy"*. Work began simultaneously on both the Cooper Bridge to Huddersfield and on the Stalybridge to Huddersfield sections. The ceremonial cutting of the sod took place near Huddersfield on 10th October 1845. Throughout the length of $21^{3}/_4$ miles, the sounds of picks, shovels, explosions and stationary steam engines accompanied daily life at such places as Stalybridge, Mossley, Diggle, Marsden, Golcar, Slaithwaite, Huddersfield and the short stretch in the parish of Kirkheaton. This clamour of activity was no less tangible in areas lying closest to Uppermill in

The magnificent Saddleworth Viaduct sweeps the line through a 40-chain curve whilst encountering a 1 in 175 gradient over the Uppermill valley. Some 320 yards long, with a height of 65feet, the twenty arches, each of 30 feet span - including three on the skew - enabled the railway to pass over the Huddersfield Canal without affecting the waterway's alignment. Beyond the viaduct is Saddleworth station followed by the shallow Brownhill cutting, hewed some 45 feet deep from the hillside. An LMS-built 'Black Five' is descending through the station with an Up express (westbound) formed of ex-LMS open and corridor coaches in carmine and cream livery, while a Class 5MT 'Crab' climbs to Standedge with a train formed of ex-LNER non-corridor suburban stock. The picture is believed to be of 1954 vintage and appeared on the cover of the February 1955 *Meccano Magazine*. The then Reverend Treacy is subsequently reputed to have commented that this had become his 'most requested picture' following publication of the magazine.

Revd E Treacy/E M Johnson collection

Saddleworth. Prominent here was a large-scale excavation round the foot of Wharmton Hill thereby bearing the railwayround its eastern flank in a deep cutting, and the erection of Saddleworth Viaduct which spanned the Tame Valley.

Progress of the work was sometimes hindered during these three years due to disputes with navvies, landowners, and dissatisfaction with the performance of contractors (Nowell and Hattersley) To cap it all, a portion of Cocker Hill Tunnel collapsed at Stalybridge on 16 August 1847. A Change in responsibility came on 9 July 1847 when the H&M ceased to be, its place taken by the up and coming London & North Western Railway (LNWR), which had acquired it to secure its own interests.

The line between Stalybridge and Huddersfield was inspected by Captain George Wynne, the Board of trade Inspector of Railways, on 2 July 1849. This first inspection revealed shortcomings in the form of unfinished station platforms and inadequate signal arrangements. Captain Wynne returned four days later to find everything to his satisfaction, *and the line was considered safe for "the conveyance of passengers"*. A private opening of the line occurred on 13 July with two trains involved, both departing from Huddersfield and destined for Manchester London Road station. The Manchester Examiner and Times providing a comprehensive account of the event.

The first train consisted of 29 carriages drawn by "two large engines", the pilot engine driven by Mr. Roach, Superintendent of the Locomotive Department, whilst on the Tender rode William Aldam (the Company Chairman), Mr. Dixon (Assistant Engineer), and Alfred Jee. On the return journey, the occupants of the first train alighted outside Standedge Tunnel, Diggle, and engaged in a picnic by the side of the railway. A fare of sandwiches, buns and biscuits, porter and wine, sated the party until the sound of the second train brought the party to an end. The *Manchester Examiner* and Times's report continued with a revealing account of the railway down to Mossley: *"On emerging from the*

Standedge Tunnel, the little village of Digley, in the township of Quick, is reached, and where the Canal has been diverted for 500 yards in length, ... the line passes for nearly half a mile until the Brownhill Cutting presents itself – a cutting of 43 feet deep in rock, and from which 65,445 cubic yards of earth and stone have been removed. At the upper end of this cutting, the Saddleworth or Upper Mill station is situated, being twelve miles from Huddersfield. The station passed, the line stretches over the Upper Mill Valley, first by embankment, and then by viaduct 320 yards long, the height being 65 feet. The number of arches are twenty, of 30 feet span, and three skew arches, two of them being 35 feet span on the square, one of them being 65 degrees skew, the third spanning the canal with an arch 40 feet span in the square, and at an angle of 50 degrees. At the upper end of the viaduct, the Delph Branch will form a junction, when directors deem it proper to avail themselves of the power of their act to construct the line....

The work deserving of notice is the Wharmton cutting, 946 yards long, from 23 to 57 feet deep. Over which a turnpike road passes on a bridge of 30 feet span and on a skew of 40 degrees. The quantity of earth removed from this cutting is 216,113 cubic yards. In the cutting the Greenfield station is placed, on the upper side of the bridge above described, the distance from Huddersfield being 13 miles. The line then proceeds over embankments and through cuttings until Hobhole cutting is met with, 286 yards long, 40 feet deep in hard rock, from which 41,593 cubic yards of stone have been removed".

The 1st August 1849 saw the opening to public trains of the Huddersfield-Stalybridge section of the L&NWR Standedge route and the inauguration of a through service from Leeds Central to Manchester Victoria. At the same time the link from Heaton Norris Junction to Guide Bridge was opened so that with the help of running powers over the Guide Bridge-Stalybridge branch, the Standedge line was connected to the rest of the L.N.W.R. network via Stockport.

A report in the Leeds Mercury (4 August 1849) noted that " On Wednesday the first inst., the Huddersfield & Manchester section of the London & North Western

Railway was opened for passenger traffic," and that " During the day, the trains were nearly all behind time in consequence of the large influx of parties anxious to obtain a ride on the first day of opening, and the great numbers of passengers that passed over the line to and from the Agricultural Show at Leeds. The last train to Manchester in the evening was due at Huddersfield at 8.32 but did not arrive until 10.15".

At Greenfield station the following services were available in March 1850:

Weekdays (to Manchester); 8.04am;
          12.34pm; 7.29pm; 10.04pm;
Sundays: 7.49am; 2.49pm; 8.31pm.
Weekdays (to Leeds): 7.16am; 9.19am;
10.58am; 1.46pm; 3.45pm; 9.16pm.
Sundays: 8.56am; 2.46pm; 9.16pm.

Note the gap between trains on Sundays for both directions. This can be explained by the so-called "Church Interval", the time in which church-attending people were at worship, a time avoided by conscientious railway companies at first so as not to incur the wrath of the Sabbatarian movement which condemned the running of trains on the Sabbath. The weekday Up service was not particularly generous considering the "pull" of Manchester. Fares were: First Class – 2s 6d; Second Class – 2s; Third class – 1s 3d, Greenfield to the big city.

It is amazing how soon the newly opened railway became part of the local scene. Throughout 1850, the first full year of existence, a variety of incidents occurred, and these were reported by the Huddersfield Chronicle. Saddleworth was, of course, part of the West Riding of Yorkshire and so it is not suprising that news items affecting the district found space in the town's newspaper. On 29 June the Chronicle reported: "Last Tuesday afternoon an axletree of a luggage wagon, forming part of a heavy train, on the London & North Western Railway, broke as the train was travelling between the Saddleworth and Greenfield stations. The accident caused several wagons to get off the rails and one of them rolled down the precipitous bank towards the canal into which it would have fallen had its course not been arrested by a tree. One wagon fell over on the opposite side. This was

heavily laden with earthenware articles all of which were broken to pieces. Two wagons were completely smashed to atoms". Axletrees (or axles) were at that time made of wood or cast iron, as were the wheels that were attached to them. Excessiveweight and constant use resulted in the fracture of both axles and wheels, often with disastrous consequences.

Excursion trains were already popular on other railways and the LNWR was no exception. On 7 September the Chronicle informed its readers that "On Monday 26th ult., a monster train started from Mossley Brow station soon after 6am, calling at Greenfield, Saddleworth and Diggle stations, to take passengers for a cheap trip to York. Twelve hundred persons were on the train... ... Much time was lost owing to there being only one engine to the train...." Towards the close of 1850 the Chronicle reported a fatal accident to a Porter going about his duties, although it is unclear what he was actually doing. "On Monday 7th inst., Ellis Hannah, a porter at the Greenfield railway station of the London and North Western Railway was endeavouring to move the traverser table close to the tope of a wall, six or seven yards high, when the iron crowbar which he was using slipped, causing him to fall very awkwardly down the whole depth of the wall. He was immediately taken to the adjoining inn where he now is. His sufferings are great and he is not expected to survive."

Greenfield before 1850 comprised a loose collection of cottages and farms. With the arrival of the railway, buildings tended to cluster close to the station so that the village was in fact centred on the station. Even today, distances by road and footpath are measured to and from the station, the historical focus of settlement. The line between Greenfield and Saddleworth Viaduct was to be the only stretch of main line over which Oldham to Delph trains would eventually pass.

THE DELPH BRANCH

The parliamentary act sanctioning the mainline also allowed the London & North Western Railway to construct a line 1 mile 33 chains in length from a point west of Saddleworth Viaduct to the small textile district of Delph. However,

DELPH
TO
GREENFIELD
AN ILLUSTRATED REVIEW

This must surely be the most familiar image of Delph terminus as seen from the goods yard. One of the 'breadvan' 2-6-2Ts No **40059**, so-called because of their hot cabs, is at the end of the branch with a typical push-pull train from Oldham in 1954. The driving trailer from which the driver would 'drive' the train back to Oldham was the very first purpose built push-pull saloon built by the LNWR in 1911 and was based on the body design of their steam railmotors. The other coach was of LMS origin, a vestibule open third converted in 1951 for push pull use and painted in carmine & cream livery. Despite the vegetation spreading from the sidings through the cobbled yard, goods services would last another twelve years. *J Davenport*

after the vast expenditure of time and money it had involved, the railway company was in no mood to incur additional outlay on a branch line of so little potential importance especially in view of the depressed economic climate which at that time prevailed. To the inhabitants of Delph, and in particular one prominent textile merchant and manufacturer, James Lees, this simply wasn't good enough. Lees, whose residence at Delph Lodge overlooked the space earmarked for the terminus of the branch, persevered tirelessly to persuade the LNWR to construct the single-track railway. Lees forwarded a letter to the chairman in attempt to urge the Company to come to a decision. The letter referred to a resolution *"passed at a meeting... on the subject of the Delph Branch of the*

Huddersfield and Manchester", to which a reply from Mr. Glyn (the LNWR Chairman), dated 21 Jul 1849, had intimated that *"the resolution will without doubt fail to be laid before the next board of the LNWR Railway company"*. Lees was even willing to travel to London and present further local information if needed. His persistence eventually paid off for it was sated in a further letter from Lees that *"We have at length an active commencement of the Branch line of railway from Brownhill to New Delph"*.

Eight tenders for constructing the line had been obtained as early as April 1849, the most expensive being that of Longden & Sons at £11,304 10s 5d, and the least costly that of Knight & Co., at £8,246. It was reported on Board Minutes (29 June 1849) that the

Directors of the LNWR were not ready to sanction a contract for the branch. It is not certain which contractor was eventually hired to construct the line, or if it was built by direct labour. Work commenced on building the line to Delph from a junction with the main line at Moorgate occupation crossing. The actual junction was three-quarters of a mile north of Greenfield Station at Moorgate, just short of Saddleworth Viaduct. On the 24th July 1851 Captain George Wynne arrived to inspect the completed line on behalf of the government. His report, dated 25 July 1851, was forwarded to the Commissioners for Railways, London. It read thus: *"Sir, I have to report for the information of the Commissioners that I yesterday arrived .yesterday................continued on page 12*

.yesterday................continued on page 12

(Right) The remains of Delph Stationmasters residence in November 1959, which to the delight of bus drivers and other large vehicles, was demolished on 4 June 1963 to make way for road improvements incorporating a new junction with Delph New Road and Huddersfield Road. Notice the 'spur' stones to the bottom right of the picture, installed-with as much beneath the ground as above it-either side of the gate post to offer protection from passing vehicles. *J Wells collection*

(Below) Delph station on 19 April 1954, showing the Gentleman's Waiting Room, Ladies Waiting Room, Booking Office Waiting room and station exit. Beyond the platform is the gable end of the Stationmasters house which backed onto the public road. Whilst the large signs over the doors were of LNWR origin, the Delph station signs were in corporate black and yellow LMS colours. The basic character of the station as rebuilt in the 1880s remained to the end, as did the gas lighting.

R M Casserley (K.Miles collection)

continued from page 11.............*and inspected the Delph branch of the London and North western Railway. This short branch which is but 1 mile 33 chains in length, commences near Saddleworth Station of the Manchester and Huddersfield Railway; the line is single, and there are no works of any importance on it. The Directors anticipate such a small amount of both goods and passenger traffic that they have made arrangements for working the line with horse power. Occasions however may occur to render it necessary to use an engine, and as there is no turntable at Delph, guards have been fitted to the tender of the engine, which may be called into service, so as to lessen as much as possible any danger that might arise from working the engine tender foremost. As the line is so short, and traffic not of a nature to render*

it probably that a high speed will be attempted, I do not apprehend danger from working the engine in this manner. I am of the opinion that the line is in fit state to open for conveyance of passengers".

The public opening took place five weeks later on 1st September amid local celebration. The LNWR on the other hand, remained less than enthusiastic about a branch line it viewed as a new liability.

The *Huddersfield Chronicle*, 6 September 1851, always on the ball as regards events in Saddleworth, referred to the opening of the line on Monday, 1 September. Its report considered the branch *"Had been a long time in progress"* and that *"A train consisting of a small engine and three or four carriages plied half-a-dozen times between the Delph and Saddleworth stations; but*

with the exception of a large number of passengers who took their fares to the latter place merely for the sake of riding back again, there was nothing remarkable". Nothing remarkable, but at least the Branch provided the village with a rail connection thereby removing all reliance on the few rutted roads and cart tracks which travellers to and from Delph had previously endured.

An early plan of the proposed branch shows the junction was to be immediately south of Saddleworth Viaduct (referred to at this time as Uppermill Viaduct), but this was later changed so that a more convenient and safe junction could be made at what became Delph Junction. Slater's Directory of Saddleworth (1852) mentions Delph and its railway connection: *"A branch was opened in 1851, from Saddleworth station.......**continued across***

(Above) Hauling the same stock as on page 9, BR Class 2 No **84010** stands at Delph in October 1954 having worked in with the 7.48am from Clegg Street. This loco had only recently been allocated to Lees shed as replacement for a Fowler 2-6-2T. These little engines with their rocking grates and ash pans were universally liked wherever they went. A story that went around Lees shed in 1960 was that an over-zealous engineman had once rocked both sides of the grate to show a passed-cleaner how easy it was before realizing he had dumped all the fire in the ash pan. Some quick moves were required to rock the ash pan then drive the engine off the blazing ash pit! **84010** ended its career at Fleetwood and was earmarked to go to the Isle of Wight in the mid 1960s, but the project was abandoned in favour of electrification of the islands railways for the use of old London Transport underground stock.   *G Whitehead*

(Below) BR Standard 2-6-2T No **84015** was another new transfer to Lees in the autumn of 1954. It is seen at Delph after arriving with the 12.06pm from Clegg Street on 30 April 1955. No doubt the brick-built block would have helped arrest the progress of any runaway train, although whether it was built for that purpose in not known. Trains had once gone beyond Delph with construction materials during the building of Castleshaw reservoir, but all this was long ago and Delph station would close its doors for the final time before this day was out.   *L Goddard collection*

.......*on the main line of the Manchester and Huddersfield Railway to Delph, where a handsome station-house has been erected. The establishment of a coal depot, and the erection of a convenient warehouse, which has just been completed, will greatly facilitate the transit of both coal and general merchandise"*. The coal depot referred to consisted of six shoots facing onto Delph New Road. A plan states the *"LNWR permit J.Lees to construct and maintain a coal shoot with sidings, etc, on his own land as compensation for damage to his adjoining property"*. The agreement dated 16 August 1851. It was not until May 1852 that the *Huddersfield Chronicle...***continued on p. 14**

*continued from page 13.........*published a
Delph Branch timetable as shown by the
following details:

Departures from Delph	Arrivals at Delph
6.53am	7.50am
10.30am	11.12am
5.17pm	5.47pm
7.25pm	8.00pm

There was no Sunday service. The destination of each departure from Delph was Greenfield, although the timetable did not make this clear. Greenfield station was chosen as the natural terminus of the line so avoiding the need for reversal at the junction with the main line (Delph Junction) in order to reach the closest station at Saddleworth. The initial passenger service was sparse, using just one set of rolling stock. Nevertheless it provided connections at Greenfield with mainline trains from Yorkshire and Lancashire.

The population Census of 1851 showed that the village possessed 1,077 inhabitants; many of whom were employed in the local woollen mills. Not only was the transit of coal and merchandise the life-blood of Delph but so too were the short-term and long-term movements of people in and out of the area. Extra trains were put on for the annual September exodus, when local textile and other industrial establishments in the locality shut down in unison for the 'wakes' holidays. Large numbers of people left the district on excursion trips to such places as Belle Vue and Liverpool. Thus the branch provided a new outlet for holidaymakers and day-trippers to leave the area at this period. Sadly not everyone approved of this annual depopulation and local traders rallied against the railway company for allowing cheap fares to take all the money out of the district! The following sequence of news items appeared from time to time in

the *Huddersfield Chronicle*:

9 September 1854: *"On Monday and Tuesday large numbers left the district by excursion trips to Belle Vue and Liverpool, and on Wednesday most of the mills again resumed work...."*

4 September 1858: *"On Monday the district became nearly depopulated, most of the adults having left by cheap trips either to Belle Vue of Liverpool, and loud and long were the murmurs heard amongst the wakes-loving people against the railway companies for allowing cheap trips to take all the money out of the district at Wakes time".*

Not all was well, however, and complaints were not confined to the inadequate local service. They encompassed a host of other shortcomings from high expense of travel to jolting of passengers *"daring enough to travel on the line".*

Historical Summary resumed on page 32

40059 runs alongside Delph station platform, in the shadow of the eight-storey Bailey Mill, with the 5.22pm push pull train from Clegg Street on 19 April 1954 (Monday). Despite the unanimously held belief that train services were an insult to Delph people before the introduction of push pull trains in 1912, at least once a year during Saddleworth Wakes the trains were packed. Ticket returns for the year 1909 were: Blackpool 142, Douglas 45, Llandudno 21, Morecambe 30, Liverpool 69, New Brighton 21, Bridlington 8, Southport 8, Scarborough 16, total 360. Returning to our view above, completion of the 6³/₄ miles from Clegg Street would have required keeping to a schedule of twenty-eight minutes with the train calling at all stations/halts apart from Measurements. The service was still operating the seven days of the week, but at the end of the 'summer' timetable *(14th June to 19th September inclusive 1954)*, the Sunday provision - nine trains each way - was withdrawn and would never be repeated. For passengers travelling to and from Manchester, fares had remained fairly static, being just short of Six shillings (30p) for the return journey. Bradshaws Manchester ABC indicated that the distance from Delph to Manchester via Oldham was one mile shorter than via Stalybridge; the fare however remained the same! **H C Casserley**

Continuing on from the view opposite (bottom of page), another 'shot' of **40059** as it slows to a halt at Delph, giving a clearer view of the vacuum controlled (VCR) gear secured to the smokebox side enabling push-pull operation. 40059 remained as a Lees based engine until August 1954. After moving, first in an easterly direction to Hull, the LM Region reclaimed the asset and transferred it south. However, the wanderer returned north for a final stint just short of two years to Heaton Mersey, from where it was withdrawn in 1959. The coaches were low-roof non-driving trailer 3425 of 1916 and driving trailer 3419 of 1913 vintages.

H C Casserley

Fowler Class 3 2-6-2T No **40059** was one of the first of its type sent to Lees shed in 1939 to replace the ageing LNWR Coal Tank 0-6-2Ts. Much was expected of these smaller versions of the highly successful Fowler Class 4 2-6-4Ts but, like the Fowler 'Austin Seven' 0-8-0s also allocated to Lees, they shared the dubious honour of being amongst the least successful of all the LMS designs. This fact didn't look as if it bothered the men of Lees. 40059 plodded between Oldham and Delph for fifteen years, and the footplate crew looked relaxed as their steed simmers at Delph in 1954.

J Davenport, courtesy *B K B Green*

Although Delph was a modest station in prototypical terms, the station plan might have been lifted from the pages of a 1960's issue of Railway Modeller. In modeller's terms, the layout featured some very interesting pointwork; it could handle comprehensive freight and passenger services and there was the obligatory private siding to a factory! *(See page 18)* Of course, the real Delph complex was not nearly so interesting. There was but one goods train a day to bring in coal, oil, textile needs and farming machinery and take out manufactured goods and coal empties, while the passenger service consisted of an engine and two coaches working on the push pull principal. Fowler class 3MT No **40012** is waiting to depart with the 5.33pm to Oldham with coaches M15846M and M3484 on 19 April 1954.

R M Casserley (K Miles collection)

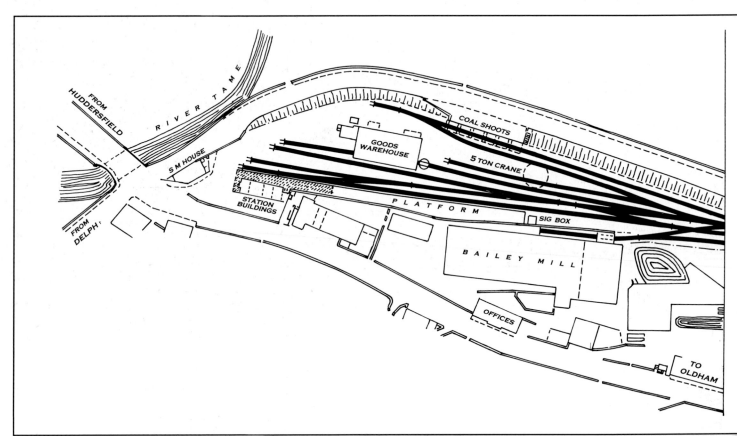

This October 1954 view of Delph looking towards the end of the line shows the goods yard and part of the goods shed. An oil tank wagon and three coal wagons are in view though no doubt more wagons are positioned near the coal chutes. The daily goods train used the engine release road as a matter of course, but it was also used by non push pull fitted locomotives that were required to run round their trains for the return run to Oldham. The *Working Timetable of Freight Trains covering the section (F) for period 9th September 1963 to 14th june 1964 (or until further notice)* detailed the schedule of the daily goods. Leaving Oldham Glodwick Road at 9.20am, the train would proceed to Greenfield (arr 10.38), from where it departed for Mossley (arr 10.48). Switching to the Down line, an 11.10 departure was followed by some ten minutes of shunting at Royal George Siding (11.15 - 11.25). Arrival at Greenfield was scheduled for 12noon, followed by a 12.7 departure for Delph (arr 12.15). By all accounts, not much time was wasted at Delph as the Up working (destination Oldham Glodwick Road) had to maintain a 12.30 departure time, allowing seven minutes to get to Delph Junction. The view above includes a push-pull local standing in the platform headed by BR class 2MT 2-6-2T No 84010.   *G Whitehead*

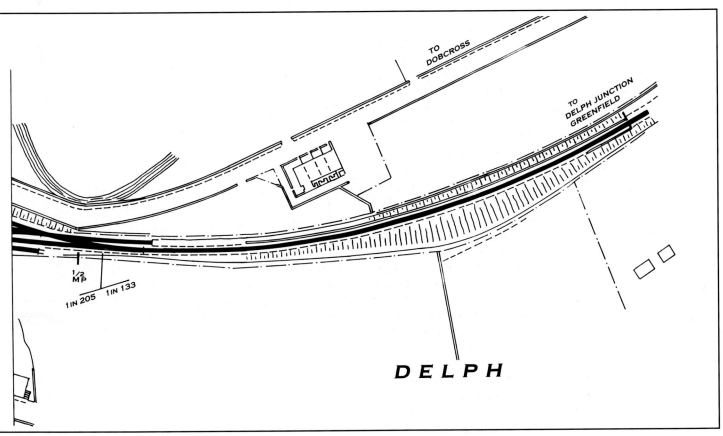

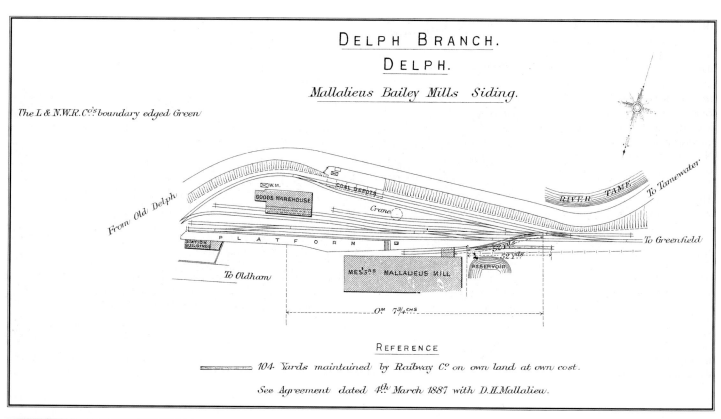

DELPH BRANCH.

DELPH.

Mallalieus Bailey Mills Siding.

The L & N.W.R. Co.'s boundary edged Green

From Old Delph

GOODS WAREHOUSE

COAL DEPOTS

Crane

RIVER TAME

To Tamewater

PLATFORM

STATION BUILDINGS

To Oldham

MESSRS MALLALIEU MILL

RESERVOIR

To Greenfield

0ᴹ 7³⁄₄ᶜᴴˢ

REFERENCE

104 Yards maintained by Railway Co. on own land at own cost.

See Agreement dated 4ᵗʰ March 1887 with D.H.Mallalieu.

LNWR 'Watford' 0-6-2T No **398** has completely derailed while entering the loop at Delph with empty stock or possibly an excursion train, while the assisting 0-6-0 has remained on the track. The time-honoured way of re-railing a locomotive using wooden blocks is in use. This incident may have occurred in the 1920s seeing as the 0-6-2T was not renumbered 6907 in the LMS series until 1928, by which time it was allocated to Buxton shed. It was withdrawn from Buxton in 1933. Note in the foreground the ¹/₂ mile-post (1¹/₂ from Delph Junction). Cast-iron numerals faced the running line whilst the unique shaped point gave a visual indication.   *L Goddard collection*

(Right) Winter on the branch, and the main thoroughfare between Delph and Saddleworth is clearly in view below the railway as Fowler **40057** propels its Oldham bound train towards Measurements shortly after leaving Delph in the early 1950s. The driver is controlling the train from the leading compartment of push pull saloon No 3421, built to Diagram M17. This carriage arrived on the Delph branch in 1951 and was withdrawn in July 1953. The other coach is No 3423.
J Davenport/B K B Green collection

(Below) This pastoral view shows BR Class 2 2-6-2T No 84010 propelling its train past Measurements in June 1954. It highlights the short distance from Delph; note Baileys Mill and chimney at the extreme upper right of the picture. The accommodation on the two-coach push pull trains became inadequate for the workers at Measurements and Mr Fred Hurst approached the LNWR for extra carriages to be put on. This request was refused on the grounds that the Branch was too tightly curved. When the problem of overcrowding in the rush hours surfaced again in November 1920, the LNWR was more obliging, but said it would be necessary for three halts to be extended. Extra coaches were only put on when the threat of bus competition reared its head.

J Davenport

(Above) Another of the Lees 'breadvans' fitted for' motor' working, **40060**, is seen passing the platform serving Measurements on 2nd August 1954 with a Delph bound train. The presence of the oil lamp is interesting as it would be only during the winter months (hours of darkness) that it would be required, given the morning and early evening nature of train timings. It is also very noticeable how clear of vegetation the platform surface is, as well as the track and lineside. Also of significance is the utilitarian wooden-post and rail fencing (of LNW design) in use both as roadside fencing and offering protection as a bridge parapet. *B Hilton/R K Blencowe collection*

(Centre) On the north side of the branch, alongside Delph New Road, sprang up Hirst Bros' Measurements factory in 1919. This unusual structure possessed a floor space of 54,000 square feet divided between five floors. Designed by local architects, the re-inforced concrete and glass structure arose from experiences Alfred Hurst had had in America; the large window space permitting the maximum daylight for the employees to work in. It was opened for the manufacture of watches and clocks, and employed a workforce which travelled in from Oldham and surrounding districts. This view was taken August 1965.
Reporter Group of Newspapers

(Right) Measurments Halt was eventually installed by the LMS and opened on the 18th March 1932 solely to serve the needs of the workers at the Hirst Bros. Works. It was a boon to the mill's employees most of whom lived in Oldham, although it is likely that some workers, especially those who resided on the Waterhead side of Oldham not served by railway, eventually turned to buses for transport. Class 3MT 2-6-2 No **40056** shuttles non-stop past the single timber platform on its way to Delph.
J Davenport/B K B Green collection

Measurements Halt, circa 1952. On a beautiful summers day, Lees based Fowler 2-6-2T No **40057** propels its train away from Measurements at 5.35pm after calling to pick up workers from the factory after which the Halt was named. Measurements was in effect a private halt and very few trains were booked to call there. The fireman is leaning out of the cab soaking up the fresh air and probably trying avoid the heat in the cab, for these engines were not nicknamed 'breadvans' for nothing. The driver is controlling the train from a special compartment in the leading coach, one of the six driving trailers built by the LNWR to Diagram M49 in 1911/1912. The non-driving trailer behind the engine was built as a one-off vehicle to diagram M47 in 1913; its deeply recessed entrances clearly evident even from this viewpoint. Booked to reach Oldham Clegg Street at 5.59pm, the train will soon pass Bankfield Mill before reaching Dobcross Halt, the only other intermediate stopping place on the Delph branch. A lone figure walks up the lane, probably heading for home after a long day at 'tMill'.

K Field/J Wells collection

Before reaching Dobcross Halt, the line passed Bridges No 4, 5 and 6 in quick succession from the Greenfield direction. Bridge 4 was close to the junction of Delph New Road with Wall Hill Road. Bankfield Mill siding lay in the cutting here, its chief use being for the reception of coal. The LNWR Appendix for April 1916 recommended that, *'Trains must not stop at these Sidings on the journey from Greenfield to Delph; and any wagons there may be for the Sidings will be taken forward to Delph where the engine will run round them and take them back to the Sidings. The Delph porter must accompany any Train which may have to stop at the Sidings'*. Bridge 5 crossed Wall Hill Brook and Bridge 6 carried Wall Hill Lane over the line.

The two views here are from each side of Bridge 6, a skewed stone arch of some 15 feet span and 107 feet in length. The top picture illustrates the view towards Delph. To the right a look in the opposite direction towards Dobcross. Both; **D Ibbotson**

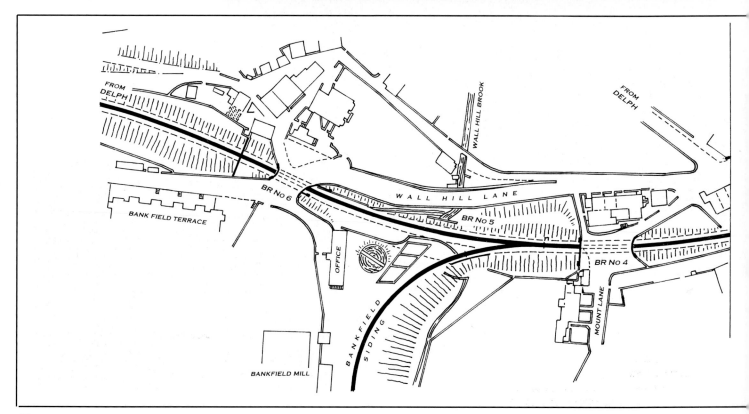

This undated picture shows the junction of Delph New Road, lower right, and Wall Hill Road climbing up over Bridge 4. Bankfield Mill is clearly seen in the distance. In the 1960s, Oldham Corporation buses worked the rush hour P service from Oldham to Delph Station then carried on empty to reverse at Wall Hill before going back along Delph New Road to pick up workers from the various mills along the bottom road. This duty often drew one of the narrow bodied heater-less 'Utility' buses delivered just after the war, which on a winters day could leave the conductor's feet frozen to the platform! *M Schofield*

DOBCROSS

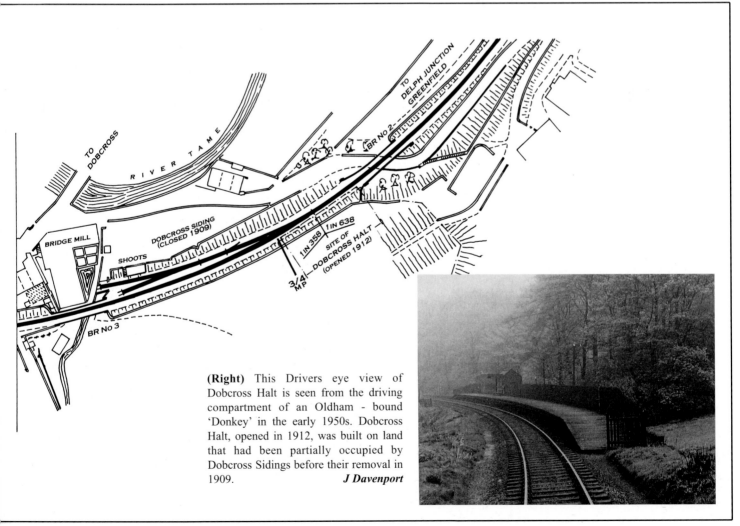

(Right) This Drivers eye view of Dobcross Halt is seen from the driving compartment of an Oldham - bound 'Donkey' in the early 1950s. Dobcross Halt, opened in 1912, was built on land that had been partially occupied by Dobcross Sidings before their removal in 1909. *J Davenport*

(Right) With the allocation of LMS Ivatt and BR Riddles motor-fitted Class 2MT 2-6-2T's to Lees Shed at the end of the end of the 1954 summer timetable, the motor-fitted Fowler Class 3MT 2-6-2T's were all transferred away to Hull (Botanic Gardens) in the autumn. One of the Ivatt variants, No **41282**, with its cylinder drain cocks open, propels an Oldham-bound train away from **Dobcross Halt** on 22 September 1954.

G Whitehead

(Below) This evocative view taken near Dobcross in the early 1950s, illustrates the vast difference between Delph Branch trains and the trains that passed Delph Junction on the Standedge main line. It also points up the varied nature of the push pull stock in use at that time. Fowler 2-6-2T No **40012**, unusually facing westward, is propelling M47 and M49 saloons away from Dobcross towards Delph Junction on the afternoon of 12 August 1954. Saddleworth station, high above the valley floor, is visible at the end of the viaduct. 40012 has an improved front end with large diameter chimney and a casing that incorporates the outside steam pipes and later form of vacuum controlled regulator gear for push pull operation.

B K B Green

The wheels of **40057** groan as the loco negotiates the 7 chains curve leading away from the main line and heads down the valley of the River Tame to Delph in 1950. Both carriages differed from other push-pull coaches on Delph trains in having side corridors leading to compartments. The leading coach is trailer No 3432, and was only 8ft 6ins wide. The difference between this and the 9ft wide corridor-driving trailer No. 3407 is clearly noticeable. The latter coach had all its internal corridor to compartment doors missing.

J Davenport/B K B Green collection

LADCASTLE

(Left-lower) **One of the 'breadvan'** 2-6-2Ts propels an Oldham bound train off the sharp curve by Saddleworth viaduct in 1950. Original plans show the branch was to form a junction just to the west of the viaduct, a juncture considered to be all too dangerous at some point in time, thus the 'deferred' junction nearer Moorgate occupation crossing. Ladcastle Quarry exchange siding was sited directly to the left of the train. The quarries were served by a singe narrow gauge layout on which trucks loaded with stone could be manually pushed to the exchange siding where blocks and ballast could be loaded into standard gauge wagons. A weighing machine, stone crusher and office completed the scene. This infrastructure was removed about 1919. On this bleak February day the exceptionally warm locomotive cab would be most welcome, although the driver would have to depend on the effective-ness of the carriage steam heating in his driving compartment while travelling in the Oldham direction. *J Davenport*

Shortly after being allocated to Lees shed, Ivatt Class 2P 2-6-2T No **41280** begins to curve away from the Huddersfield - Manchester line with its Oldham-Delph train in the autumn of 1954. Push pull coaches Nos 3484 and 15846 are in use on this particular day. Uppermill lies in the deep valley below.

J Davenport

LOCK No 22

HUDDERSFIELD CANAL

FROM HUDDERSFIELD

BR No 31 (SADDLEWORTH VIADUCT)

TO GREENFIELD

P L HUT

OFFICE

BR No 30

FROM DELPH

1/4 MP

L A D C A S T L E   Q U A R R Y

(Right) One can almost hear the three-cylinder music of 'Jubilee' Class 4-6-0 No **45709** *Implacable* as it roars through Delph Junction with the 2.20pm Liverpool Lime Street to Newcastle express in the early 1950s. Three out of the eight LNER wooden bodied coaches on this train carry BR carmine & cream while the remainder carry varnished teak. All the signals at this location were built tall for sighting purposes and to make them visible to enginemen from a distance.

J Davenport

(Right-centre) The main line to Standege played host to a diversity of trains, and this Mirfield - based Fowler Class 4MT 2-6-4T No **42406** is passing Delph Junction with what the photographer described as a Mirfield to Congleton parcels working, circa 1950. The leading six-wheeled van suggests a fair amount of parcels traffic and the three bogie non-corridor coaches are presumably loaded with parcels too. The Delph line is on the left and ran parallel with the Down main line for a distance of 440 yards on a rising gradient of 1 in 182. **J Davenport**

(Below) This shot was taken from Delph Junction signal box and shows 'Black Five' 4-6-0 No **45232** of Newton Heath shed passing with a westbound train in the early 1950s. The leading coach is a late period Midland Railway brake first, of which only two were built to D1285 in 1922/3. The whole junction appears to have received some recent attention from the permanent way gang and part of the Up line has been relayed with flat bottom rail. Note the burning embankment by the home signal. *J Wells collection*

(Right) One of Lees' Fairburn Class 4MT 2-6-4T's No **42114** is probably covering for one of the Class 3MT 2-6-2T's as it shuttles through Moorgate Halt with the 3.55pm Halifax Town to Stockport 'express' circa 1952. The loco looks as if it hasn't seen a cleaner for a while. An LYR open third coach, that wasn't as ancient as it looked, is sandwiched between two LNWR non-corridor brake thirds. *J Davenport*

DELPH JUNCTION

(Left) Fowler Class 3MT 2-6-2T No **40060** slows to a halt at Delph Junction as Signalman Bill Hogson prepares to hand the Delph branch single line staff to driver Tommy Evans on an Oldham-Delph train in 1950. Prominent in the foreground is one of two bells positioned on each side of the level crossing that rang loudly to warn of approaching trains. The loco still carries the short-lived 1937 block style LMS lettering but the original number has been painted over to make way for the BR number. *J Davenport*

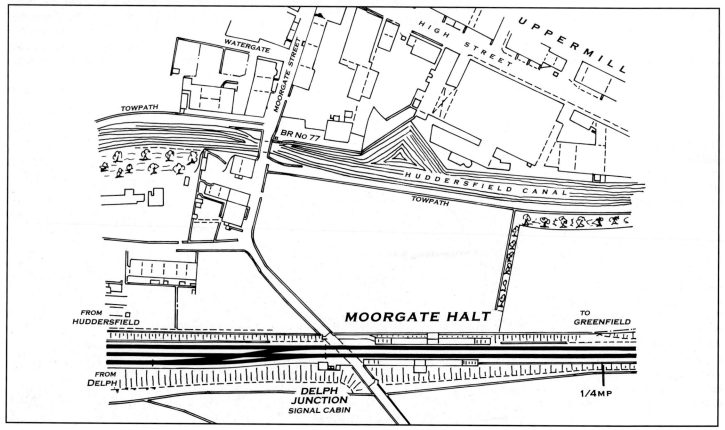

During 21/22 June 1960, the Royal Train bearing the Queen Mother took advantage of the Delph branch as an overnight siding facility. "Deepdene 155W" was BR's code for this illustrious train, the whole episode being organised with military precision. Weeds were cleared and stonewalls repaired within view of the train, and new uniforms were issued to staff, to be returned after the Royal train had departed! At 11.5pm on Tuesday 21, Class 5MT 4-6-0 arrived chimney first at Delph Branch with generator van and brake van. At 1.45am on Wednesday 22nd, the Royal Train arrived from York with five carriages (188 tons) and was propelled onto the Branch by Class B1 engine. This engine left two minutes later and proceeded to the North East. Class 5MT No **44687** arrived on the Branch tender first from Stockport at 9.15am. This engine departed with Royal train at 10.5am for Stockport. The Class 5 with generator van followed the train to Stockport at 10.25am. In this view of Delph Junction overlooking the weed-strewn platforms at Moorgate Halt, 44687 is coming off the Delph Branch onto the Huddersfield-Manchester line. Interestingly, Great Western designed coaches' top and tailed the Royal coaches – probably the only time GWR stock traversed the Branch.

G Whitehead

(Right) Looking towards Greenfield, **40056** rolls into Moorgate Halt with a mid-morning train from Oldham Clegg Street in June 1951. When changes in motive power for push-pull trains took place in 1954, this engine became the first of the Class 3 2-6-2Ts to be transferred away from Lees in the four week period ending 14 August. Coach No 3425 leading, was the last of the purpose-built push pull saloons built in 1916, its design reflecting the style of Oerlikon multiple unit electric stock then being constructed for the London suburban area. The modern-looking Driving trailer was No 3424. It had worked Oldham-Delph services since before the war but left for pastures new in 1953. *J Davenport*

(**Above**) It is difficult to see why main line trains between Lancashire and Yorkshire did not serve **Moorgate Halt**. Positioned as it was off High Street in Uppermill, it was far better placed to serve this large village than the outlying stations at Greenfield and Saddleworth. Bus operators had a field day! Back in April 1951, No **40012**, with a good head of steam, waits for the guards whistle amid the gas lamps, shelters and wooden platforms of Moorgate. From here the train will make a quick dash along the main line to Greenfield Junction before diverging for a leisurely run along the Oldham Branch. The war had ended six years before this scene was enacted and yet it could easily have been 1939, such was the quiet and unhurried way of life around Saddleworth. *J Davenport*

(**Below**) This delightful view of **Moorgate Halt** shows the driver of a Delph-Oldham train giving up the single line staff in time honoured fashion while passengers wait eagerly for the train to enter the platform. BR Class 2MT 2-6-2T No **84015** is propelling the train, on the last day of service, 30th April 1955. The Branch would continue to see goods trains but no more would the station's gas lamps be lit or waiting rooms swept out. All the effort put into linking the village of Delph with the outside world a century before had come to this, but by 1955 the Delph Branch was an anachronism as charming as the 'Titfield Thunderbolt' of Ealing Films fame, and the public had simply discovered more convenient ways of getting into Oldham.   ***D L Chatfield***

(Right) A set of LNWR lower-quadrant signals protected Greenfield Station at its east end until the mid 1950s. Stanier 4MT 2-6-4T No **42463** passes the Delph Junction Distant signal soon after departing Greenfield with a Stockport to Leeds train routed via the Oldham Branch. The three coaches visible are LMS flush-sided Period III non-corridor coaches.

J Davenport

GREENFIELD

(Below) Here we are at Greenfeld Station on Monday 19 April 1954. This scene portrays my (L.G.) most vivid memories of the 'Delph Donkey'. Amid the hustle and bustle was the noise of the locomotive's blower, which on the push-pull locos had a sort of humming sound. There was none of the typical slamming of carriage doors….......these elderly push-pull coaches had large recessed wood

panelled doors and passengers closed them as if they were living room doors! Driving trailer No 3419, nearest the camera, arrived on Delph services in 1954 and generally ran with non-driving trailer No 3425. At 4.53pm, class 3MT 2-6-2T No **40059** will make its departure and deliver the workers to various points along the Oldham Branch before arriving at Clegg Street at 5.08pm. It tends to be forgotten four decades on that within minutes of the departure of this train, connections would be available to transport passengers east with an all stations to Leeds service (arr 6.31) and west to Stockport (for Crewe and Euston).

H C Casserley

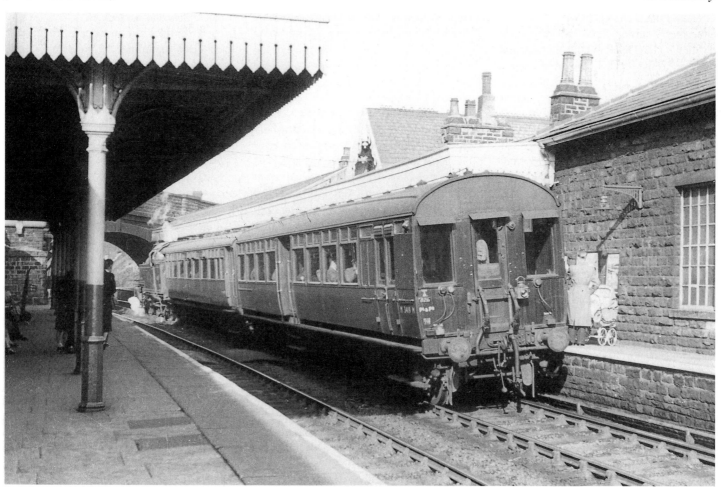

Greenfield station a decade later in October 1964. This view from the westbound platform shows the skew built overbridge, which gives the appearance of carrying the road on a gradient when in fact it is almost level. Prominent in the foreground is the subway roof. Prior to 1874 passengers simply walked across the tracks. There is also a flight of stairs behind the water tower but I suspect the door at the bottom was kept locked unless the station staff wanted it otherwise. If there were time, locomotives would replenish their tanks at the water tower before proceeding to Delph. Of note is the white board behind the signal arm to make it more visible against the soot blackened stone bridge. Some alterations to the canopy in front of the main building have taken place and guttering has been added to stop rainwater spilling onto the track and subway. The latter was prone to flooding. When BR officials approached the staff in the 1970s to enquire if they had any suggestions for the subway, one of the signalmen suggested they lay duckboards! The station got a footbridge instead. *Reporter Group of Newspapers*

HISTORICAL SUMMARY - CONTINUED

GREENFIELD JUNCTION

Greenfield station held an important position on the Delph to Oldham route. Its nearness to the junction conferred upon it a major status; every day its platforms were swept by fast expresses, drawn alongside by local passenger trains, and passed by slow-moving goods trains. A double tragedy at Greenfield was reported in the Huddersfield Chronicle, 25 May 1866: *"On 22 May as the train from Manchester, due at Greenfield at 4.22pm, was approaching the station, a points man, Charles Blomiley, who was engaged in oiling and clearing the points, was caught by the approaching trains and killed on the spot. On the same evening of the same day, about 11.45pm, as an excursion train from Belle Vue was returning and was about to take water in Greenfield, a young woman put her head out of the window of the carriage, and the wind blew her hat off. She immedietly got out before the train came to a stand and was drawn between the train and the platform. She was cut in two and killed on the spot".*

The shunting of wagons and carriages at Greenfield Junction often coincided with the arrival and departure of local trains eager to avoid blocking the paths of non-

stop expresses. On a spring Saturday evening, things went wrong. The *Oldham Chronicle* of 4 April 1874 printed the following report: *"On Saturday night the line between Greenfield and Oldham was blocked for some hours by the overturning of a number of empty wagons. About 8 o'clock a goods train was shunted onto the Oldham Branch at Greenfield to leave the main line clear for the express. The goods train was setting back to the main line when the guard's van was caught at what is called a 'diamond crossing' and was overturned together with about half a dozen wagons. The line was completely blocked, and passengers to Oldham had to walk from the station up the line before they could get onto the train. The line was not cleared until 12 o'clock".*

It was not until 1874 that the LNWR considered the danger to the public while crossing the tracks at Greenfield. It was observed that workers had been engaged in carrying out a much-needed improvement, namely the construction of an underground passageway from one side of the line to the other. The *Oldham Chronicle*, 12 September, argued that a bridge would have been preferable to a passage, but conceded that a subway would be a great

convenience to passengers.

Greenfield station came in for further criticism regarding the time passengers were kept waiting in cold weather, and the uncaring attitude of the station staff. A letter appeared in the Mossley and Saddleworth Reporter, 29 March 1879: *"Who has not been at the above station at evening to come Oldham way by the train timed to leave at five minutes past eight? For years it has been a standing source of complaint by the passengers as to the cool and callous way the officials and the station will detain a train in the sidings long after the expired time for despatch. Wednesday evening was bitterly cold and the train from Yorkshire steamed out of the station towards Mossley at eight o'clock, leaving margin of five minutes for passengers to cross, if any – yet it was thirteen minutes past eight when the train was sent off, this time having all been taken up by the shunting, etc, the engine of the passenger train always being pressed into this service. You may make enquiries. You may complain, but it is no good; the shunters send the train off just when they like, the business and comfort of the passengers being not considered, and the guard of the train not heeded, however*

This part of Greenfield station was added when the Oldham Branch was built, although the branch also had its own bay as well. Looking west from the eastbound platform, one can see the narrowness of the Up platform where it ran beside the goods shed. Wagons standing by the shed doorway appear to be carrying old ballast from some track relaying in the area. 19th April 1954.   *H C Casserley*

angry he might get. Wherever the fault lies, it is a standing reproach on the Company, and the comfort of their fares should be worth better treatment than is meted out to them at Greenfield".

The LNWR came in for further criticism for not managing its affairs properly at Greenfield station during the winter of 1891-2. Several of the waiting rooms had been without fires, but when the company officials were appealed to, they could only say they were without coals.

DEALINGS AT DELPH

Delph station also came in for much criticism, much of it levelled at poor access and the lack of station facilities, but almost a decade passed before station buildings were extended to include a separate ladies room and improved station access. These works also included the installation of a yard crane with sufficient capacity to lift heavy weights, an enlarged warehouse and more siding space. The substantial improvements of 1885 caused the Mossley and Saddleworth Reporter to acknowledge that *"it is now the best and*

most comfortable station in Saddleworth. The waiting room accommodation is much better than formerly and the narrow, short and dirty platform of the past has given way to a new one that is much extended and is nicely asphalted".

An accident at Delph was reported in the Mossley and Saddleworth Reporter, 30 June 1894. For whatever reason a village publican had taken his horse and cart to the station yard, his trouble for doing so ended in tragedy. William Kershaw had been the licensee of the Pack Horse Inn, Delph from 1884. *"On Tuesday morning a terrible accident befell Mr William Kershaw, a Delph publican at Delph Station, and one which resulted fatally. Mr. Kershaw was at the station with his horse and cart, and it chanced that shunting operations were being carried out at the time. For some purpose or other, the unfortunate man attempted to cross the metals when he was caught between buffers of two wagons.... The accident was witnessed by several persons and Kershaw was warned of his danger but evidently too late".*

As late as 1895 the railway company had still not conceded a late evening service on the line. The last departure from Delph on a weekday, the 7.45pm, was certainly an improvement over the 1880s position but was still early enough to rouse the wrath of the local council. Final victory came in 1899, some fifteen years after pressure had first been applied, when three extra return trains were granted, one reaching Delph from Oldham at 10.40am, and a second reaching Delph at 2.35pm. A third reached Delph at 9.15pm and left for Clegg Street fifteen minutes later. The yearly exodus continued unabated and both private bodies and the railway company organized trips to Belle Vue Pleasure Gardens in Manchester and to Blackpool, Rhyl and Liverpool with as many as 600 people packing into such excursions. Liverpool's popularity was mainly due to the Manchester Ship Canal, which was under construction at this time. It was not all one-way traffic either. The sheer beauty of the Saddleworth area and surrounding hills attracted hundreds of people away from the industrial murk of Oldham.

FREIGHT

On the freight side, passenger trains were regularly called on to carry goods wagons until at least the 1880s. There was also a daily goods train (Sundays excluded) from Manchester Longsight that reached Delph around 8am. Generous timings allowed it to shunt the branch's three intermediate sidings at Ladcastle Quarry, adjacent to the main line, at Bridge Hill, Dobcross and at Bankfield Mill near Delph. There was also traffic in and out of sidings at Bailey Mill. Trains were not allowed to stop at these sidings on the journey from Greenfield because of the danger of runaways heading off downhill towards the mainline. Materials destined for the sidings had to be taken forward to Delph. There the loco could run round its wagons and drop them off on the return from Delph. The originating points for goods vehicles were varied, but the majority were dispatched from Greenfield Huddersfield, Dewsbury, Liverpool, Bradford and London. This indicated the branch's importance to the woollen trade as a carrier for raw materials and finished products. Coal was also another of the line's staple traffic for powering the textile mills as well as for domestic consumption. This was the period of expansion for the local textile industry and extra traffic came to the Delph line in

the form of steel girders and timber, for example, for building extensions to existing mills.

Freight operations over the Delph branch reached a peak when this small railhead came alive with the construction of Castleshaw Reservoirs. Oldham Corporation, as conductor of the work, built a standard gauge tramway from an end on junction with one of the sidings in Delph yard and along Huddersfield Road to the site of the two reservoirs. Construction materials were conveyed to Delph by the daily freight and were carried forward by contractor's locomotives. Several runs were made each day to the site commencing in 1887. When this traffic ceased a few years later with the completion of the project, its loss marked the start of a steady decline in freight of all types, which was to erode the line's already flimsy prosperity in the new century.

MICKLEHURST LINE OPENS

Increasing traffic had imposed severe strains on the capacity of the mainline through Greenfield by the 1880's and so the L&NWR set about quadrupling the entire line from Leeds to Stalybridge. Engineering difficulties made it impractical to do this between Diggle and Stalybridge, so the L&NWR elected instead to build a completely separate

double-line railway between these two points, running broadly parallel with the old line, but on the eastern side of the valley. The new line commenced just east of Stalybridge station and rejoined the old line at Diggle. An additional twin bore tunnel opened through Standedge in 1894. The Micklehurst line, as it became known, opened for goods traffic on 1st December 1885 and provided a valuable relief line from the Manchester area to Yorkshire. A passenger service commenced from 3rd May 1896 serving four intermediate stations serving Staley & Millbrook, Micklehurst, Friezland and Uppermill respectively.

The virtual monopoly that railways had over transport in Britain was to change with the coming of the electric tramcar. Company owned horse-drawn and steam-hauled trams had served parts of Oldham since the 1880s, but the lease of the Oldham lines expired in 1901. The Oldham Corporation Act, 1899, gave the Corporation powers to build and run its own electric tramway system and convert existing lines to electric traction. Having obtained its powers, Oldham lost no time in setting about the establishment of a network of lines to its boundaries at Hathershaw, Hollinwood, Chadderton, Thornham, Shaw, Grains Bar, Waterhead and Lees. ....*continued on page 36*

Diggle junction, just over a century after the opening of the Huddersfield & Manchester line by the L&NWR on 2nd July 1849. Having just run through one of the earlier tunnels tunnels beneath Standedge, 'Black Five' 4-6-0 No **44896** of Farnley Junction passes by Diggle junction signal box, extreme left, with a westbound fitted freight in February 1952. A Belpaire boilered 'A' Class, probably from Lees shed, stands in the goods yard behind the water tower, while Diggle station is visible in the far distance. Of the main lines in view, a result of the 'quadrupling' between Huddersfield and Manchester, those to the left are on the original alignment from Greenfield whilst those to the right (the Up line which is occupied by the train) were provided for the Denton & Saddleworth Railway - more commonly known as the Micklehurst Loop.

J Davenport

(Right) This view of Class 5 4-6-0 No **45202** passing through Greenfield with a Manchester Exchange-Leeds express in the early 1950s is a driver's eye view of the station from the driving compartment of a push pull coach. As soon as the Down main line is clear the signalman will raise the right-hand signal to indicate to the driver of the 'Delph Donkey' that he may proceed across the junction onto the Oldham Branch. Greenfield Junction box is just visible through the mist. Of note is the section of platform open to the elements between the two platform canopies and separate station buildings. *J Davenport*

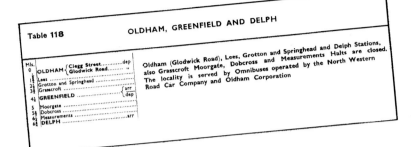

Table 118	OLDHAM, GREENFIELD AND DELPH	
Mls.		
0	OLDHAM { Clegg Street...............dep	Oldham (Glodwick Road), Lees, Grotton and Springhead and Delph Stations,
	{ Glodwick Road...... "	also Grasscroft Moorgate, Dobcross and Measurements Halts are closed.
1¾	Lees	The locality is served by Omnibuses operated by the North Western
2¾	Grotton and Springhead	Road Car Company and Oldham Corporation
3¼	Grasscroft .... { arr	
4¼	GREENFIELD .... { dep	
5	Moorgate	
5¾	Dobcross	
6¼	Measurements	
6¾	DELPH ....arr	

(Left-centre) With the fireman in the cab of class 2MT 2-6-2T No **41281** and the driver in the leading push-pull coach, the train is ready to proceed to Oldham. If the engine begins to slip while departing, the driver will not be aware of this so it will be up to the fireman to bring the slipping under control. It is clear from this angle just how much the LNWR purpose built push-pull saloon coaches differed from ordinary stock. This particular coach had grey and black upholstered back-to-back seats, which were far more comfortable than the tram-like seats to be found in driving trailers. *G Whitehead*

(Right) Taken at the same time as the picture above, the driver has been given the signal and 41281 makes a steamy departure for Oldham in October 1954. Surprisingly, for a threatened service, Saturdays still gave the population of Delph and district a choice of twelve return workings to and from Oldham. An additional five trains on the Oldham branch boosted services to and from Greenfield. Although the Delph-Oldham service had seen its last summer of operation, it would appear in the national passenger timetable after withdrawal the following May. It would be the 'winter' publication of 1955/56 which acknowledged that the service had been withdrawn and was advertised by the accompanying reproduction above. *G Whitehead*

NEW CENTURY, NEW PROBLEMS

Like many other railway stations across the land, the one at Lees was some way out from the centre of the village, whilst people living on the main thoroughfare between Lees and Oldham had no access to the railway at all. All had reason to be grateful for the coming of the electric tram in 1903.

By 1905, the Mondays to Friday's service consisted of ten trains each way between Delph and Oldham, with extra trains on Saturdays. Although the Micklehurst line carried much freight and passenger traffic, the intermediate station at Staley & Millbrook and at Micklehurst were not doing so well and closed in 1909. By the following year, there were only four trains booked to stop at Uppermill and Friezland.

The Pennine hills have always been subject to severe weather conditions in winter. So bad were the conditions following a snowstorm in 1909 that the Mossley and Saddleworth Reporter, 25 December 1909, commented on the effects it had on railways and on people; *"The storm was so violent on Tuesday night and Wednesday morning that the branch line of the London and North Western Railway from Greenfield to Delph was blocked for several hours. The first two trains on Wednesday morning were unable to get to Delph and the result was that scores of passengers were greatly inconvenienced. Some waded through the slush and snow to Saddleworth station – a distance of two miles – but the majority waited until the line was cleared. It was ten o'clock in the forenoon before the first train could get through".*

Increasing road competition and rising costs was forcing many railway companies into seeking fresh ways of modifying the traditional steam train to a more economical form. One attempt was the self-contained steam-railmotor; a combination of a small locomotive portion with a passenger carrying area. It appeared to offer the perfect solution. Railmotors were cheaper to build and cheaper to operate than conventional trains of locomotives and carriages but, as things turned out, they were only viable so long as they did not generate more patronage. Attaching an extra coach often overburdened the rather feeble engine

portion. LNWR steam railmotors were in fact capable of hauling a trailer when required, nevertheless, when it came to providing a steam railmotor for the Delph branch in 1910, the LNWR built a more powerful unit, No. 5507 with a dedicated trailer No 1777. Both vehicles were 60' long. However, the steam-railmotor service to Delph was a short-lived affair. It was not popular with those who travelled in it, quickly earning the sobrique *"The Potato Roaster"*, due to the heat in the passenger saloon. The technology was soon overtaken by the push-pull concept of using conventional locomotives and specially adapted driving trailers.

PUSH-PULL TRAINS TAKE OVER

Push-pull trains, or Motor trains, as the LNWR preferred to call them, were introduced on the line on 1st January 1912. On the same date, three new stopping places were opened at Dobcross, Moorgate, and Grasscroft. Saddleworth Council had taken the initiative by reminding the LNWR that its Greenfield to Delph service would be more viable if it were to recognise the two sizable and growing settlements at Moorgate, a spot close to Uppermill, and Tamewater, an area near Dobcross village. For once, the council's aims coincided with those of the company. Dobcross Halt was chosen in preference to Tamewater, and was situated about a mile from Delph. Moorgate Halt was adjacent to Delph Junction and its platforms flanked the main line. Grasscroft Halt was 2¾miles from Delph and was situated in a cutting on the Oldham Branch. When the push-pull trains were worked 'single motor', that is with a loco and two coaches, it was generally engine first to Delph and then push them back to Oldham. When two coaches were attached on either side of the engine, as on Saturdays, it was referred to as working 'double motor'. Some LNWR Webb 4' 6" 2-4-2T locomotives were equipped with mechanical push pull linkage and returned to the line to work the Motor Trains, but they were eventually replaced by Webb 0-6-2T 'Coal Tanks'. Further expansion of passenger services accompanied the introduction of push pull trains and by 1914; the weekday total of services from Oldham to Delph was thirteen, with

twelve in the opposite direction for either Greenfield or Oldham.

Rail travellers on the mainline, perhaps riding in old arc roof stock, must have looked enviously at the new push-pull trains provided for Oldham-Delph services. Externally at least, the new push pull saloons looked very modern, but this was to belie the interiors! The driving trailers had slender tram-like seats that could be swung over to face direction of travel, although first class accommodation provided conventional fixed high-back seating. The non-driving trailers had back-to-back seats for third and first class passengers.

Freight traffic suffered a decline when coal deliveries to Dobcross siding ceased in 1909 and when Brownhill quarry lost its connections around 1919, even so substantial quantities of wagons were still conveyed by the daily goods train. The 1914-18 war brought few changes, and life went on pretty much as normal for a time, but as the conflict went into its third year the committee controlling the railways on behalf of the Government ordered cuts in passenger services. These measures, which were intended to be purely temporary, also included the closure of stations and even full branch lines. Thus, the remaining two stations on the Micklehurst line closed their doors on 31st December 1916. They would never re-open.

After the Great War, Mossley and Saddleworth Councils urged the railway to re-open the passenger stations on the Micklehurst line, by which time the stations were in a neglected condition, with partial removal of some buildings, but the railway rejected the idea. Saddleworth Council also returned to lobbying the railway company for improvements on the Delph line and turned its attention to the platforms at Delph Station, which it considered were too low. Again nothing was done. Meanwhile, under the railway grouping of 1923, the Oldham-Delph line came under the newly formed London Midland & Scottish Railway (LMS)). It was the LMS that raised the height of the platform at Delph in 1925, a date that is not without some significance considering new competition from buses............

.........*continued across*

(Above) What a difference a year makes! BR Standard Class 2MT No **84015**, working the 11.33am Oldham Clegg Street to Delph, comes off the Oldham Branch and joins the main line at Greenfield on 30 April 1955. Trains terminating at Greenfield always used the bay platform on the right, but Delph-bound workings could also use this bay if the main line platform was occupied, regaining the main line via the crossover in the foreground. Some rationalization had taken place by this date with the removal of the canopy over the Oldham platform. The gas lamps appear to have been re-hung from new concrete posts. Greenfield Junction signal box is on the left.
R J Buckley

BUSES FOR TRAINS

Formed from the BAT Peak District Committee in April 1923, the North Western Road Car Company's (NWRCC) first expansion away from its home territories of Cheshire and Derbyshire took place in Saddleworth, where it started running local bus services in 1924. It was an obvious opportunity. Many of the scattered villages around Saddleworth lay some distance from railway stations and were outside the areas of operation of the local municipal undertakings. North Western's appearance here and its persistent attempts to gain access to the city of Manchester and surrounding towns, and the consequent threat to their tramway systems, was one of the stimuli that caused the municipalities of the North West, led by Manchester with considerable encouragement from Oldham, to

set up a network of express bus services. The first commenced in April 1927 and, always a realist, North Western decided that, if it was to survive, it had better cooperate rather than fight. Meanwhile, in 1925 the LMS agreed to introduce a 5.45am departure from Delph to Greenfield to connect with a train to Yorkshire to provide for the many local residents who worked as mill operatives at Marsden on the east side of the Pennines. Yet another concession at this time was the granting of Saturday afternoon cheap fares from Delph, Dobcross and Moorgate stations to Oldham.

In August 1927, North Western and Oldham Corporation entered into an agreement for joint operation of bus services from Oldham to Greenfield and Uppermill. These were in competition with the Delph - Greenfield - Oldham

Branch of the LMS Railway. On 1st March 1928 North Western became a full partner in the express bus network and a week later cross-city express services from Gatley, in the south of Manchester, to Greenfield (service 10) and Uppermill (services 13 and 14) commenced. The networks grew and prospered and nowhere else in Britain were such operations as extensive and successful. Despite the fact that the 13 and 14 buses ran parallel with the Delph line for much of the way, the L.M.S. clearly thought it worthwhile to install a new halt at Measurements between Dobcross Halt and Delph. Measurements Halt opened on 18th July 1932, its name derived from the factory it was built to serve, and trains only stopped there at peak hours as follows: 7.14am and 7.50am from Oldham and the 12.04pm (Saturdays only) and the 5.33pm back from Delph.

The LMS abolished first class on many of its push pull-operated services in 1930, consequently passengers on the Oldham-Delph trains were able to take advantage of the plush first class accommodation on offer in some of the open composite coaches. The timetable for 1933 showed 22 trains running between Greenfield and Delph, and 21 in the reverse direction on weekdays with one less train each way on Saturdays.

The threat of further road competition raised its head in 1936 when the North Western applied to the traffic commissioners to insert a bus stop at Duckworths Corner, a short distance from the Woolpack Inn stop and close to Dobcross Halt. It is probably no coincidence that the LMS made big reductions in fares from Saddleworth to Oldham at around this time. Delph continued to be the place of embarkation for people travelling away on holiday and traffic of this kind in the inter war years showed no signs of subsiding despite locally advertised coach outings. Traditional destinations throughout the 1930s continued to be places such as Blackpool, Southport and Llandudno.

Many years later at the age of 97, Charlie Harrison recalled the 1920s and 1930s in the days when he had advanced into the link that operated the Delph motor trains. I am grateful to Keith Miles for allowing me to use his recorded interview with Charlie. *"... 06.25 in the morning were t'first train to Delph and they were going every half hour all day long; out into t'country where there was no b*****. Buses didnt have t'people on a Saturday; we had 'em".* This was a reference to competition from such as the North Western Road Car Co. *"On Saturdays we used to work what we called double motor, two coaches each side of th'engine. The driver was at t'other end all day long; I only saw him when he walked past! Yes, on Saturdays I used to do all t'lot. When we set off from Clegg Street I'd got the firebox half full and the footplate full up with coal just so I could get into t'cab. By the time we'd done one trip I'd taken all that off the footplate and I'de still got a full bunker. By gum, I know I'd got that to empty before I'de finished work but, d'y' know, I loved every minute of it".* The push pull sets went to Stockport once a week for cleaning. Sometimes they'd

return the wrong way round, in which case the engine would have to couple onto the Oldham end instead of the usual Delph end.

SECOND WORLD WAR

The outbreak of World War Two meant a stay of execution for many life-expired locomotives, trams and buses and it affected public transport operations in several ways. The most obvious sign of change was the imposition of blackout. Restrictions on lighting made it a requirement to paint white bands on platform edges, canopy support columns and corners of station buildings, while on the roads, the white paint was apparent on the mudguards of vehicles, kerbs stones near bus stops and crossings, and on lamp posts etc. Increased employment on essential war-effort production and the decline of private motoring due to fuel rationing caused a marked rise in bus and tram travel. Many tram-replacement projects had to be abandoned, and the restrictions in the consumption of fuel resulting in mileage reductions led to the curtailment of many stage carriage routes. Single-deck buses had worked the 10, 13 & 14 limited stop services into Saddleworth, but growing wartime

The photographer has captured a quiet spell at Greenfield in April 1954 with no traffic signalled on the mainline and no passengers in view. Fowler Class 3 2-6-2T No **40014** simmers in the Oldham Bay platform while the footplate crew take the opportunity to relax in between duties. This engine was one of two 'breadvans' allocated to Lees not fitted for push pull working. Their duties included this working from Greenfield to Stockport (arr 6.21pm), which departed at 5.40pm, calling at Mossley, Stalybridge, Ashton (Park Parade), Dukinfield Central, Guide Bridge, Denton, Reddish South and Heaton Norris. However, it is difficult to explain the presence of the train in the Oldham bay when there was no direct access to the Up Main. Must one assume that an ECS movement would be required to cross the lines? The canopy over the Oldham platform is still intact at this date.   *Neville Stead collection*

passenger loadings probably led to the operation of double-deckers for the first time on 5th November 1941. Fewer buses carrying greater numbers of passengers led many people to return to the railways. Even so, by 1940 there were eighteen return Mondays to Friday's workings along the branch, a reduction on pre-war timetables.

POSTWAR YEARS

The October 1945 timetable showed the day's first departure from Oldham Clegg Street was the 5.45am to Leeds City followed by the first Motor Train (push pull) of the day this being the 6.25am departure arriving at Delph at 6.54am. Two minutes were allowed at Greenfield to take water. The 6.58am from Oldham Clegg Street terminated at Greenfield but the 7.12am 'Motor' again went to Delph. The 8.00am from Stockport to Greenfield was the next train, then there was a gap until the 10.20am 'Motor'. This train was followed at 10.33am by a light engine from Mumps to Lees shed. On Saturdays-only there were three Clegg Street departures quite close together at 11.09am to

Greenfield, 11.33am to Delph, and 11.45am to Greenfield. The first two were 'Motor Trains'. The 12.10pm went 'Motor' to Delph, followed by the 12.20pm (SO) Ashton to Greenfield. The 12.48pm (SO) was a 'Motor Train' to Delph as was the 1.10pm, the 1.55pm(SO), the 3.27pm, and the 4.20pm, but the 4.35pm terminated at Greenfield. At 4.48pm there was a light engine to Greenfield followed by the 4.53pm and 5.22pm 'Motor' to Delph. The 5.08pm from Stockport followed as far as Greenfield, and then there was a gap until the 6.15pm 'Motor' to Delph and the 6.40pm(SO) 'Motor' to Delph. The 7.10pm from Clegg Street was a 'motor Train' on weekdays as far as Delph, but was non-Motor on Saturdays and terminated at Greenfield. There was then a 7.30pm Oldham-Delph 'Motor' followed 15 minutes later by the 7.05pm Stockport-Greenfield. The 8.52pm, 9.20pm(SX), 9.25pm(SO) and 9.54pm all went to Delph while the 10.25pm went only as far as Greenfield. All ran 'motor'.

The first eastbound departure was the 6.09am Greenfield to Clegg Street empty

stock while the first passenger train left Delph at 6.57am. Motor fitted trains kicked in with the 7.45am and 8.25am from Delph followed by a non-motor working from Greenfield at 9.12am. The 11.01am from Greenfield to Lees was a light engine movement and the 11.40am(SO) was a Motor train to Oldham. The 12.08pm(SO) 'Motor' from Delph was booked to call at Measurement while the 12.27pm(SO) from Greenfield went to Stockport. There was a 12.42pm(SO) Delph – Oldham and a 12.45pm(SX) Delph-Greenfield. The 1.18pm Delph-Oldham was non-Motor while the 2.01pm(SX) went as far as Greenfield, but on Fridays-only continued to Oldham and Saturdays-only worked as a Delph-Oldham train. Next departure was the 2.47pm Delph-Oldham 'Motor'. Empty stock left Greenfield for Oldham Glodwick Road at 5.17pm(SO) whilst on weekdays it ran passenger to Stockport. The 5.33pm Delph-Oldham 'Motor' was booked to call at Measurements, and this was followed by the 5.57pm Delph-Oldham 'Motor'. There was a 6.18pm Greenfield-Stockport, then a 6.25pm(SX) Delph - Oldham 'Motor', a 6.43pm Delph - Oldham 'Motor', a 7.30pm(SO) Delph - Oldham

'Motor' and a 7.39pm(SX) Delph.-Oldham 'Motor'. In between there was a light engine movement from Greenfiueld to Lees at 7.35pm. The 8.21pm and 9.20pm departures from Delph were both motor trains to Oldham as were the 9.50pm(SX) and 9.55pm(SO). The final train of the day left Delph at 10.23pm for Oldham followed by a light engine from Greenfield (10.50pm) to Lees.

There was no Sunday service on the Delph branch but there was a Sunday service to Oldham worked by Motor Trains with departures from Greenfield at: 3.20pm, 5.45pm, 6.10pm, 7.15pm, 8.25pm and 9.56pm. Down departures from Oldham Clegg Street were: 12.40pm, 3.00pm, 3.20pm, 6.15pm, and 9.38pm. The 1947 timetable showed no significant changes but of interest was a 5.00am Greenfield-Stalybridge push pull train, and an 8.20am Greenfield-Ashton (Oldham Road) train.

The Second World War had been difficult period for the railways, but they acquitted themselves well in the national interest. A large backlog of maintenance made recovery a slow process but continued fuel rationing brought with it even bigger demands on public transport. As if this was not enough, the election of a Labour Government in 1945 was to have far reaching consequences for British transport as a whole and the railways entered the post-war era in the shadow of Nationalization. The traveller from Delph saw little change in the first few years following the war, either at the railway station or at the adjacent bus stop. The necessity to keep road vehicles in service because of war had shown operators that buses could last much longer than the common pre-war seven-year span, and many buses built in the early 1930s were still in daily use. Residents of Delph, Uppermill and Greenfield were fortunate that only the fittest buses were used on the 10, 13 and 14 services due to the hilly retain and the relatively long distances involved.

Manchester Corporation's Queens Road depot continued to put its very capable 1939-built Leyland Titans on the limited stop services, with the occasional Crossley Mancunian thrown in if they were stuck. Many of Manchester's buses were still in streamlined red and off-white livery. North Western continued to use it's luxuriously appointed Bristol K5G's; their coach type seats were said to be the most comfortable ever fitted to double-deck buses. Oldham's contribution to these jointly run services

were this operators relatively new TD5s with Roe bodies. The Corporation had purchased no less than 47 Leyland Titan TD5 buses for tram-replacement before war started and these vehicles comprised almost the whole output of the Charles Roe body works during the first three months after the outbreak of war. Oldham had put many into storage for a while and they represented this operator's front-line fleet together with new buses delivered in 1946/7.

NATIONALIZATION

British Railways began life with 1941 prices and 1948 costs, unlike all other industry. Whilst B.R. was unable to obtain the limited raw materials authorised in Government's Economic Plans, road transport - year after year, was allowed to exceed the limits that they had been given. Hence, they soon had a modern post-war fleet, whilst B.R. had to lumber on with war worn vintage rolling stock. While modernization of bus fleets really began to show by 1950, the country branch lines carried on pretty much as they had before the war. The LNWR motor-fitted saloon coaches still ruled supreme on Delph services, while non-motor trains to Stockport etc continued with a mixture of pre-group and early LMS non-corridor stock. The withdrawal of motor trains in other areas of the London Midland Region led to a surplus supply of ex-LNW push pull saloons. A few were overhauled and sent to Delph in 1952-3 to replace worn out vehicles, but apart from a fresh coat of paint or varnish, there was nothing to distinguish them from the coaches they were sent to replace. A solitary exception was non-driving trailer open third No. M3484M, one of three LMS Period II coaches converted to push pull operation in 1951. This coach carried carmine and cream livery, better known as blood and custard, and added a touch of colour to the line. It ran coupled to a driving trailer that remained in LMS maroon livery.

While the railways as a whole struggled with a backlog of maintenance on locomotives, rolling stock and infrastructure, Lees also struggled to maintain sufficient push pull fitted Fowler 2-6-2Ts to cover its Delph and Greenfield services. Heavy on maintenance and particularly springs, they were not the most proficient locomotives ever built. When things got desperate, elderly LYR 0-6-0 freight engines were pressed into service on the Greenfield passenger turns. No one batted an eyelid when these engines worked goods trains, but

when seen heading the 'Delph Donkey', some rail travellers suspected Stevenson's Rocket had been resurrected! The footplate staff were not best pleased either because of the added irritation of having to uncouple to run round their train at each end of the line, which of course the push pull trains had eliminated many years before. In 1953, Lees was forced to borrow three ex-LYR push pull fitted 2-4-2Ts in order to maintain services. All these problems were finally solved when three LMS and three BR design 'Mickey Mouse' Class 2 2-6-2Ts arrived at Lees in August and September 1954 to replace the motor-fitted Fowler tanks. On paper, the replacement locos were less powerful than the Class 3 Fowler engines, but they were far more modern and were fully in command of their jobs. The first of the Fowlers to go was 40056 on 14 August, followed by 40012/57/59/60/61 - all of them moving to Hull Botanical Gardens MPD on the North Eastern Region.

The timetable at this time was offering fourteen return trips on weekdays and some twenty trains on Saturdays. As before, not all trains went through to Delph. An innovation, at least as far as the Delph branch was concerned, was the introduction of a Sunday service in the summers of 1953 and 1954. All previous Sunday trains had terminated at Greenfield. With nine departures from Oldham Clegg Street reaching Delph approximately every hour from 12.10, the trains gave the residents of Oldham every opportunity to venture into the beautiful Saddleworth countryside and get their fill of fresh air.

THE END AND BEYOND

When the summer timetable of 1954 ended, the winter timetable showed a much-reduced service of fourteen trains in each direction although the Saturday service was quite generous. In 1954, British Railways formally sought permission to close the passenger service and on 9th March 1955, it was on the agenda of a meeting of the North West Transport Users Consultative Committee. As was to prove some years later during the Beeching closures, there was a huge gap between the perception of the line's worth to the local communities it served and the incredible indifference of the rest of the world. Arguments about inadequate alternative bus services gained nothing against the stark reality that trains were losing around £28,000 a year. The committee supported BR's view that passenger services should be withdrawn and the date earmarked for the withdrawal of the Oldham-Delph service was 2nd May 1955, although the final trains actually ran on Saturday 30th April. On 30 April 1955 the Oldham Chronicle announced te impending demise of the Branch: "From next Monday, Grotton Station will be closed for all traffic and Oldham (Glodwick Road), Lees, Grasscroft Halt, Measurements Halt, Dobcross Halt and Delph will be closed to passenger traffic. Parcels and passenger train merchandise will be accepted or delivered from Oldham (Mumps) and Greenfield stations and Oldham (Glodwick Road). Lees and Delph will continue to deal with freight traffic". The continuance of goods traffic was a sort of reprieve at the time.

The last working left Clegg Street for Delph at 11.10pm with some five to six hundred passengers packed into four coaches. It is said the small number of regular passengers looked on with bemused silence as the host of newspaper reporters, Members of Parliament and railway enthusiasts delivered an impromptu display of sentiment. If only trains were always this full…!

When the train arrived at Delph a cheering mass besieged the driver Edward Richards and his fireman Harold Freeman, for their autographs. The assembled crowd sang choruses of Aulde Lang Syne, and a donkey even put in an appearance. The train was supposed to leave Delph for Lees as empty stock but such was the tide of enthusiasm that locomotive No.41281, a Class 2P 2-6-2T, carried its passengers back to Oldham. It thus became the last regular passenger train to depart Delph. The 'Delph Donkey' was no more.

Replacement bus services commenced running on 2nd May, but it was soon apparent that reservations raised at the closure meeting concerning inadequate bus services had some validity, for within a few months the bus operators were pressing for service reductions. A sudden increase in car ownership might have altered the balance, but such things just did not happen in the mid 1950s. Bus operators had simply over-egged their case to ensure victory, a pattern that was to become familiar during the Beeching-led railway closures of the 1960s.

The residual freight traffic was largely comprised of coal for Bailey Mill at Delph and domestic coal merchants. The presence of this mill with its singe short siding had for a long time played a dominant part in the fortunes of the Branch. For eight years after closure to passenger traffic, the goods yard and mill siding continued to function as a reception for incoming coal supplies,

but with diminishing use. Bailey Mill Siding, along with the goods yard, was closed on 4 December 1963, having reached beyond useful life. However, passenger trains continued to traverse the Delph Branch in the form of enthusiast specials. The 'Old Manchester Rail tour' of the Stephenson and Manchester Locomotive Societies ran a railtour over the line on 12th May 1956. A less spectacular rail tour was worked by Ex-L&Y 0-6-0 No. 52275 of Lees shed hauling two brake vans loads of enthusiasts in 1962.

During 21 June and 22 June 1960, the royal train bearing the Queen Mother took advantage of the Delph branch as an overnight facility, secure in the Royal Train in between engagements at York and Chester. "Deepdene 155W" was BR's code for this illustrious train, the whole episode being organized by BR with military precision. The following is an outline of the regal stop-over.

On Tuesday 21st June, Class 5MT engine arrived at Delph Branch running chimney first with a generator van and brake van at 11.5pm. On Wednesday 22nd, the five-coach Royal Train arrived from York at 1,45am, and was propelled onto the branch by Class B1 engine. This engine was detached and left the branch at 1.47am.

Black Five No.44687, the last of the class to be constructed, arrived on the branch from Stockport at 9.15am and departed with the Royal train at 10.5am for Stockport, arriving there at 10.45am. The Class 5MT with the generator van and brake van left the branch at 10.25am for Stockport.

On 10 April 1964, the Branch played host to the last goods train to run the 3½ mile journey between Oldham and Greenfield. The trip began at Mumps, leaving there at 9.15am with a brake van conveying twenty members of the Locomotive Club of Great Britain (LCGB) on board at 4 shillings per head. *"The train chugged slowly along"*, explained the Oldham Chronicle three days later *" and the driver obligingly made several stops while his enthusiastic passengers got off and took pictures of the train entering and leaving tunnels, passing signal boxes and standing in derelict station".*

The train picked up mineral wagons on its journey and was drawn by Ivatt 2-6-0 No. 46452. At Greenfield, the train ran to Mossley and back before returning to Oldham. From Greenfield, the brake van was propelled to Oldham, which must have given the LCGB members a gusty ride through Lydgate tunnel!

The LMS found it hard to compete with a bus route that ran parallel with that of the 'Delph Donkey' from Mumps Bridge and had nine intermediate bus stops between there and Grotton. Trams to Lees operated for the last time in 1928, replaced by a new bus service extended beyond Lees to Station Road at Grotton. Barely twelve months separates these two Oldham Corporation buses yet advances in design are readily apparent. The second bus is fleet number 14, a Leyland Titan TD2 with English Electric body delivered to Oldham in 1933. It looks completely outdated compared with the leading bus, fleet number 58, a Leyland Titan TD3 with English Electric body. Its paint barely dry, No 58 leaves Oldham Market Place on the Lees and Grotton route in the summer of 1934. *Leyland Vehicles*

GREENFIELD
No 8

SMITH
ELPH

A railway between the busy Lancashire mill town of Oldham and the delights of Greenfield was proposed by Alfred S Jee in 1845, but it was not until 18 August 1846 that a branch was authorised as the Huddersfield and Manchester (Oldham Branch) Act. In addition to the main 3³/₄ - mile route, it was intended to include a secondary branch from Springhead (lying just inside the Yorkshire boundary) to Mossley. This was not, however, proceeded with. There followed a lengthy period of gestation during which a number of alterations and deviations to the proposed route were incorporated into a new Act of 9 July 1847, the very same date that the Huddersfield and Manchester Company was subsumed under the London & North Western Company. Yet further delay hindered the start on construction of the branch. A fourth and final survey was completed by Joseph Locke on 1 July 1852, at which point lands over which the railway would pass were purchased. The definitive Act of 4 August 1853 rejoiced in the name *"LNWR (Oldham Branch Deviation)"*,

THE OLDHAM BRANCH
GREENFIELD TO LEES
AN ILLUSTRATED REVIEW

and from this date, preparations began to move forward.

Extracts from LNWR Minutes throw some light on the progression of developments between February 1854 and July 1856. It was agreed on 8 February 1854 that Joseph Locke and John Errington should both be in charge of engineering the branch. Thirteen tenderers bid for the

contract in June 1854, the Company requiring comparative estimates for a single and double line. The most expensive tender for a double line was £127,355 5s 0d; this came from Joseph Gregson & Robert Humphries. The cheapest was that of James Dickson (of Wellington, Shropshire) whose tender of £87,471 for a double line must ....*continued on page 44*

....*continued on page 44*

(Above) Greenfield Junction, an early 20th Century view showing the Oldham Branch in the foreground. An L&NWR six-wheel composite and a bogie brake third are stabled in the siding; the Standedge main line from Huddersfield to Stalybridge running behind the coaches. The very prominent viaduct carries the Mickelhurst Loop line across Chew Valley and the centre of Greenfield.

E M Johnson collection

continued from page 43.......appeared very inviting. The Company vetted the credentials of short-listed contractors and chose Messrs. Tredwell, a well-known and reliable firm whose tender of £95,258 for a double line was accepted on 26 June 1854. This supports the view that it was not necessarily the cheapest tender that found favour: just as important was the security of competency and reliability.

Work started in the autumn of 1854 and construction seems to have continued without much interruption. A blot on Mr.Tredwell's copybook merited a comment in the Minute Book for 25 June 1855, where Mr.Brook (one of the Directors) reported that Mr.Tredwell had begun carrying an embankment through a Mr.Cooper's reservoir at Springhead without removing the soft material from the bottom first. Accordingly, Mr.Locke and Mr.Errington were to be informed. The enormity of this misdemeanour probably elicited strong words for the contractor. Messrs. David and john Cooper owned land on the north side of the railway at Springhead; their reservoir lay on the southern side very close to the course of the railway.

The *Huddersfield Chronicle*, 9 December 1855, reported a fatal accident that befell a worker at Grotton who for some reason attempted to couple two dirt wagons together whilst they were being pushed along temporary rails by a group of men. From this foolhardy action, the man's family (if he had one) would have been denied any monetary compensation.

Company Minutes reflect the anticipation of the opening of the Branch in 1856. In March it was expected that two coupled tank engines would be required to work the Branch on opening day, whist in the same months, plans for stations at Mumps, Lees, Buckley (Grotton), and alterations to Greenfield to accommodate Oldham Branch traffic were approved. On 9 June 1856, it was announced that Captain Henry Tyler was to inspect the line in two days time. This he did on Wednesday, 11 June. Tyler's report furnished a few details of the line as he found it on that summers day: *"This Branch, which is double line, is a little less than 4 miles in length, and extends between Mumps and Greenfield.............. The permanent way is laid in a substantial manner, with rails from 18 to 21 feet in length, and weighing 10lbs to the lineal yard, connected by fish joints, and supported in cast iron chairs, upon transverse sleepers, 2 feet apart at the points, and 3 feet 3 inches from centre to centre elsewhere. The works are heavy, containing a tunnel, 1,332 yards long, through the coal formation. The gradients are severe and the curves sharp. The bridges are 19 in number, 9 over and 10 under the railway"*. Tyler concluded his report by cementing that *"All these works appear to be substantially constructed; and I am of the opinion that this line may be opened without danger to the public using the same"*.

The tunnel referred to was the Lydgate Tunnel, which carried the railway through a prominent physical barrier between Grotton and Grasscroft. Less well known was the 210-yard long cut-and-cover tunnel between Moorhey Street and Glodwick Road, ...*continued on page 46*

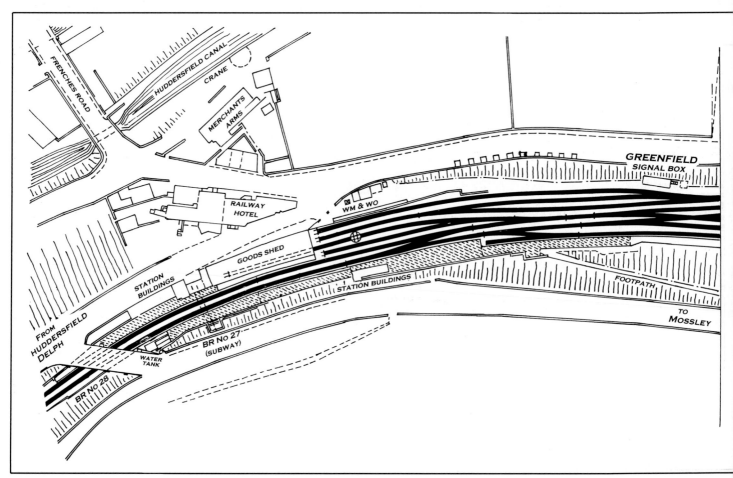

A sunny spring afternoon in 1953 sees Fowler tank No **40057** on a Delph bound train drifting slowly down the 1 in 75 gradient from Grasscroft Halt to Greenfield Junction. This view towards Grasscroft is very pastoral and the footplate crew would see the valley of Greenfield opening out before them. Out of sight and running deceptively close to the branch on a lower level is the Huddersfield & Manchester main line. Such was the nature of this service covering the 6¾ miles (Clegg Street-Delph) that the maximum journey time between any of the stations/halts was five minutes, that particular statistic belonging to the Glodwick Road-Lees section.   *J Davenport*

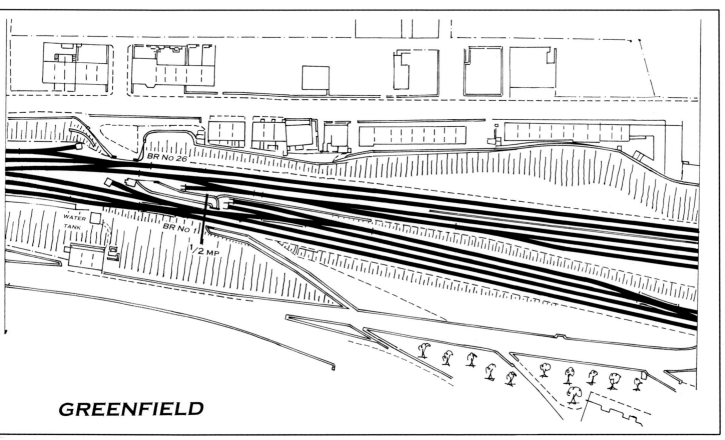

GREENFIELD

continued from page 44.......... Oldham. This particular section of the Branch must have been a difficult one to construct, as it passed through an area congested with mills and reservoirs. An 1879 plan indicates the tunnel clearly and shows that no buildings or highways were built over it. Judging by the amount of compensation paid out by the Company to local landowners, this section probably proved to be an expensive one. The tunnel was opened out in 1898, leaving the railway confined within two high stone retaining walls.

Before the opening day, two trials were made along the branch on 12 April and 1 May 1856. Details of the second trial caught the attention of the Oldham Chronicle, 3 May: *"On Thursday afternoon the contractors of the Oldham and Saddleworth branch of the London and North Western Railway, invited a number of their friends to accompany them on a trial trip from Oldham to Greenfield. Accordingly, a party of about 120 persons, from various points along the line, was conveyed to the junction with Greenfield, and back again. The engine and tender with two carriages containing the passengers were under the direction of Mr. Godsell, the foreman of the works, and of Mr. Wrigley the agent of the contractors, Messrs. Tredwell. The line will afford to Oldham many advantages of a commercial character, and will also be the means of opening up to the inhabitants an easy access to the very romantic and healthy district of Saddleworth".* The cold and raw weather failed to dampen the trippers who *"seemed much pleased with their trip to Greenfield and back again".*

The opening day (4 July 1856) was a cause for celebration in Oldham. The Oldham Chronicle carried a report of the event under the banner, *"OPENING OF THE NEW RAILWAY".* Part of the account is worth reproducing. *"On Friday (yesterday) the Oldham and Saddleworth Branch of the London and North Western Railway was officially opened. The day was fine, and the bells rang out joyously as the time approached for the proceedings to commence. At about twelve o' clock the procession began to form at the town Hall, and consisted of many gentlemen who feel an interest in the commercial prosperity and railway communication in the district. The procession having formed, proceeded from the Town Hall along High Street, down Manchester Street, along King Street, and Union Street, down Bottom of moor, up Lees Road, and down Harrington Street to the New Station of the Oldham Branch at Mumps, this circuitous course being rendered necessary by the refusal of the Lancashire and Yorkshire Line, to allow any parties to cross their line. The company having taken their seats in fifteen first class carriages, the train moved on, amid the shouts of the assembled multitudes who lined the embankments on either side of the railway, in the direction of Greenfield. On arriving at Lees the train stopped for a few moments to take in another portion of passengers, after which it moved to Greenfield, and afterwards to the Diggle Station, where, after about half-an-hour's pause, the company returned to Oldham. The line is a very well constructed one, and as smooth and level as could be desired; forming, in this respect, a marked contrast with some others in this neighbourhood, under the able management of C.Cooper Esq., the superintendent of this division... There were two locomotives to the train which were hung with garlands and under the superintendence of Mr. J. Ramsbottom (shortly to take on responsibility for LNWR locomotive affairs) . The trip was a very pleasant one, and many were the good wishes expressed by the passengers for the prosperity of the new branch railway, which puts Oldham into direct communication with the busy hives of manufacturing industry in Yorkshire".*

When the L.N.W. opened its Greenfield to Oldham line (known as the Oldham Branch) on 5th July 1856, the working of the Delph branch was combined with that of the new line. The Oldham line served intermediate stations at Grasscroft, Grotton & Springhead, and Lees. The traveller from Delph now enjoyed a wider number of destinations and could seek work further afield. A weekday service of ten trains in both directions was available, the earliest leaving Oldham being 7.20am; the latest 6.40pm. On Sundays, four trains plied in both directions. The two weekday trains which were Delph-bound left Oldham at 8.40am and 2.45pm. From Delph, three trains left for Oldham.

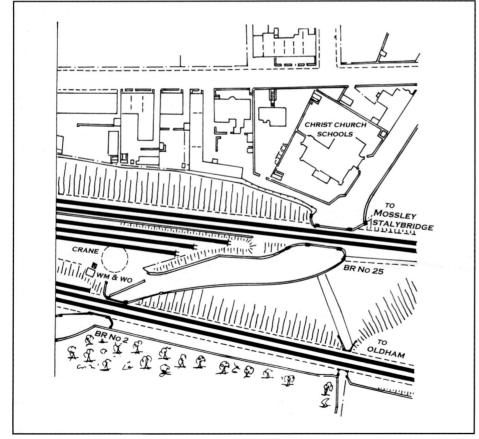

Delph(Dep)	Lees	Oldham(Arr)
9.20am	9.40am	9.50am
2.10pm	2.30pm	2.40pm
4.35pm	4.55pm	5.05pm

Any cause for celebration was short-lived, however, as by the following year the already meagre service was reduced to just two trains in each direction between Delph and the original terminus of the Oldham Branch at Mumps. Glodwick Road station, built opposite Christ's Church, Glodwick, replaced Mumps (LNWR) station when it opened for passengers on 1 November 1862. In 1878, the L.N.W. opened a loco depot at Lees to replace an earlier one at Mumps. In the same year, three additional trains were added to the timetable running between Delph and Greenfield, although they were soon extended through Oldham Clegg Street Station, with one train running through to Stockport on the MS&L/LNWR joint line via Park Bridge.

Extract from L&NWR Time Table for October 1st 1889

LYR 'A' class 0-6-0' No **52099** approaches Greenfield along the Oldham Branch with the local breakdown train in May 1953, indicating a 'spot of bother' somewhere in the area. This class of loco was introduced in 1889 and the LYR Birdcage roof brake third coach wasn't much older, so the pair made a perfectly matched period ensemble. Some of these elderly coaches saw further service as non-passenger carrying vans after 1933 and this one became Lees' tool van. Although the maximum speed limit for the line was a modest 40mph, it is most unlikely that this venerable duo would have been required to attain or keep to such a stipulation.

J Davenport

(Above) The driver appears to have company in his driving compartment, probably the guard, as it heads an Oldham bound train towards Grasscroft in 1955. The coach is No 15846, the first of the purpose built push pull saloons to be built in 1911. Its design closely followed that of the last-built LNWR steam rail motor, which had been tried on the Delph branch in 1910. *J Davenport*

(Below) A view of No **84015**, this time departing Grasscroft. The hill in the background is known locally as 'Pots & Pans'. It has long been a favourite with hikers and the casual walker, but the hill took on a more sinister prominence for a while after a passenger aeroplane crashed into it just after the Second World War. *J Davenport*

(Above) A native of Waterhead, Jim Davenport took up railway photography in the 1940s and recorded the local railway scene on film at a time when other photographers headed for more exotic locations. This isn't to say Jim didn't get around, for he took some wonderful pictures on Shap and on the West of England main line as well as in the London suburbs and around Scotland. But he also saw beauty in the industrial suburbs of what we now call Greater Manchester. On 30th April 1955, he was at Grasscroft Halt to record the passing of BR Standard Class 2MT 2-6-2T No **84015** with a Delph-bound train.

J Davenport

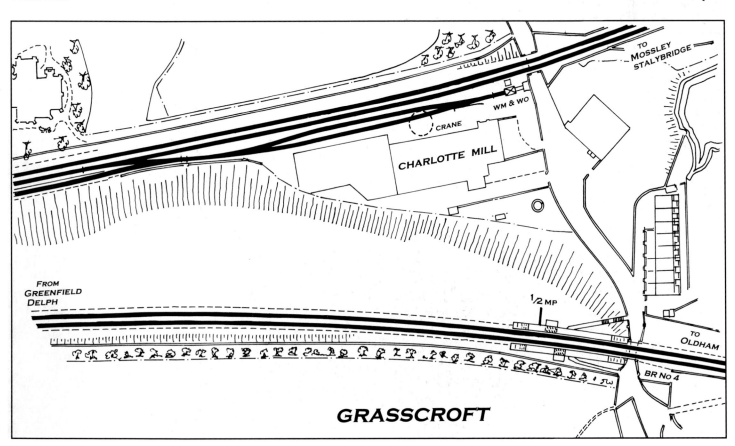

TO MOSSLEY STALYBRIDGE

WM & WO

CRANE

CHARLOTTE MILL

FROM GREENFIELD DELPH

1/2 MP

TO OLDHAM

BR No 4

GRASSCROFT

Grasscroft Halt in all its splendour amid the rolling hills of Yorkshire in the spring of 1955. Access to the Halt could be made via a set of stone steps to the Down platform and a sloping footpath to the Up platform on the right of this view. The station name or 'running-in' board is pure LNWR as are all the station signs; in fact it is unlikely the station saw any alterations during its life apart from a change of colour on the waiting shelters. The waiting shelters again highlight the lengths to which the LNWR would go to customise a range of 'standard' buildings. Originating as a range of portable buildings to a design authorised by Mr (F W) Webb, these eight-feet wide buildings would be provided in whatever length was thought necessary and appeared in all manner of small buildings used in goods yards, station buildings, signal boxes, etc., The buildings at Grasscroft were embellished by canopies in a similar manner to Dobcross. The coaches are No 15846 nearest the camera, and No 3407. BR 2-6-2T No **84012** is working the train.   *J Davenport*

On the final day of passenger services, **84015** rolls down hill into Grasscroft on 30th April 1955. The distant signal on the left provided the photographer with a convenient perch from which to take the panoramic view above. The lineside or 'Fogman's' hut beside the telegraph pole was placed opposite the distant signal (fixed) - note the absence of the lower spectacle - and equipped with a telephone. A Handsignalman, usually a ganger 'passed-out' for 'fogging duties' would be in charge of this cabin during thick fog and included in his duties were the laying of detonators on the rails to warn enginemen of their location and to give them instructions. By this means, the railways were able to remain operational when other forms of transport had given up. Thick fog in Grasscroft often meant thick choking smog in Oldham.

D L Chatfield

BR class 2MT 2-6-2T No **84012** reverses out of Grasscroft and propels its train towards Lydgate tunnel on 29th September 1954. With the engines exhaust well be behind him, the fireman of will have no need of a handkerchief over his mouth when passing through the 1,332 yards long tunnel. *G Whitehead*

APPROACHING
LYDGATE
TUNNEL

(Centre-right) From leaving Grasscroft, the landscape becomes harsher as the line approaches the eastern portal of Lydgate tunnel and heads under physical prominence of Lydgate hill. This view is from the driving compartment of a Delph to Oldham train.

(Below) Just clear of the east end of Lydgate tunnel, the crew of class 3MT 2-6-2T No **40059** will welcome the fresh air after breathing in the foul damp atmosphere within the tunnel. The look of this unappealing cutting is not helped by the pile of 'debris' between the tracks, the likelyhood that it consisted of bricks either recovered or for repairs to the tunnel lining. This was a notoriously damp tunnel and continued to eat into the engineers resources long after it ceased to be operational. Unfortunately, this Delph bound train is negotiating what must have been the untidiest section of track on the whole line! The steep cutting gradually opened out on one side near Grasscroft Halt to leave the line running on the side of a hill.

Both; *J Davenport*

(Left) At the western end of Lydgate tunnel, only a short distance from the station at Grotton, Fairburn Class 4P 2-6-4T No **42115** emerges into the light with driver John Waterhouse at the controls while working the 12.27(SO) Greenfield to Stockport train on 30th April 1955. As the service, inclusive of the Delph-Oldham trains, was withdrawn from the 2nd May (the following Monday), this was the last day of operation. Whilst there were a handful of trains which worked through to Stockport, the service was split between the *Oldham, Greenfield and Delph* timetable and the *Stalybridge, Rochdale, Oldham and Manchester (Victoria) to Stockport* timetable, usually being shown as a TC (Through Carriage) facility.

J Davenport

(Left-centre) Moments after the above picture was taken, another photographer fired his shutter and captured not only the same train but also a youthful Jimmy Davenport ahead of him on the embankment. Photographers seldom visited Grotton judging by the dearth of photographs at this location, but for some reason it was favoured with their presence on the last few days of services. *P Hutchinson*

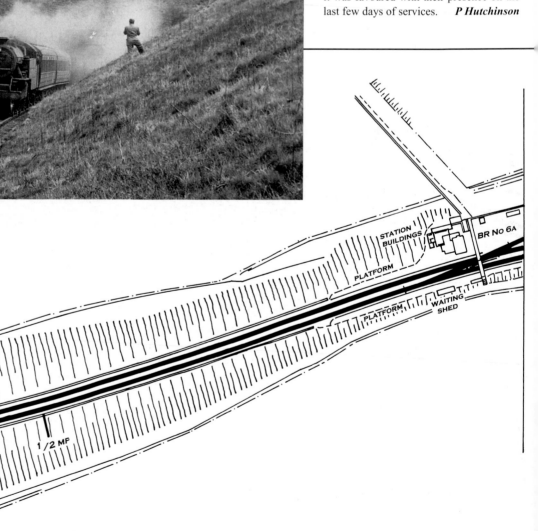

A sunny teatime at Grotton & Springhead station, and 2-6-4T No **42115** is seen on another occasion departing with a Greenfield to Stockport train, watched by three children on the footbridge. The cobbled level crossing in the foreground leads to the goods yard but there is no sign of the trailing crossover from the Down line entering the yard. The yard had in fact been simplified some time before cessation of passenger and freight services and the yard loop ended at buffer stops on the Lees side of the level crossing. *J Cocker*

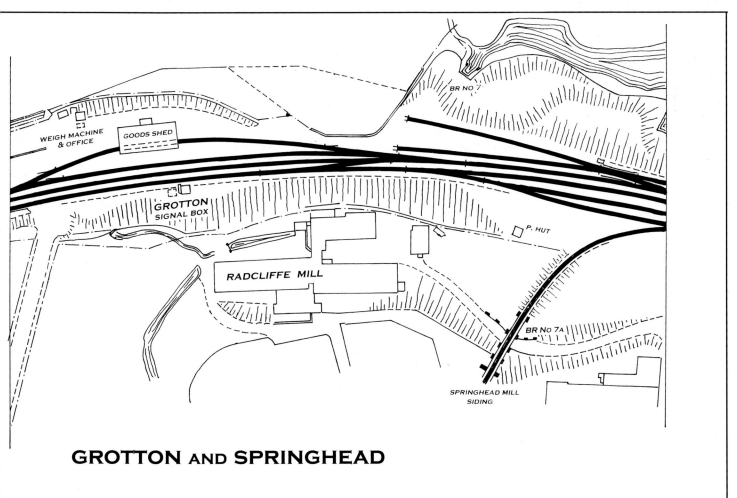

WEIGH MACHINE & OFFICE

GOODS SHED

BR NO 7

GROTTON SIGNAL BOX

P. HUT

RADCLIFFE MILL

BR NO 7A

SPRINGHEAD MILL SIDING

GROTTON AND SPRINGHEAD

(Right) Photographed from Grotton Signal box, an LNWR 0-6-2T Coal Tank enters Grotton & Springhead station with a four-coach push-pull working in the mid 1930s. The train consists of a diagram M18 driving trailer, a diagram M11 non-driving saloon, a Diagram M75 cove roof corridor third on the other end of the loco, and another (unidentified) driving trailer. Beyond the GWR and LMS wagons in the goods yard stand the weigh machine and goods office. *N Wisenden collection*

(Below-centre) Twenty years on and non-driving trailer No 3427 was still in service coupled with diagram M49 driving trailer No 3416. Fowler Class 3 2-6-2T No **40014** is propelling the coaches away from Grotton with the driver controlling the train from his compartment in the leading coach. The term "controlling" is applied very loosely on this occasion because No 40014 is not fitted for push pull working but is being used as if it was to avoid the chore of running round the train at Delph! The fireman, who remains on the loco, is regulating the trains progress according to his mate's gestures and his own route knowledge of the line, although the driver could apply the brakes by destroying the vacuum. *J Davenport*

(Bottom) Class 2 2-6-0 No **46452**, based at Lees from January 1964 until April 1964, heads the very last goods train over the Oldham-Greenfield line on 10th April 1964. The line closed completely the following day. At the rear of the train was a special brake van carrying members of the Locomotive Club of Great Britain. *I G Holt*

Smoke from BR Class 2MT 2-6-2T No **84010** blows back across the fields towards Springhead Club, a meeting place for locals and popular in the late 1950s with teenagers and author LG who played in a rock group there. No 84010 approaches Grotton with a morning train from Oldham Clegg Street on 30th April 1955, the final day of local passenger services on the Oldham and Delph branches. While quite a lot of people turned out to witness the last day of trains, for most people the event passed un-noticed. Come Monday morning, the terraced streets of Oldham would resonate to the sounds of Reginald Dixon's cheery organ melodies, while rag-men traded rags for donkey stones and *Dolly* the horse consumed crusts of bread while her master doled out milk, not in bottles but straight into waiting jugs on windowsills. Life carried on as before but the passenger train service between Clegg Street and Delph would be but a memory.

J Davenport

Fowler 2-6-2T No **40014** heads through Springhead after passing under Oldham Road. The appearance of this engine on an Oldham-Greenfield short working might indicate there was an absence of push-pull locos fit for duty. These engines were said to be a throwback to pre-1923 Midland Railway ideology, for when a proposed 0-6-2T was cancelled by the LMS in 1928 because its axle load was too high, the old Midland men resurrected their 2-6-2T designs with glee; No 40014 displays the post-war fittings of large diameter chimney and outside steam pipes, conversions that were intended to improve the performance of these appealing but ineffective machines.

J Davenport

Driving trailer No 3419 and trailer No 3425 head for Oldham under Oldham Road Bridge propelled by Ivatt Class 2 No **41280** in the autumn of 1954. From open countryside, we suddenly enter a complex consisting of Lees engine shed, railway station and goods yard, all crammed in between this bridge and one at St Johns Street, and dominated by a large goods warehouse. Station Street can be seen on the elevated ground to the left while departure tracks forming the eastern exit from the goods yard lie in the foreground.

J Davenport

LEES

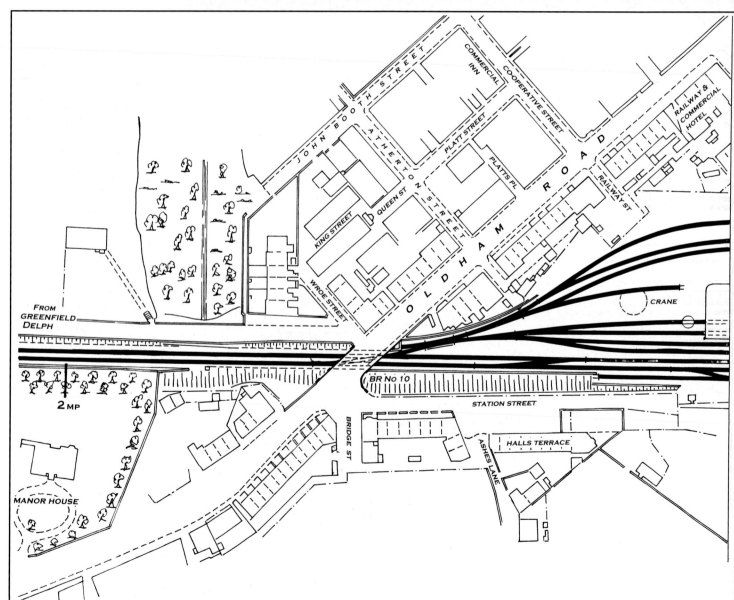

(Right) A Greenfield to Guide Bridge local hurries under Oldham Road Bridge behind LYR 'A' Class 0-6-0 No **52248** circa 1953. These engines were considered maids of all work at Lees and this one appears to be putting up a very spirited performance despite its age. The three non-corridor coaches are of LMS origin but the first two coaches give rather better accommodation especially in relation to toilet facilities. A wooden coal wagon is in the shed head shunt while 16-ton mineral wagons are visible in the goods yard. *J Davenport*

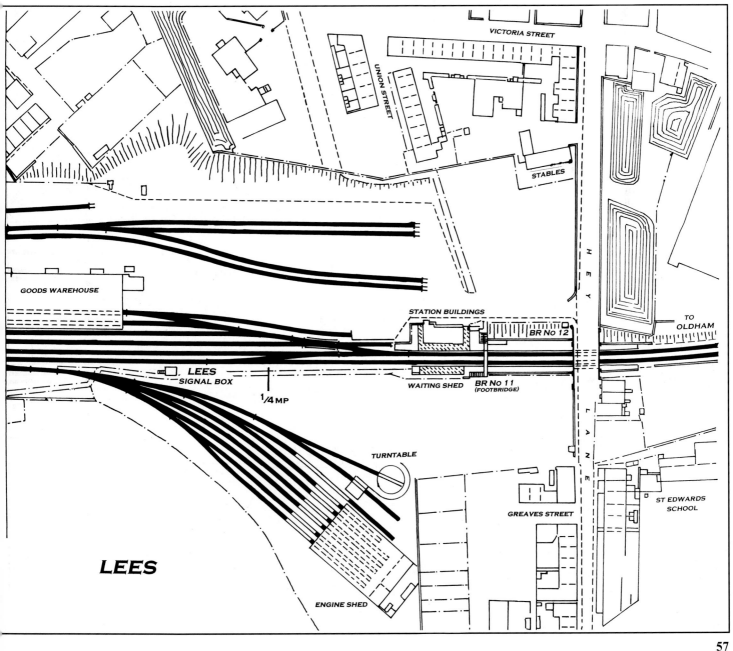

VICTORIA STREET

UNION STREET

STABLES

GOODS WAREHOUSE

STATION BUILDINGS

BR No 12

TO OLDHAM

LEES SIGNAL BOX

¼ MP

WAITING SHED

BR No 11 (FOOTBRIDGE)

HEY LANE

TURNTABLE

GREAVES STREET

ST EDWARDS SCHOOL

LEES

ENGINE SHED

(Right) Lees-based Stanier Class 4MT 2-6-4T No **42551** is passing the western exit of Lees goods yard with the 12.27pm (SO) Greenfield to Stockport local on a cold day in 1954. The train is non-corridor consisting of a brake third and a lavatory third, both built by the LNWR. The huge goods warehouse overlooks the yard, its shadow preventing a scattering of snow from melting, while Rome Mill dominates the skyline. A Fowler 2-6-2T is just visible on Lees Shed.

(Centre) A good deal of through traffic was diverted off the Huddersfield - Manchester main line onto the Oldham Branch and back onto the main line at Ashton after travelling via Park Bridge, this diversionary tactic taking pressure off the direct route into Manchester. Hughes/Fowler 'Crab' 2-6-0 No **42565** of Bolton shed races through Lees with a Leeds to Blackpool Relief in the early 1960s, long after the line had ceased to carry a local passenger service. Note the overgrown goods yard.

(Below) Lees 'A' Class 0-6-0 No **52365** is piloting Low Moor-based Class 5 4-6-0 No **44946** on a Bradford – Oldham football excursion through Lees in the early 1950s. The LYR loco was probably attached at Huddersfield to assist the train over Standedge. Apart from the leading LNWR non-corridor coach, the remainder of the train appears to be LMS mainline stock in carmine & cream livery.

All (3); J Davenport

(Left) Early evening at Lees in the late summer of 1954 and 'Black Five' No **45200** is seen leaving the station on a Newquay-Greenfield relief. The first two coaches are ex-Great Western corridor thirds, with an ex-LMS articulated twin open third and open brake bringing up the rear. An Ivatt 2-6-2T is leaving the Up platform with a push-pull train for Oldham. These West of England Summer/Wakes workings were detailed in an earlier Foxline publication, *Scenes from the Past 42, Part One - The Oldham Loop.* It would be interesting however to discover how a locomotive allocated to Blackpool found itself on the last leg of West of England to north-west England train.

(Left-centre) Fairburn 2-6-4T No **42115** of Lees is assisting LNER Class B1 4-6-0 No **61049** on yet another Footex or football excursion, this time from Darlington to Oldham. The train is wasting no time in getting its consignment of supporters to Clegg Street station where Oldham Corporation buses will be waiting to take them to the 'Latics' ground at Boundary Park. I wonder who won?

(Below) Fowler Class 3MT 2-6-2T No **40014** approaches Lees bunker first with the 11.5am Greenfield to Oldham Clegg Street in the summer of 1953. This non-push pull loco could not operate with push pull coaches and would have to run round them at each end of the line. The carmine & cream coach on the back of the train brought a touch of mainline comfort to these trains for a couple of years.

All (3); *J Davenport*

(Right) An 'A' class with Class A lamps up! Driver Frank Bottomley and Fireman Frank Hallam are in charge of LYR class 3F 0-6-0 No **52248** standing in Lees Sidings before leaving with empty stock to form an Oldham Clegg Street to Skegness Relief train in the late 1950s. This annual pilgrimage only took the 'A' class as far as Guide Bridge. The fact that 70-year-old engines were regularly used on trains of eight coaches shows they were deemed capable of handling such assignments. If only diesels were so dependable! The five-storey goods shed, located on the Up side of the line, was served by two through roads and six 30cwt hand operated cranes built on an end to end stage. The cotton bales, baskets of yarn, machinery, food stuffs and other produce to keep Lees at work and fed were accommodated under this one roof. *J Davenport*

(Centre) Bunker first working of a different kind on what Jim Davenport described as a lousy day, though whether he meant weather-wise or operationally we will never know! For some reason, Fowler 2-6-2T No **40012** has found itself assisting Fowler Class 7F 0-8-0 No **49509** on the 11am Diggle–Oldham Freight. The train may possibly have been unusually heavy this particular day, but judging by the exhaust, No 40012 is doing most of the pulling as it passes Lees. *J Davenport*

(Right-lower) Until the mid 1950s, Lees had an allocation of LYR 3F 0-6-0s with Belpaire fire-boxes. These ungainly looking machines always looked top-heavy and out of gauge, and lacked the grace of the original un-superheated 'A' class locos. No **52360** grinds to a halt in the goods yard opposite Lees signal box. The 11am Diggle-Oldham Glodwick Road goods is made up of cattle wagons and goods vans on this day in 1951.

J Davenport

(Above) LYR 'A' class 0-6-0s No **52427** has nothing to collect or drop off in Lees goods yard as it rolls through with the 11am Diggle-Glodwick Road goods in June 1955. This loco was re-allocated to Lees from Bury in late 1953 and withdrawn from Lees shed in June 1958. A Fairburn 2-6-4T is waiting to go off shed. *J Davenport*

(Right) Two 'A'class 0-6-0s for the price of one, ready to work all the way to Healey Mills with a special freight from Oldham in the mid 1950s. The driver of No **52365** is going round his loco filling the sand boxes while the crew of No **52099** are probably in Lees signal box discussing the train with the signalman. It is not known why the covered goods van roofs needed tarpaulin sheets for added protection.

J Davenport

(Right) Not much on the 11am Diggle goods this day! LYR 0-6-0 No **52427** and its train enter the confines of Lees goods yard circa 1954, back-lit by low winter sunlight forcing its way through a smoke polluted haze. This location was unusual in that the county boundary between Yorkshire and Lancashire struck across the area, so that the massive goods warehouse and signal box were in the white rose county while the engine shed and passenger station were located in the red rose county. Lees goods yard had the merit of taking up land in both counties!

J Davenport

LEES

(Below) It wasn't much different on the 8.55am Glodwick Road-Delph goods on some days. Ivatt Class 2MT 2-6-2T No **41206** of Hellifield is running as engine and brake van through Lees station. The boundary fencing behind the delightful LNWR lower-quadrant signal indicated a foot-way that linked the station with the east end of the complex at Springhead.

J Davenport

The push-pull apparatus mounted each side of the smokebox of this BR class 2MT 2-6-2T will not be of much use on a train of coal wagons nor indeed any working at Lees Shed, for No **84014** was transferred to Lees after the Delph passenger service finished. The loco finds itself on the 8.55 Oldham Glodwick road to Delph goods. The coal is doubtless destined for Mallalieu's Bailey Mill at Delph. A GWR 'Toad' brake van brings up the rear of the train as it passes slowly through the platforms of Lees station.   *J Davenport*

Viewed from the carriage landing siding at the end of Lees station Up platform in 1953, the 'Delph Donkey' rolls into Lees led by driving trailer No 15846 and propelled by an unidentified Fowler 2-6-2T. LNWR non-corridor stock is stabled in the goods yard. A public footpath ran behind the Down starting signal that is 'off'. This path connected Hey with Springhead at the opposite end of the complex and ran from the station footbridge, on past the signal box, across the throat of the engine shed tracks on into Station Street. Rome wallpaper mill is clearly seen in the background.   *J Davenport*

(Right) LYR 0-6-0 No **52099** was another 'A' Class that had a tender with no coal rails, and therefore reduced coal capacity. Coal that had lain at the very back of the tender around the water filler for months would eventually find its way into the firebox when things got really desperate! Once again, we see the 11am goods from Diggle, this time leaving Lees yard for the final leg to Oldham Glodwick road yard. *J Davenport*

(Centre) Not one of ours! Fowler Class 3MT 2-6-2T No **40063** was based at Newton Heath, and has arrived in Lees sidings with a Sunday engineers train of rails and ballast. These engines were quite versatile despite their well-documented weaknesses and, like all Derby products; they were well proportioned engines despite the rather puny boiler. They also looked particularly attractive in BR lined black livery. No 40063 had a life of thirty years and was withdrawn in August 1962. *J Davenport*

(Below) With the driver, fireman and guard posing for the camera, one wonders if the somewhat smoky departure from Lees was put on especially for the photographer! Class 3MT 2-6-2T No **40060** is on a Clegg Street to Greenfield working in the early 1950s. In place of a push-pull set, the coaches on this train are LMS-built non-corridor suburban stock. The leading brake third retains LMS livery although all the third class markings have been obliterated, but the all-third coach is in BR unlined carmine livery. Lees Shed loco coal stock is piled high behind the fence on the right. *J Davenport*

(Right) What with boiler washouts and a sudden increase of repairs, availability of the Fowler 2-6-2Ts reached an all time low in the spring of 1953 and Lees MPD was forced to ask other sheds for assistance. In the interim, its non-push pull locos were pressed into service on local passenger trains to the irritation of loco crews who had been used to the convenience of push pull operation. LYR Class 3F 0-6-0s No **52248** plods away from Lees on an Oldham Clegg Street to Delph service with push pull corridor coaches Nos 3432 and 3407 which, needless to say, will have to run round at each terminus.   *J Davenport*

(Centre) Help arrived from other districts in the form of LYR Class 2P 2-4-2Ts dating from the 1890s, and No **50731** was one of the non-superheated examples that had been rebuilt with belpaire boiler and fitted by the LMS for pull-push working. The new recruit propels its train into Lees in April 1953. These engines were standard motive power on local passenger turns on virtually every corner of the old L&Y system at one time, and several members of the class had been shedded at Lees in the 1930s and during the Second World War.   *J Davenport*

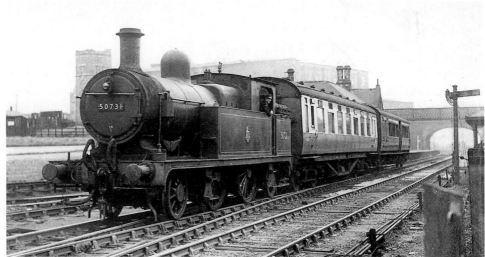

(Below) LYR Class 2P 2-4-2T No **50648** in near original condition is departing Lees with an Oldham Clegg Street to Delph train with coaches No 3432 and 3407 in tow. Of note are the extra coal rails and shed code painted on the smokebox door in the non-standard fashion. Both locos were loaned from Bolton (26C). A Fowler 2-6-2T can just be seen in steam beside the water tower so perhaps things were just getting back to normal.   *J Davenport*

Ivatt tank No **41282** leaves Lees in 1954 hauling push pull saloons 3427 and 3416. One can only speculate as to what was being said at Control about Lees' loco shortage. It is not beyond the bounds of possibility that the "emergency" use of LYR 2-4-2Ts on the 'Delph Donkey' showed these old timers to be better machines than the Fowler 2-6-2Ts! Whatever, changes were put in motion, three Ivatt Class 2P 2-6-2Ts Nos 41280-82 arrived in August 1954, followed by three BR class 2P 2-6-2Ts 84010/12/15 the following month. Delph trains lost some of their character when the six push pull Fowler tanks departed Lees for Hull Botanic Gardens shed in the same period. *J Davenport*

Steam is issuing from the steam heating pipe on the driving trailer as Fowler 2-6-2T No **40014** waits to leave Lees station in the 1950s. This loco and 40062, were not fitted for push pull working, nevertheless, they frequently turned up on Oldham-Greenfield turns such as on this occasion They stayed on at Lees after the push pull Fowler 2-6-2Ts had been transferred to Hull, but were eventually transferred to Newton Heath on 20th October 1955. The Down platform waiting shelter was a rather rudimentary affair and was virtually open from end to end. The only other structure on this platform was the all-important Gents urinal; important because Oldham was reputed to have a public house on every street corner and the 'Delph Donkey' had no toilets. *J Davenport*

(Right) This shot of Lees station taken on 22nd June 1960 is as I remember it (LG) while working at the nearby loco depot. Most of the station amenities were on the Up platform in one large building and consisted of a booking office (nearest the camera), general waiting room, ladies waiting room and porters room. Beyond the footbridge was a gent's toilet. A public footpath led from St Johns Street (Bridge No 12) to the Up platform and continued via the footbridge (Bridge No 11) behind the Down waiting shelter and on past Lees loco depot. The long grass growing around the main building gave it a sort of abandoned 'wild west' appearance, and it is hard to imagine the scene in 1881 when one hundred and ten operatives of the Livingston spinning company crowded this platform waiting for their special train to Belle Vue, Manchester. The building had numerous similarities

with those designed for stations on the Huddersfield to Manchester line. The indication is that the low platforms which came with the original station were replaced sometime during WW2, utilising LMS concrete components manufactured at Newton Heath. *G Whitehead*

(Below) Lees station viewed looking east from the Down platform. Although no trains had stopped here for six years, it witnessed much activity, particularly Monday to Friday with engines arriving and departing Lees shed at regular intervals around tea-time. LYR Class 3F 0-6-0 No **52271** has just left the shed to take up pilot duty at Mumps in the spring of 1961. It had not long been at Lees and was one of a batch transferred from Newton Heath in 1961, giving Lees the largest concentration of LYR 0-6-0's in the country. Even at this late date, the station remains pretty well intact with canopies and footbridge. The footbridge was built in 1881 after the Lees Local Board remonstrated with the LNWR saying the village had been cut in two by the railway and people were risking life and limb by walking across the tracks as a right-of-way in order to reach Springhead. *L Goddard*

The road over the arched bridge at the west end of Lees is shown on early LNWR drawings as Hey Lane, but it is perhaps better known as St John Street. BR Class 2MT 2-6-2T No **84015** propels the 12.06pm Delph-Oldham Clegg Street under St John Street Road Bridge on 30th April 1955. Three weeks later on 21st May, this engine would be transferred from Lees to Rose Grove shed. The original Lees station name board consisting of metal letters screwed to a wood backing is still in place, in fact, none of the stations, apart from Oldham Clegg Street, Greenfield and Delph, ever got LMS metal signs. The platform wall appears to be whitewashed, a legacy from wartime blackout days. Atop the embankment is the pathway leading to the station, and beside it the cobbled road leading to the goods yard, while the small building is presumably the coal office. Stamford Mill towers over the area in the background.

R J Buckley/Initial Photographics

Non-push pull operation of push & pull stock lasted right up to the penultimate day of operation. Fowler 2-6-2T No **40014** heads away from Lees station with a Greenfield-Oldham Clegg Street working on Friday 29th April 1955. Here we have an excellent view of driving trailer No 15846, which typifies the substantially built LNWR motor fitted open stock built in 1911/12. With louvres above every window for ventilation, the smallest windows could be lowered to give extra ventilation and to clear tobacco smoke, although in later years some were sealed up to prevent draughts. The recessed doors with their long brass vertical handrails allowed passengers to make a right royal exit from these distinguished carriages!

P Hutchinson

LEES
A MOTIVE POWER CHRONOLOGY

This view of the shed shows the type of engines allocated to Lees circa 1953. On the left, Fowler Class 3MT No **40061** is down by the side of the shed having taken water and had its fire and ashpan cleaned. The wooden coal wagon, with its side down, is there to collect ash. Beside it is Stanier Class 4MT 2-6-4T No **42551** with a Fowler 0-8-0 behind it just inside the shed (probably on boiler washout). The three other locos on view are LYR Class 3F 0-6-0 No **52099**, Fowler 2-6-2T No **40056** and Fowler Class 7F 0-8-0 No **49662**. The shed roof is being repaired after suffering from enforced wartime neglect. Beyond the 0-8-0 can be seen farmland, very old properties on Den Lane and Austerlands atop the hill.   *J Davenport*

LEES MOTIVE POWER DEPOT

The branch from Greenfield to Oldham opened on 5th July 1856 and in that year a tender for £1052 10s 0d was accepted for the construction of a loco shed at Oldham Mumps. This opened in 1857 as a sub shed of Longsight. According to reports, five locos were kept at Mumps. This shed only lasted a short time, closing in 1878 when a new and larger shed was opened at Lees on the outskirts of Oldham. The first mention of the intention to erect a new shed appeared in the LNWR Locomotive Committee Minutes, dated 21 September 1877, entitled *"Removal of the Engine Shed from Mumps",* and refers to a plan of the proposed shed. It was *"recommended that a shed to hold 12 engines, together with a coaling stage... and a turntable laid down ast an estimated cost of £4,620, exclusive of excavations and permanent way"*. Lees shed was a standard L.N.W.

brick structure with north light roof and had six roads, each 125ft long, capable of holding about 12 locos, and was situated on the north side of the Oldham to Greenfield line. Associated with the shed building in LMS days were workrooms for fitters, offices, stores, messroom, drivers lobby, booking-on room and a sand-dryer. Alongside the south wall was an ash pit road for fire dropping and smokebox cleaning, the ash and clinker being shovelled from the pit to ground level, then shovelled again into empty wagons standing alongside on No 1 shed road. This antiquated practice continued until the shed closed and was a good muscle-building exercise for passed cleaners! A large water column was situated just beyond the ash pit. The shed once boasted a turntable, initially 42ft and replaced with a larger one, but it was removed years before the Second World

War, possibly even in L.N.W. days. Thereafter engines turned at Ashton Moss or Miles Platting triangles. After it became a sub shed of Newton Heath, Lees went to great lengths to avoid its engines visiting the parent shed for turning on one of its two turntables, and a trip to Hillhouse shed in Huddersfield was regarded as quite normal despite the double journey through the three miles of Standedge Tunnel! Offices for the shed master and foremen, and for clerical staff, were at the back of the shed, while toilets and stores were around the side. A canteen was built in later years behind the main shed.

Lees was transferred from the LMS Western Division to the Central Division in 1931, and given the shed code C15. In the 1935 changes, Lees came under Newton Heath with shed code 26F. On 8th October 1955 the shed became 26E and

(Left) When the shed opened in 1878, the principal passenger services for which it was responsible were, Oldham to Greenfield & Delph, and from Oldham to Stockport. The 4ft 6ins 2-4-2Ts were the mainstay of these services in the Webb era, the first of the class being built in 1879, the year after Lees opened. 4ft 6ins 2-4-2T Nos 298, 998, 1056 and 1358 were at the shed in 1912 and by 1917 it had Nos.977, 1358 and 1444. No **1444** is seen at Manchester London Road. It was withdrawn in November 1924 and may never have carried its allotted LMS number 6560.

J M Bentley

(Right) 0-6-0 'Coal' engines and 0-6-0 'DX' goods engines would have handled much of the goods traffic and shunting duties in the latter part of the 19th Century. Longsight, of which Lees was a sub shed, had a large number of these engines. 'DX' No **3086** was working from Lees in 1917 and is seen here at an unknown location. It never carried its LMS number.

J M Bentley

continued from page 69..........the final change occurred in September 1963 when Lees returned to the control of Longsight with shed code 9P. The shed closed the following year on 13th April.

The principal passenger services for which Lees was responsible were from Oldham to Greenfield and Delph and from Oldham to Stockport. Normal trains, with locos running round their trains at each terminus, had operated the Oldham to Greenfield line from its opening in 1856. There is little information available about the locos that were supplied to Lees Motive Power Depot for working these services and those to Delph, but it is known LNWR 2-4-0Ts Nos 83 and 84, built under Francis Webb's superintendence, worked the Delph trains. These were built at Crewe in 1856 and were re-numbered 483/84 the following year. In the Webb era, the 4' 6" 2-4-2Ts were the mainstay of passenger services, the first of the class being built in 1879 around the time Lees Shed opened. In a bid to stave off the rising cost of operating the line, the LNWR sent its latest 60' steam railmotor to Delph in 1910. The railmotor was to Diagram M6 and was paired with an unpowered 60' trailer to diagram M44, but this train did not prove popular. Many of Britain's railways were using steam rail motors at this time for similar economic

reasons but push pull motor trains superseded them when it was realized the latter were far more flexible in their operation. For instance, a separate locomotive was not overtaxed when additional coaches were added to trains at busy periods, plus it could be put to other uses when not working push-pull trains. Webb 4' 6" 2-4-2Ts and 0-6-2T 'Coal Tanks', with mechanical push pull linkage, worked these motor trains.

Much of the goods traffic would have been handled by "DX" Goods 0-6-0s in the latter part of the 19th Century, and Longsight had a large number of these numbered from 1500-12 and 1533-99. Webb Coal Engine 0-6-0s would also have been used, and in the early 1900s, some of the 0-8-0s were provided for the longer distance freights that were handled by the shed. The Dudley Whitworth records for 1917 show 14 engines were at Lees: -

0-8-0 Class B (Compound)	No. 1066, 1281
Class D	No. 1865
Class G	Nos. 1271, 1887
0-6-0 Coal Engine	No. 3398
DX Goods	No.3086
2-4-2T 4' 6"	Nos 977, 1358, 1444
5' 6"	No. 408
0-6-2T Coal Tank	Nos. 850, 2457
0-6-0 Saddle Tank	No. 3064

The next allocation is from the records of C.E. Williams in the NRM at York, and is dated January/February 1928, by which time the motor trains were worked exclusively by 0-6-2T Coal Tanks. This was at the time when the LMS was allocating blocks of engines with consecutive numbers to sheds: -

4-6-0 19" Goods	Nos. 8857/58/59
0-8-0 Class G1	Nos. 9288/89/90/91/92
0-6-0 "Cauliflower"	Nos. 8349/50/51/52/53
0-6-2T "Watford" Tank	Nos. 6888/89/95/97/98
0-6-2T Coal Tank	Nos. 7550/51/52/53/54/55/56

When control of the shed was transferred to the Central Division, LYR 'A class' 0-6-0s replaced the LNWR "Cauliflowers" and the LYR 2-4-2Ts took over from the LNWR 0-6-2T "Watford" tanks. LYR 0-6-0 saddle tanks also appeared at the shed for shunting duties at this time. The three LNWR 19" 4-6-0s had gone by April 1934 when the sheds allocation was as follows: -

0-8-0 ClassG1 Nos.9288/89/90/91/92/97
0-6-0 A Class Nos. 12196, 12216, 12222, 12314, 12378, 12438
2-4-2T Class 5 Nos 10670, 10680, 10752, 10821
Class 5A No. 10872
0-6-2T Coal Tank Nos.7553, 7555, 7627, 7796, 7640
0-6-0ST Saddle Tank Nos. 11401, 11462, 11489, 11503

The work at Lees was sufficient to operate a 'link' system, and the main freight workings between the wars were to Crofton (Wakefield), and to Mold Junction and to Rowsley, which involved lodging overnight. The Mold Junction turn ended during the Second World War from when the men only worked to Warrington Arpley, then returned home from Warrington Central 'on the cushions'. The Rowsley turn involved working via Stockport and Buxton with a 0-8-0, but lodging ended at the beginning of 1947. Rowsley men also worked to Lees, usually with a 4F 0-6-0. Locos from Wakefield, Farnley Junction and Stockport were also to be seen at Lees. Other long distance freight jobs were lost to Newton Heath when the shed was transferred to the Central Division, although on the credit side Lees got some LYR pilot jobs and trip workings at such places at Mumps and Royton Junction. A major change came in 1939 when four motor-fitted (Vacuum Control Regulator or VCR) Fowler 3P 2-6-2Ts arrived at Lees from Newton Heath to replace Coal Tanks 27553, 27627, 7773 and 7796. 2-6-2T No.58 was first noted on Oldham-Delph service on 3rd April, and was followed during the next four weeks by Nos. 59 to 62. All but No.62 were VCR fitted. Nos 56 and 57 arrived at Lees soon afterwards, and Coal Tanks 27553, 27555 and 27627 were transferred away. Of the others, 7773 was withdrawn. The influx of larger motive power left most of the 0-6-2T Coal Tanks either stored or transferred to other sheds, but at the outbreak of war in September 1939 No. 7796 was still working passenger services on the Greenfield line. By the end of the year the Fowler 2-6-2Ts were working most of the passenger turns and continued thus throughout the war.

In July 1939, there was a change on the freight side when all the LNWR 0-8-0s were transferred to Wakefield and were replaced by LMS Fowler Class 7F 0-8-0s Nos 9508, 9509, 9511, 9593 and 9596. These powerful looking engines were destined to be the mainstay of Lees' freight operations for the next 18 years. Seventeen different Fowler 0-8-0s were based at Lees as follows:
9508 July 1939 to December 1957.
9509 July 1939 to April 1943.
9511 July 1939 to February 1942.
9593 July 1939 to May 1951 (withdrawn).
9596 July 1939 to August 1939
9507 December 1939 to March 1940
9548 December 1939 to December 1951 (withdrawn)

............*continued on page 72*

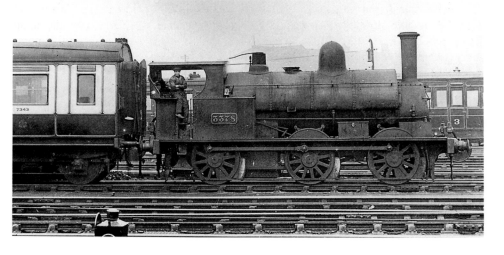

(Left-upper) Lees had Ramsbottom/Webb 'Special Tank' 0-6-0 saddle tank No **3064** on its allocation in 1917. Designed in 1870 for shunting duties, some were painted in lined black livery from 1890 onwards for shunting passenger stock in station areas. Carrying this livery for shunting at Stockport Station, No 805 starting life as No 1751 but was renumbered No 3041 in December 1891, No 805 in April 1909 and No 3611 in January 1919. It was scrapped in October 1925 without ever carrying its LMS number 7234.

(Left-lower) This is what Lees's 'Special Tank' 0-6-0ST No 3064 would have looked in 1917. No **3378** is seen with LNWR corridor third class carriage No 7343 while engaged on carriage shunting duty at Manchester London Road station sometime after 1908. This engine became LMS No 7297 after 1923.

Both; *J M.Bentley*

(Right) This picture shows what Oldham-Delph trains looked like before 1910, with Webb 0-6-2 Coal Tanks and 2-4-2Ts hauling little 4 and 6-wheel carriages. These carriages, which had dominated services for so long, were swept aside in 1912 when push-pull trains were introduced and 57ft long bogie carriages took over. Coal Tank 0-6-2Ts were based at Lees in December 1912 to work these trains and No **2457** (seen here at Nantlle) was based there in 1917 when equipped with push-pull apparatus. The Coal Tanks would dominate 'Delph Donkey' services until the arrival of Fowler 2-6-2Ts in the early years of the Second World War. *J M Bentley*

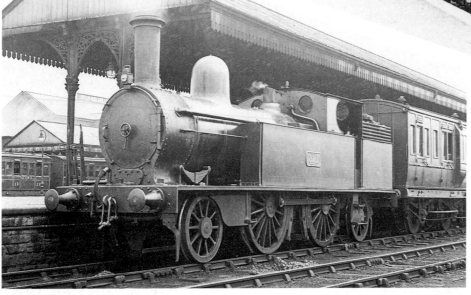

(Left) Besides having 4ft 6ins 2-4-2Ts in its allocation, Lees had Webb 5ft 6ins 2-4-2T No 408 for a time. Sister loco No 371, in LNWR livery, is seen at Stalybridge on a local passenger train in the mid 1920s. The leading 6-wheel carriage is in LMS livery but the loco has yet to be renumbered 6720. *Real Photographs*

.....continued from page 72
9668 October 1947 to December 1957.
9590 January 1949 to May 1951 (w/dn)
49598 March 1951 to November 1951
49608 May 1951 to June 1953 (w/dn)
49618 May 1951 to December 1957
49536 June 1951 to October 1957 (w/dn)
49563 February 1952 to June 1952 (w/dn)
49662 June 1952 to December 1957
49578 March 1954 to December 1957
49505 December 1955 to December 1957

Twenty-three locos were based at Lees when the Second World War broke out in 1939, and comprised five Fowler 0-8-0s, five LYR. 'A class' 0-6-0s, six Fowler 2-6-2Ts, four LYR 2-4-2Ts, two LNWR. Coal Tank 0-6-2Ts and a solitary LYR 0-6-0ST. However, by the end of the year the LYR tanks were stored out of use inside the shed. In a surprise move, three LMS Stanier 8F 2-8-0s were transferred to Lees in May 1947. Nos 8425, 8444 and

8446 joined the Fowler 7F's on freight work, and although they were mainly used on the Crofton coal workings, they must have been a sight to behold when they also appeared on 2-coach passenger trains between Oldham and Greenfield. Lees probably kept these splendid locos busy in a futile bid to keep them. Whatever, they were transferred to Agecroft after only five months. In may 1947 the VCR equipment from Fowler 2-6-2T No 58 was fitted to No 12, which then went to Lees and No 58 departed for Patricroft. In addition to the six Fowler 2-6-2Ts with vacuum control gear for push-pull workings, Lees also had Nos 14 and 62 without this facility for working Stalybridge - Leeds, Leeds - Huddersfield, Huddersfield - Stockport and Stockport - Oldham diagrams. There was also a Greenfield-Stockport, Stockport - Manchester and Manchester Victoria - Royton diagram on Saturdays. The Fowler 2-6-2Ts were reputedly heavy on

maintenance and tricky to fire. They also had "cabs like ovens", and it was not long before Lees men nicknamed them Breadvans. The sheds allocation on the eve of Nationalization in December 1947 was: -

0-8-0 7F 9509, 9548, 9593, 9668
0-6-0 3F LYR 12248, 12326, 12378, 12387, 12389, 12464, 12545, 12469, 12586, 12607
2-6-4T 4MT 2550
2-6-2T 3P 12, 14, 56, 57, 59, 60, 61, 62

LEES SHED UNDER BRITISH RAILWAYS

Under the general British Railways numbering scheme of 1948, the numbers of L.M.S. steam locomotives were increased by 40000, although some engine were completely renumbered. As renumbering was carried only as locomotives visited main works, it was some time before all locomotives carried their new numbers. The engines allocated to Lees at 14th June 1952 were: -............*continued on page 74*

(**Above**) The famous '18in. Goods' or Cauliflowers' were intended for express goods work. They had a fair turn of speed and were frequently used on passenger trains. No **461** pauses at Greenfield with a local passenger train on 26th April 1907.

E M Johnson collection

(**Centre**) Lees had five 'Cauliflower' 0-6-0s, Nos 8349-53, on its roster in 1928. No **8350** has been rebuilt with a Belpaire boiler and carries pre-1928 plain black livery with 14inch numbers and round cornered cab panel.

Real Photographs

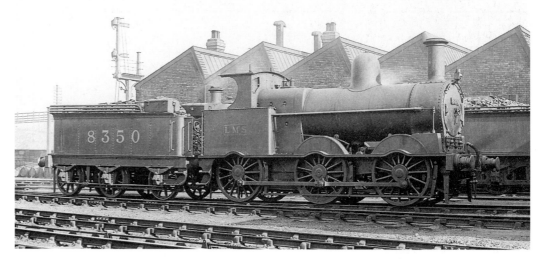

'CAULIFLOWERS'

(**Right**) 'Cauliflower' No **8352** was also based at Lees until the mid 1930s. This engine has the 'H' spoke driving wheels off one of the earliest built engines, and a Belpaire firebox. The latter was an LMS innovation and was fitted after 1923. Lees was transferred from the LMS Western division to the Central division in 1931, and when the shed came under Newton Heath in 1935, the LNWR 'Cauliflowers' were gradually replaced by LYR 'A' Class 0-6-0s.

J M Bentley

......*continued from page 72*

2-6-2T 3P   40012, 40014, 40056, 40057,
        40059, 40060, 40061, 40062.
2-6-4T 4MT 42550.
0-8-0 7F 49509, 49536, 49608, 49618,49662,
        49668.
0-6-0 3F LYR 52099, 52248, 52360, 52365,
        52549, 52615.

LMS Stanier 2-6-4T No 2550 was the first of this type allocated to Lees. It was joined later on by two Fairburn 2-6-4Ts Nos. 42114 and 42115. There were odd occasions in BR days when the motor-fitted tanks were unavailable for work due to repairs and boiler washouts, and 40014, 40062 or one of the LYR 0-6-0s would step into the breach. In April 1953, things got so dire that LYR. motor-fitted 2-4-2Ts returned to Lees for a short while. These locos had not been seen on Oldham-Greenfield-Delph services since before the war, although they had been a common sight on the Oldham Loop services despite the availability of Stanier 2-6-4T's. By the end of November 1953, engines allocated to Lees were: -

2-6-2T 3P   40012, 40014, 40056, 40057,
        40059, 40060, 40061, 40062.
2-6-4T 4MT 42114, 42115, 42551.
0-8-0 7F 49509, 49536, 49598, 49662,
        49668.
0-6-0 3F LYR 52099, 52248, 52365,
        52427, 52569.

It can be seen that even within an 18-month period, engines at Lees were in a state of flux. 2-6-4T No.42551 had replaced 42550.

The Fowler 2-6-2T domination on Delph workings finally ended in the autumn of 1954 when three LMS lvatt 2-6-2Ts Nos 41280-82 and three BR 2-6-2Ts Nos 84010/12/15 arrived at Lees. Some rebuilding of the shed began in April 1955 and it was re-roofed. The front of the shed got a new brick façade carrying the date '1955'. When Delph passenger services ended that year, the only Fowler 3P's that remained at Lees were Nos. 40014 and 40062. Both were transferred to Newton Heath on 20 October 1955; meanwhile the three BR standard 2-6-2Ts were transferred to Rose Grove, while the three Ivatt 2-6-2Ts moved away in December 1955; No.41280 went to Chester Northgate, and 41281/2 to Royston. BR standard Class 3 2-6-2Ts Nos 84013/14 replaced these locos. Ex-Lees No 40060 ended up at Rhyl in 1957. It occasionally worked over the Denbigh to Mold line where some of Delph's push pull open driving trailers had once operated.

The Fowler 0-8-0s continued hauling freight until December 1957 when they were replaced by WD 'Austerity' 2-8-0s. The first to arrive was 90140 in November 1957, ...*continued on next page*

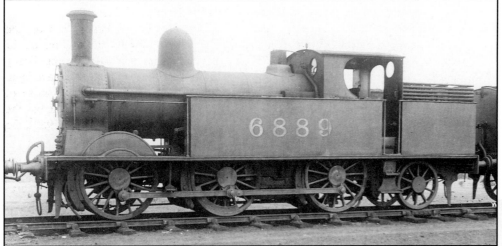

(**Left**) Eighteen years after the introduction of the 'Cauliflowers', a tank version was produced for local passenger train work. No **6889** was one of five of these fast running 0-6-2Ts that were allocated to Lees in LMS days to replace the LNWR 2-4-2Ts. It is seen at Crewe on 21st July 1928. None were fitted for push-pull working so they would have worked the same duties that would in later years be worked by Fowler Class 3P 2-6-2Ts and the Stanier/Fairburn Class 4P 2-6-4Ts.

Real Photographs

'WATFORD'
TANKS

(**Right**) 0-6-2T No **6898** (LNWR No 280) was also based at Lees from 1928 and is seen at Crewe that same year. These engines were commonly known as 'Watford Tanks', though they were to be found all over the LNWR system. The livery is something of a hybrid style. The 18-inch numerals and circular LMS coat of arms are those usually associated with red engines, but in the case of 6889 and 6898 the locos are plain black.   *Real Photographs*

(Right) For its longer distance goods trains, Lees was provided with some of the Webb 0-8-0s in the early 1900s. Class B Compound 0-8-0 No 1281 is seen hauling a goods train into Chester. The piano-like lid covering the rocking arms gave rise to the nickname 'Pianos'. In 1912 the shed had Class 'B' Compound No 1094, Class 'D' No 1865, and Class 'G' Nos. 1299, 1556 and 2014. Five years later the 0-8-0s were; Class 'B' Nos 1066 and 1281, Class 'D' No.1820 and Class 'G' Nos 1271 and 1887. *J M Bentley*

.......closely followed by 90123, 90141, 90271, 90306, 90402 and 90589 the following month. The next closure to affect Oldham came on 2nd May 1959 when the last trains ran to Guide Bridge and Stockport over the LNW/OA&GB line. No.84013 worked passenger on the last day before being transferred to Bolton. The sixteen locos based at Lees in April 1960 were nine 'Austerity' 2-8-0s, five LYR 'A class' 0-6-0s and two Fairburn 2-6-4Ts. One notable withdrawal at this period was LYR 0-6-0 No.52322, now preserved at Bury on the East Lancs Railway. Many of Newton Heath's remaining LYR 0-6-0's were transferred to Lees in early 1961, giving Lees possibly the largest concentration of these engines in the country. With much of the work gone, all these 0-6-0s were replaced by five Ivatt Class 2 2-6-0s, although the Ivatt engines were no strangers to Lees men. The shed also had several Diesel shunters, although all were allocated to Newton Heath but were worked by Lees men. The first was 12113 in January 1956 but 12115 replaced it soon after. They had been used on maintenance work in Standedge Tunnel. 204 hp diesel mechanical shunters built by the Yorkshire Engine Company were employed at the new Clegg Street Parcels Depot In 1960, but it was considered they did not have enough brake power for the work involved and 350 hp Class 08 shunters soon replaced them.

The Fowler 3MT 2-6-2Ts and the LMS and BR 2MT 2-6-2Ts that replaced them, worked Oldham - Delph, Oldham - Stockport and Stockport-Stalybridge services plus some freight workings. After the Delph

Pilot duty was put in the Motor Link, a day's duty commenced with working the 8.05am Middleton Junction – Mumps passenger train, then the 9.15am Glodwick Road goods to Delph. The return run left Delph at around 11.00am and terminated at Lees. However, by the 1950s the diagram worked an Oldham-Delph and Delph-Oldham passenger train, then the 8.55am Oldham Glodwick Road to Delph goods. From Delph it worked to Mossley and back to Greenfield before finishing at Lees. The trip to Mossley was necessary in order to gain entry to the private sidings of Oswald McCardell & Co. Ltd., soap manufacturers, to drop Crosfields Chemical tanks from Warrington. Officially known as Royal George sidings, they were only accessible from the down Stalybridge-Huddersfield mainline. This diagram was being worked by Fairburn 2-6-4T's by the late 1950s. Another diagram was Oldham-Stockport-Greenfield in the morning, then Oldham-Greenfield-Oldham at lunchtime. The loco then ran light-engine to Stockport to work Stockport to Stalybridge, Stalybridge-Stockport, and Stockport-Greenfield.

The Stanier and Fairburn 2-6-4Ts had two diagrams on weekdays. One was Lees via Greenfield to Stalybridge, then passenger to Leeds and empty stock to Huddersfield. The loco worked Huddersfield-Stockport-Greenfield in the afternoon then returned to Lees shed. The second worked Stalybridge-Stockport-Manchester Victoria-Oldham Mumps in the morning. In the afternoon, it worked Oldham Clegg Street to Leeds City passenger, and then fish train to Manchester Exchange. One Saturday diagram was Greenfield-Stockport-

Manchester Victoria-Royton, then shed. After the opening of Clegg Street Parcels Depot, more locos were allocated to parcels services and they worked parcels to Stockport, Manchester Victoria, and Wakefield. One turn went light engine to Middleton and worked a passenger train to Victoria, then a parcels train via the Park Bridge line to Clegg Street.

The Fowler 0-8-0s and, later on, the WD Austerity 2-8-0s principal reason for being at Lees was for moving heavy freight from yard to yard and loop to loop, and heading endless clumping trains of forty or more wagons of coal across the north of England. In the early 1950s, the duties included:

1) Light engine Lees to Diggle to work 4.00am to Ashton Oldham Road. It then acted as pilot at Ashton before working 12.10pm to Oldham Glodwick Road.

2) Light engine Lees to Guide Bridge to work 11.20am to Stalybridge Millbrook with power station coal. Then 1.30pm empties Millbrook to Healey Mills. Light engine to Mirfield shed.

3) 10.35am Mirfield to Diggle and 2.20pm Diggle to Stalybridge (alternating with a Mirfield engine).

4) Micklehurst Pilot, then 12.40pm Greenfield to Healey Mills and 5.05pm Crofton to Diggle.

5) 5.05pm Lees to Heaton Norris (Jubilee Sidings), working nearly all sidings en route. Turning and watering at Stockport shed,.......................*continued on page 77*

continued on page 77

(Above) After the grouping of the railways in 1923, the LMS started allocating blocks of engines with consecutive running numbers to sheds. Ex-LNWR 'G1' 0-8-0s Nos 9288 – 9292 were based at Lees in 1928 and No 9297 had joined them by 1934. Lees' sphere of operation was wide for such a small shed. The Rowsley run, for instance, was a lodging turn until 1947, which involved working via Stockport and Buxton with an 0-8-0. Lees' No **9288** is seen on a down goods train near Chapel-en-le-Frith on 23rd May 1929. The engine appears to be struggling and the driver has gone forward to look at something between the frames. ***J M Bentley***

(Centre) The LNWR 'C' Class 0-8-0 locos had been fitted with larger boilers between 1906 and 1909 to produced the 'D'class, and one of these, No **1865**, was based at Lees in 1917 for long distance goods trains. Pictured here after rebuilding at an unknown location. This loco became No 9068 in LMS days. ***Real Photographs***

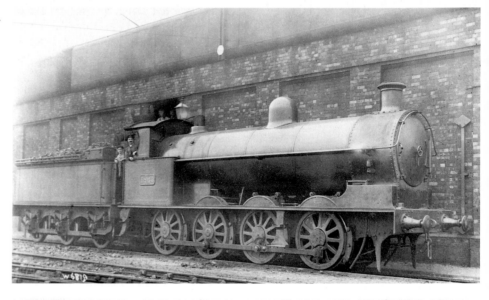

(Right) The Micklehurst Loop was no stranger to Lees men as they worked over the line calling at Millbrook and Uppermill sidings, generally with their largest freight engines. The line continued to see much goods and excursion traffic up until its closure as a through route in 1964. An unidentified LNWR 'G1' 0-8-0 wheezes its way towards Uppermill goods yard with an Eastbound goods train in June 1946. These rugged no-nonsense engines were an important class in LMS days. Their ability to handle heavy trains led the LMS to progressively develop the type through various rebuilds, and the boiler became the basis of the LMS standard class 7F 0-8-0. The latter design could have been very good had in not been stymied with inadequate axle boxes and springs. ***J Davenport***

(Right) Up until 1934, Lees had three LNWR '19inch' Goods 4-6-0 engines on its allocation, Nos 8857/58/59. The three 4-6-0s are the only locos of this wheel arrangement known to have been shedded here. No.8859 is seen at Springs Branch shed in March 1938. These engines were the goods equivalent of the 'Experiments' but whereas the latter had gone by 1935, the 19inch Goods didn't become extinct until 1950. ***Real Photographs***

......*continued from page 75*.........then 9.50pm Adswood to Oldham Glodwick Road and Greenfield.

6) 9.15pm Royton Junction to Moston and 3.35am Brewery to Royton Junction, via Rochdale in each direction.

These locos also had workings on the LYR Oldham-Rochdale line such as the 8.45pm Mumps to Royton Junction, 9.15pm to Moston via Rochdale and 1.10am Brewery Sidings to Mumps via Rochdale. There was also a travelling pilot diagram on the Micklehurst line between Stalybridge and Diggle. More work came in the form of Ashton Moss-Brindle Heath trips and pilot work, Woodstock sidings and Royton Junction, and materials into and out of Park Bridge iron works on the OA&GB line.

The LYR 0-6-0s and their Ivatt Class 2 2-6-0 replacements worked pilot duties at Mumps, Royton Junction and Shaw along with trip workings between each of these major sidings. They also worked 5.50am Glodwick Road-Diggle empties, shunted at Diggle and then worked the 11.00am Diggle to Glodwick Road freight. In the afternoon, they worked 3.10pm Glodwick

Road - Ashton Oldham Road freight, shunted in the Ashton area and returned light engine to Lees shed. The LYR 0-6-0s also had a passenger turn, the 7.40am Greenfield to Stockport, alternating Tuesday and Friday with a Stockport 4F 0-6-0. On arrival at Stockport the loco went light to Edgeley shed, did trip work in the area and returned next day with the 6.52pm Heaton Norris to Diggle freight.

Lees was a shed that worked many of its turns with other people's engines and the engine variety was quite astonishing under British Railways. Lees needed larger engines to work passenger specials to Blackpool, Morecambe, North Wales and Southport, and extra engines were always needed during Oldham Wakes holidays. The lines around Oldham were remarkable in having a multiplicity of loops, forks and spurs, giving alternative routes. These became exceedingly useful at Whitsuntide, and at the annual "Wakes" holidays, in that they allowed of excursion trains to Blackpool, Southport &c., to be

worked in either direction. The numerous "specials" could be worked either way, this traffic being operated with equal facility via Manchester or via Rochdale, Bury and Bolton. Thus, one series of trains started at Royton Junction calling at Mumps, Central, Werneth, and Hollinwood, and the other series started at Hollinwood, calling at the same stations in the opposite direction. Others took the Park Bridge line, which was always regarded as a valuable relief route in and out of Manchester. Sometimes, excursions were simply worked as far as Stockport or round the Oldham loop, stopping at selected stations until they reached Rochdale or Manchester Victoria. There the Lees engines were replaced by something more suitable for a long run. Since anything that could turn a wheel was deemed suitable for these short-haul jobs, the WD Austerity 2-8-0s regularly stretched their legs hauling passenger excursions around the Oldham 'loop'. The sight and sound of a WD 2-8-0 in harness with a LYR 0-6-0 in flight towards Rochdale will long remain in the memory of those who witnessed these trains! ....*concluded on page 78*

THE '19 INCH GOODS'

(Left) It is thought these LNWR 4-6-0s were used on the job to Mold Junction, but not surprisingly they were equally at home on passenger trains where high speed was not an essential requirement. No doubt Lees found their 4-6-0s very useful during 'Wakes' week for hauling the holiday crowds. This undated picture shows one-time Lees based No **8857** working a ten-coach train of mostly LYR non-corridor coaches over Lea Road water troughs in the 1930s. ***J M Bentley***

..........Special parcels trains were worked from Clegg Street Depot during the pre-Christmas period and when new mail order catalogues were being issued, and trains worked to Carlisle, Crewe, Shrewsbury, Willesden, Wigan and into Yorkshire, often with 'borrowed' engines. Special freight's worked to various places and an annual event was the concentration of loco coal in the Oldham area prior to the colliery holidays. There were a couple of booked Sunday turns for all manner of permanent way/engineering specials and 'ballasts', which were regularly worked by passed firemen. Passed cleaners were also called on to work the Sabbath, all of which served to fatten the pay packet. Retirement and difficulty in retaining young recruits led to rapid promotion from the late 1950s onwards, and cleaners did very little cleaning once they were passed out for footplate duty.

(Above) When control of Lees shed was transferred from the Western division to the Central Division and then became a sub-shed of Newton Heath, LYR 0-6-0s replaced the LNWR 'Cauliflowers' and LYR 2-4-2 tanks took over from the LNWR 0-6-2 'Watford Tanks'. LYR Class 2P 2-4-2T, now carrying BR number **50746**, passes Lees shed with LNWR Inspection Saloon No M45032 shortly after Nationalisation. This ex-WCJS carriage was one of three that were rebuilt for such duties in LMS days. Regarding the LYR 2-4-2Ts, the survival rate was high for a design dating back to 1889, with over 100 entering British Railways stock in 1948. *J Davenport*

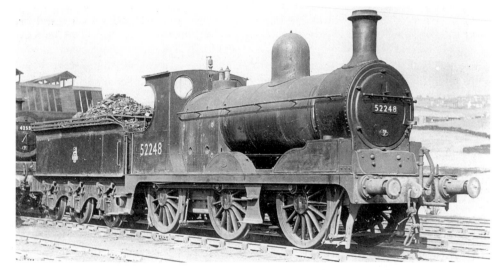

(Left) In later years Lees was really an LNWR outpost in LYR territory. The shed began its association with the LYR 'A' class 0-6-0s around 1934 when it received six of these engines. Lees also got some LYR shunting jobs in the early 1930s at places like Oldham Mumps, Royton Junction and Shaw. By the end of 1947 Lees had no less than ten LYR 0-6-0s, one of them being No 12248 seen here as renumbered by BR to **52248**. Pictured outside the shed together with newly arrived 2-6-4T No 42551 in the summer of 1952.

J Davenport

THE 'A' CLASS ON SHED

(Right) LYR 'A' class 0-6-0 No **52615** was originally an Aspinall round top firebox type that had been rebuilt with superheated Belpaire boiler. The chimney is set well forward in order to clear the superheater header. Still carrying its previous LMS ownership markings in 1952, it is pictured at Lees beside Stanier Class 8F 2-8-0 No **48500**, the first of the Darlington-built engines of 1944. The latter had arrived on shed from Longsight. *J Davenport*

(Above) Although LYR 0-6-0 No **52360** has a Belpaire boiler and resembles the loco in the previous picture, is not superheated. This 3F has obviously just come out of works after overhaul and repaint in BR plain black livery. It is standing on No.1 road with an old wagon of ash from numerous ash pans and smoke boxes. Behind the loco is the road running through the old corrugated coaling shelter and water tower. The shed roads were numbered 1 – 6 from the station side. After the rebuilding of the shed in 1955, No 1 road was truncated outside the shed to become a spare road for the ash-collecting wagon. The track through the water tower was removed along with the coaling shelter and the water tower was blocked up with sheets of corrugated iron. A new-elevated coaling stage was built more or less on the site of the old turntable road.

J Davenport

(Centre) Having just crossed over from the Down line, No **52389** is about to move forward on shed, but not before the footplate crew and a free-rider have had their photo taken. The loco has probably been working one of the pilot jobs at Mumps since the early hours and has arrived back at Lees in the late afternoon for disposal and bedding down. The date is April 1955.　　**J Davenport**

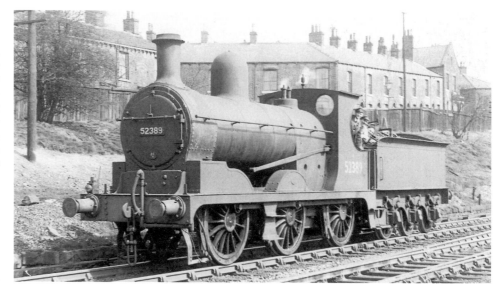

(Right-lower) The Lees breakdown train is about to go into action behind LYR 0-6-0 No **52365** in the early 1950s. The tender hand-brake is off, the regulator is open and the sound of steam can be heard rushing down internal passages, but nothing moves. A further yank on the regulator brings results as the chassis shudders and one of the coupling rods shoots to the end of its pin. As wheels begin to turn and pent-up steam escapes up the chimney, the ancient LYR 6-wheel coach tugs on the drawbar while its wheel flanges groan with torment on the sharp curves leading from the shed. Were off! The fitters were able to coax derailed engines back into the rails with just jacks and packing materials, which is all the coach carried.　　**J Davenport**

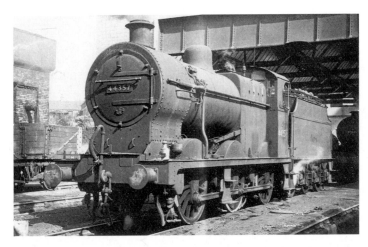

(Above) The Derby Four, or Fowler Class 4F 0-6-0 goods engine, was to the Midland what the 'A' class 0-6-0 was to the Lancashire & Yorkshire Railway. Construction of the 4F's continued up to 1941 until there were 772 of them. Longsight-based (9A) No.44357 was the first of twenty-four 4F's built by Andrew Barclay in 1926. The LH injector is on and the loco is being prepared for the road on track No 2 (old No 3 road) at Lees.

(Top right) I couldn't let this look at the LYR 'A' class 0-6-0s without mentioning a rather special member of the class, No **52322**, pictured in the afternoon sunshine at Lees. Instead of going for scrap after being withdrawn in 1960, the 0-6-0 was privately purchased by Fairclough's and stored near Chorley for eventual preservation at Steamtown, Carnforth. This loco was rather special to me too (LG) because I had the task of shovelling all the coal out of the tender. I supposed the tender was leaking at the time. It was all good arm-building exercise for a passed-cleaner!   *J Davenport*

(Centre-right) Twenty-two years after departing Lees shed, the work battered No 52322 (LYR No 1122) is seen again, this time fully restored and resplendent in Lancashire & Yorkshire livery as No 1300. It is pictured at Steamtown on 30th August 1982. This engine was one of the basic Aspinall round top boiler, saturated steam series introduced in 1889, and weighed in at 42 tons 3 cwt with a tractive effort of 21,130lb. Originally aquired by Civil Engineers Leonard Fairclough and stored in the depot at Adlington, Chorley, the locomotive, following restoration at Carnforth, has continued to perform continually ever since around the country on 'Heritage' lines, latterly in plain black livery as 52322 and based on the East Lancashire Railway at Bury.   *J Davenport*

ARRIVAL OF THE
'BREADVANS'

(Right) A major change in motive power occurred in 1939 when four push pull 'motor' fitted Fowler 2-6-2Ts, Nos 58-61, were transferred from Newton Heath to Lees to replace some of the LNWR 0-6-2 Coal Tanks on the Oldham - Greenfield - Delph services. No 58 was noted on such a working on 3rd April 1939., Nos 56 and 57 soon joined them. 4,000 was added to their numbers following nationalisation of the railways in 1948, and No **40056** is seen drawing an empty wagon off the 'turntable' road. This loco was the first to be transferred away from Lees on 14th August 1954 when the Ivatt Class 2MT 2-6-2Ts arrived. A 16ton mineral wagon is parked on the road leading through the water tower.
                                          J Davenport

(Right) Push-pull 'motor' fitted No **40057** and non-motor fitted 40014 are soaking up the mid morning sunshine on No.4 road. The BR lined black livery suited these locos well. Almost as interesting as the locomotives is the changing condition of the loco shed roof. It escaped the attentions of the German Luffwaffe, Doodlebugs and V2 rockets.

(Below-centre) The reason why No 40058 is missing is because its push pull equipment was fitted to No 40012, which then went to Lees while 40058 departed for Patricroft. Push pull fitted No **40012** passes Measurements Halt with a Delph to Oldham Clegg Street ....***continued below***

........train on a cold frosty morning in the earl 1950s. Interestingly, this loco is seen before it received an improved front end with large diameter chimney and a casing that incorporated the outside steam pipes and later form of vacuum controlled regulator gear.

(Right) Fowler push pull 2-6-2 tank No **40059** stands on number 6 road at Lees circa 1953. No 6 road was principally used for engine repairs so this engine is probably out of steam. Some restoration work has been done on the shed roof and it looks to be in reasonably good condition.

All (3); *J Davenport*

(Left) This similar view shows No 40060 on No 5 road, and once again one cannot ignore the condition of the roof! A new frame is in place ready to receive new timbers. No 40060 is still carrying a transitional livery incorporating LMS 1937 block style insignia in the 1950s.

(Centre) No 40060 is seen at a later date in BR lined black livery and the roof is still receiving some attention with new timbers already in place. These engines worked Oldham-Delph, Oldham-Stockport and Stockport - Stalybridge services. One diagram worked Oldham-Delph round trip, then 8.55am Oldham Glodwick Road - Delph - Mossley - Greenfield goods. Another diagram was Oldham-Stockport-Greenfield in the morning, then Oldham-Greenfield-Oldham at lunch time. Then light engine to Stockport to work Stockport to Stalybridge and return, then Stockport-Greenfield

(Bottom of page) Fowler 2-6-2T No 40061 was the sixth member of the class at Lees fitted for push-pull 'motor' working and was used principally on Oldham-Greenfield-Delph services. The nickname 'bread-vans' has already been alluded to, but they were also known, with some irony, as 'novelties'. No 40061 was an early BR repaint and received 'LNWR' style lining with the full British Railways insignia in use before the familiar Lion & Wheel totem was adopted. In contrast to previous locos in this class, this engine has visible snap-head rivets on its tanks and bunker rather than the flushed and countersunk type. This may have been a cost-cutting measure instigated by Stanier when he took over as CME after Fowler. The ash pit road must be busy because the loco is having its fire cleaned out on the 'tuntable' road. Prominent in the background of this April 1952 view is the corrugated iron coaling shelter and class 7F 0-8-0 No 49509.   All (3); *J Davenport*

(Right) After water has been taken, the fire, ash pan and smokebox cleaned out, and the bunker coaled in readiness for its next job, No **40061** has been moved to No.5 road. Rather unusually, the 6-wheel breakdown/tool van has been placed on No.6 shed road while a wagon of bricks has taken possession of the track on which the van is normally kept. This ex-LYR coach was later replaced by an ex-Midland clerestory bogie coach, which in turn was replaced by an ex-LNWR bogie coach. *J Davenport*

(Centre) When No **40061** went back into works in 1953, it was again given a repaint, and this is the result, looking very smart indeed in BR lined black with early totem. The sight of these little engines in Oldham started my (LG) lifelong interest in the products of Derby. And doesn't the shed roof look smart too! This picture is proof, if any were needed, that the roof was in fact repaired at some point. It is quite possible it caught fire after being repaired and was then removed completely in 1955. No view of Lees shed yard at this period is complete without a Fowler '7F' 0-8-0, in this instance No 49618. *J Davenport*

(Below) Fowler 2-6-2T No **40062** departs Lees with M47 saloon No.3423 and driving trailer No.3414 push pull coaches on an Oldham Clegg Street to Greenfield working in 1953. This loco was not fitted with vacuum regulator control and could not work these coaches in push pull mode, nevertheless, it was pressed into service when required. *J Davenport/E M Johnson collection*

LEES

7F 0-8-0's
ON
LEES SHED

(Right) There was a change on the freight side at Lees in July 1939 when the LNWR class G1 0-8-0s Nos 9288 – 92/97 were transferred to Wakefield and replaced by five LMS Standard Class 7F 0-8-0s, Nos 9508/09/11 /93/96. Class 'G1' No **9292** is pictured at Lees on 30th July 1933, with a further six years of activity at Lees ahead of it.
J M Bentley

(Below) After Lees' allocation of LNWR 0-8-0s were transferred away in 1939, the Fowler Class 7F 0-8-0s were destined to be the mainstay of the shed's freight operations for the next eighteen years. This pleasing study of one of my (LG) all-time favourite classes shows No 49662 in residence at Lees, circa 1954. These engines had a boiler that was based on the LNWR G2 boiler married to a modern 'engine' portion with Walschaerts valve gear, long lap long travel valves and multi-ring pistol valve heads. They should have been a sure-fire winner, but the combination of high piston thrust combined with high axle box loadings simply overwhelmed the grossly inadequate axle boxes. As a result, these strong engines became badly run down very quickly after passing through works for overhaul, and 70% of the class had gone for scrap by 1951. It was a great pity. They were well proportioned and looked very impressive.
J Davenport

(Right) Fowler class 7F No 49618 arrived at Lees from Mirfield (25D) in May 1951 and stayed until December 1957. This class of 175 engines was built between 1929 and 1931 during the depression years, and their overall appearance was entirely Derby inspired with the usual unfussy appearance and Fowler details. Whereas LNWR 0-8-0s waddled along, the progress of a Fowler 7F was smooth, its 18ft 3in long coupling rods appearing to move up and down with the deliberations of a whales tail. Anyone who saw these engines at work, their progress marked by huge columns of smoke, cannot fail to have been impressed. On the other hand, the cabs were very small and footplate men considered there was more room in an Austin Seven, a popular small car of the 1930s, hence the nickname 'Austin Sevens'. *J Davenport*

'AUSTIN' SEVENS

(Left) Fowler 7F No **49608** has been put out at the back of the shed near Den field, an exposed place if ever there was one. This track was unofficially known as No 7, and engines that were well run down and due for overhaul were usually left here in steam, ready to haul the breakdown van if it was required to attend some minor derailment. The modern canteen/mess room can be seen behind the tool van. *J Davenport*

(Right) At the opposite side of the yard from No 7 road was the former 'turntable' road, on this occasion occupied by 'Austin Seven' No **49563**, LYR 'A' class 0-6-0s No 52365, while another 'A' class is down by Greaves Street allotments. This track was a convenient place to clean out the grate if the ash pit road was fully occupied. Fowler 2-6-2T No 40056 is on shed. The track leading off to the left led to the coal stack. *J Davenport*

(Right) Stanier 'Big Tank' Class 4P 2-6-4T No **42551** was allocated to Lees shed in 1953 to supplement the smaller Fairburn 2-6-4Ts Nos. 42114/5. These engines worked two weekday diagrams, leaving one loco spare, one being Lees via Greenfield to Stalybridge, then passenger to Leeds and empty stock to Huddersfield. The afternoon working was Huddersfield-Stockport-Greenfield, then shed. The second diagram worked Stalybridge-Stockport-Manchester Victoria-Oldham Mumps in the morning. No.42551 is seen leaving Lees with the afternoon working; the 4.52pm Oldham Clegg Street to Leeds City, from where it will work a fish train back to Manchester Exchange. The coaches on this occasion are a LNWR brake third, LMS composite and LMS brake third, all non-corridor stock. *J Davenport*

(Centre) Fairburn Class 4P 2-6-4T No **42115** is seen on the Standedge mainline at Grasscroft after dropping off Crossfield Chemical Tanks at the Royal George sidings of Oswald McCardell & Co. Ltd soap manufacturers. This turn started as the Delph Goods. It then worked to Mossley and shunted there before calling at Royal George Sidings, which were only accessible from the Down Stalybridge-Huddersfield mainline. Author LG had been out photographing trains around Greenfield in March 1961 and got a lift back to Lees on 42115. These engines were a slightly shorter and no-frills version of the Stanier 2-6-4T, though no less capable. No 42114 and 42115 were allocated to Low Moor (25F) before arriving at Lees. *L Goddard*

Ominously, the date is Friday the 13th May 1955, and with the shed roof gone, demolition looks to be in progress at Lees! In fact, there is much going on at this time and the shed yard track layout is in the process of some reorganisation. Changes to achieve more efficient operational patterns had already been carried out when the coaling shelter between ash pit road and No.1 road was removed along with the track through the water tower, and replaced with a wagon slope to a new coaling facility. Ivatt Class 2P 2-6-2T No **41281** stands 'outside' the shed extreme left. Under the revised layout, this track would be slewed over to make a new connection with tracks to the coaling stage and siding, while No 1 road beside the ash pit road would terminate outside a yet-to-be-built shed wall to became a short siding. 2-6-4T No **42551** stands on No 2 road and 0-8-0 No **49536** is on No 3 together with two 'A' class 0-6-0s. Another 0-8-0 is on No 5 road. This view affords a clear view of Austerlands, which lies atop the hill, along with the 'Big Chimney'. The picture was taken two weeks after the demise of 'Delph Donkey' services. *J Wells collection*

(Right) Push-pull fitted Ivatt Class 2MT 2-6-2T No **41280** stands amid its new surroundings at Lees in August 1954 following transfer from Fleetwood (24F). This engines new line of work on 'Delph Donkey' services would be far removed from running push pull trains between Fleetwood and Blackpool North. After Oldham-Delph services finished, No 41280 would leave Lees for Chester shed in December 1955.

MIXED TRAFFIC
2-6-2 T's

(Left) Sister engine No **41281** arrived at Lees from Fleetwood on 11 September 1954. These engines were small but strong and were known on some parts of BR as 'Mickey Mouses'. It is seen in the siding beside the coal store while the wagon ramp can be seen to the right of the engine. A LNWR 'G2' 0-8-0 stands beside the new coaling shelter Just visible immediately behind the loco bunker is the entrance and path from St.John Street to the loco shed.

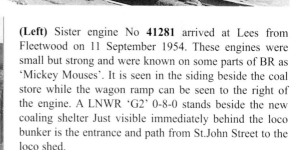

(Below) BR Standard 2-6-2T No **84015** arrived at Lees with 84010 and 84012. It is seen beside one of the two 'breadvans' (Nos 40014 and 40062) that remained at Lees after the six push pull variants had been transferred to Hull. No 84015 later carved out a new career at Fleetwood (24F).

(Above) Modernity in the shape of rocking grates/ash pans came late in the day to Lees shed but, needless to say, the men whose task it was to dispose engines welcomed the innovation with open arms. This BR version of the Ivatt 2-6-2T also arrived in 1954 to finally oust the 'breadvans'. Push pull fitted Standard Class 2MT 2-6-2T No **84012** is moving off shed over the public crossing that led from Station Street to Lees station in April 1955. It would be transferred to Rose Grove (24B) on 21st May 1955.

All (4); *J Davenport*

The icy wind of change arrived at Lees metaphorically and literally in December 1957 as the Fowler 7F 0-8-0s, which had handled the heavy freight diagrams for so long, were replaced by Austerity Class 8F 2-8-0s. This rural outpost was regularly assailed by snow and No **90306** looks as if it has been in conflict with a snowdrift! Sub-freezing weather conditions such as this took its toll as people stoked up their fires in an effort to keep warm within the home and unconsciously added yet more pollution to the freezing misery outside. The men of Lees were a hardy race, even so, the shed would be short-staffed at times like these and sick notes would continue to arrive on the foreman's desk until the thaw. *J Davenport*

There was some disbelief at Lees when Austerity 2-8-0 No **90589** arrived in December 1957 from the Western Region. The stores had to stock additional parts because this loco had been well and truly 'Swindonised' with Swindon boiler fittings and lamp brackets. This meant that Lees' normal lamps, when mounted on this loco, faced sideways instead of forward! The loco was thus given a duplicate set of London Midland Region lamp brackets on the footplate and smokebox door. Nevertheless, 90589's stay was short and it left for pastures new in July 1958. Having just come on shed, the loco will have just taken water while someone removes unwanted ash and clinker from the firebox. It would have to reverse over the ash pit to have its ash pan raked out and then go for coaling before being placed on one of the five shed roads. *J Davenport*

(Right) The Austerity 2-8-0s were useful machines and their tasks were many and varied working heavy goods, pick-up goods and on shunting duties. They also got in some passenger haulage during the Oldham Wales holiday period and Bank holidays. Lees-based No **90306** is passing Heyside with a Shaw to Blackpool excursion, calling at all stations as far as Manchester Victora. It would return light engine to Lees via Park Bridge. The coaches are no less interesting. The first three are MR Bain arc roof stock led by a Sheffield District 8ft 6ins wide brake third and two 9ft wide all-thirds. The remainder are elliptical roof non-corridor coaches of LMS and LNWR origins. *J Davenport*

(Below) Austerity No **90525** was allocated to Lees from June 1958 until the shed's closure in April 1964, and is seen between Royton Junction and Shaw working the 2pm Hollinwood-Moston freight with Driver R. Barratt of Lees in charge. Built for the Second World War effort, they had driving wheels with solid cast balance weights which made no provision for balancing the reciprocating masses but gave freedom from hammer-blow. For wartime service on track not in the best of condition, the lack of hammer blow was an advantage at a time when speed restriction not particularly important. It was all a different matter in peacetime when speeds increased and the unbalanced reciprocating masses resolved into large fore-and-aft forces, especially at speeds above 35mph. This fore and after movement between loco and tender was both noisy and uncomfortable. It would alternate with lateral swinging, which could bruise the ribs if one was unwise enough to sit down, or worse, fill the footplate with coal. The loud clanking of an Austerity running light to or from the shed was a familiar sound around Lees in the later 1950s. *J Davenport*

(Right) Diggle Junction in all its glory in the late 1930s with a LMS 'Black Five' 4-6-0 departing Diggle Station on a non-corridor train. It is about to pass more carriages stored in the goods yard together with a handful of wagons. In contrast, the marshalling yards on the left are full of brake vans and coal wagons, many in LMS pre-1936 livery with large letters. The LNER and GWR are also well represented in their later liveries and small lettering. The track, which is quite a complicated formation squeezed into a short space, is designed to allow trains to cross from the original Saddleworth line onto the Micklehurst Loop line and vice-versa. There are also passing loops to accommodate quite lengthy trains as well as connections to three separate siding complex.

E M Johnson collection

(Below) Lees-based Austerity 2-8-0 No **90671** shunts wagons of coal in the goods yard at Diggle Junction while a BR Standard Class 5 No **73164** passes with a Leeds-Manchester semi-fast in the early 1960s. This train is taking the original route via Saddleworth, the crossovers to the Micklehurst Loop line being in the foreground. Diggle Station platforms can just be seen in the background. The sidings behind the signal box are empty, a far cry from earlier years when they were often full of coal wagons and carriages there for winter storage or use on local lines at Bank holidays. *J Davenport*

(Right) Longsight based LMS Stanier class 8F 2-8-0 No **48165** is being coaled at the new coaling platform before working the 10.22am Diggle-Mold Junction as far as Warrington. On the previous day, Lees crews would have used it to work the 5.20am Guide Bridge-Millbrook and the 1.31pm Millbrook-Healey Mills. It was then stabled at Mirfield before working freight back to Diggle then light engine to Lees shed. For a short period in 1947, Lees shed had its own allocation of Stanier 8F locos, LMS Nos 8425, 8444 and 8446, which it used on the Crofton coal workings. To make it look as if Lees really needed them, they also appeared on two-coach trains between Oldham and Greenfield! *J Davenport*

(Centre) Longsight-based Hughes 'Crab' 2-6-0 No **42772** has a good head of steam and is being prepared on the short siding that had once been No.1 road at Lees. The most striking feature of these engines was the raised running plate and large cylinders, features that conjured up images of a crab with large claws, hence the nickname. *J Davenport*

(Below) Lees was used to playing host to Eastern Region locos such as Class B1 4-6-0s and Class K3 2-6-0s, but this Class 04/8 2-8-0 was a real rare bird. No **63653** is cautiously reversing up to the coaling stage in the late 1950s. It carries the post 1956 totem on its tender and has obviously received a recent overhaul and repaint. It has no shed plate so it may be en route to a new home. This loco was a Thompson rebuild of a GCR O4 in 1947, with a Diagram 100A boiler and a new double side window cab. The boiler had been introduced in 1942 for the Class B1; however, its working pressure was reduced to 180lb when used in Class 04/8. They had the distinction of being the last engines of GCR design to be withdrawn in April 1966, and were amongst the last steam locomotives in the Eastern Region. *J Davenport*

WORKING AT LEES

BY LARRY GODDARD

(Above) This is Lees shed, or to give its correct title, Lees Motive Power Depot, as I knew it when working there as a passed-cleaner in 1960. My youthful days of gazing at engines from the fence in Den field may have been behind me, but the old buzz was still there when working around them. Lees shed was basically a servicing area and base for an allocation of engines, which were balanced to operate the type of traffic that originated or had to be managed in that area. Its main occupation was one of servicing and the shed track layout was designed to permit the locomotive a smooth passage. On entering the shed complex, the loco usually went straight onto the ash pit road to take water and have its grate, ash pan and smokebox cleared of ash and other detritus. Then it would go to be coaled and then stabled on shed or placed on preparation pits ready for further duty. The whole fire would be removed if the loco was due for boiler washout and it would be set aside to cool down. Running repairs were carried out as necessary in between trips, based on driver's reports. Fitters had the use of lathes, drilling machines and other equipment to speed up repairs. This view of Lees was taken on 22nd June 1960. Far left is the 'coaling plant' where locomotives were hand-coaled from wagons standing on top of the wagon slope. This facility was built in the early 1950s when changes were made in order to achieve more efficient operation. Previously, coaling was undertaken on track that ran right through the water tower, the structure seen next to the coaling stage. In front of the water tower is the ash pit road where engine disposal took place. Ash from this pit would be loaded into the wagon standing alongside. A sand-drying plane stood just inside the shed plus piles of cast iron brake blocks. The shed had five roads plus offices at the bottom end for the foreman, clerical staff and fitters. A booking-on office and pay office stood to the right of the other offices while stores and oil were kept in outbuildings. The track on the right stored the tool van, behind which can be seen the mess/canteen. *G Whitehead*

Three years spent at the Oldham Municipal School of Arts & Crafts on Union Street from the age of thirteen to sixteen should have led to further training at Manchester Art College; however, it soon became clear my parents preferred me to start bringing in an income. Art qualifications and the school's 'Sidney Andrews' award would not be necessary for the labouring jobs I would be undertaking, so I decided to turn a handicap into an advantage and only do the jobs that took my fancy. These included firing locomotives and working on the buses, and by the age of thirty, being my own boss.

My first job was in Designs Reproduction at the Calico Printers Association in Manchester, but the call of the outdoors came when Spring arrived and I got a job at Manchester Victoria Parcels Depot delivering railway parcels around Salford. My driver, a great guy by the name of Henry Chew, dropped me off early several days a week so I could dash home to play piano with a local rock band while he went off to unload the van on his own at Manchester Central. Commuting by rail to Manchester all the while enabled me to keep in touch with the railway scene, which for the most part was steam, but in 1960, I decided to apply for a railway job at Lees Motive Power Depot.

A feeling of excitement was tinted with nervousness that spring morning as I walked between the rows of simmer-ing engines, which looked so gargantuan from ground level! Like many other loco depots, Lees found new recruits hard to come by as people looked for cleaner jobs so maybe I was a welcome sight at the Shed Forman's office that morning. Following a medical and eyesight test at Hunts Bank, Manchester, it was a case of being thrown in at the deep end, cleaning engines and shovelling ash out of the disposal pits. Training for footplate work took place at Bolton loco depot. Each morning for two weeks, I met up with a handful of other trainees and a Training Inspector at Manchester Victoria for the train journey to Moses Gate station. From there, we walked through the sidings to Bolton shed while the Inspector pointed out various railway operations on a daily basis. We discovered that firemen of LYR 0-6-0 Saddle Tanks used short handled shovels because of limited footplate space, that connections and jumper cables on push pull coaches were painted different colours, and that heavy-handed shunts had a habit of propelling wagons over the top of buffer stops!

We were expected to absorb a general knowledge of signalling, Notices, Rules, regulations, and locomotive parts, while firing lessons and changing a boiler water gauge glass were part of the hands-on training. Lessons on controls-recognition took place on rusty out-of-service Fowler class 3 2-6-2Ts and 'Austin Seven' 0-8-0s before we were let loose on engines in steam. Sheer enthusiasm and my ability to shovel coal around the firebox of an Austerity 2-8-0 with the dexterity of a champion seemed to impress our instructor so I did not tell him I was left-handed. In case the reader is wondering what being left-handed has got to do with it, most ex-LMS engines were left-hand drive so the fireman was on the right hand side firing left-handed whereas right-handed men had to learn to fire left-handed. As might be expected, the instructor was not taken in by my performance and so comeuppance arrived when the he took me aboard a right hand drive engine. My determination to fire it left-handed was matched by his equal determination that I was not, which he enforced by kicking my backside every time it faced in his direction!

Examinations were held at Bury loco depot, then we caught a local train from Bury to Rochdale headed by a Fowler Class 2P 4-4-0, but before departing Bury I was instructed to climb aboard the engine and watch everything the fire-man did. With the breeze blowing through my hair and my ears tuned to the rhythmic clanking of the coupling rods and chirruping snifter valves, this first trip was an experience I will never forget. As well as doing a spot of firing and working the injectors, I felt king of the road as we entered platforms packed with workers eager to get home. It was the one and only time I fired on a passenger turn.

Back at Lees, I received a pay-docket, joined a Trades Union and was ready for action! Passed-Cleaners spent a large proportion of their time working through the night with only one week in eight on days because the clocking-on time moved forward four hours every week. In addition, our night foreman, who I only knew as Jock, was very persuasive in getting me to work on Sundays as well. By its very nature, much of the work in an engine shed..........**continued on page 95**

continued on page 95

One of my first tasks at Lees was shovelling ash and clinker out of the ash pit, which I suppose was like asking nurses to empty bedpans on their first day to see if they'll stick the job! Engines came on to this pit for fire dropping and smokebox cleaning. Hosing down this mess of hot ash and clinker made it even more sulphurous and unbearable as the backbreaking task of throwing it up from the pit to the ground began. Such piles of ash can be seen beside of LYR 'A' class No **52248**. The ash had then to be hoisted again into the waiting wagon. By the way, the opening of that heavy metal door on the 16ton mineral wagon was carried out with caution if one was to avoid a nasty injury as it rebounded off its doorstop. Such labour was endless but it was part and parcel of an engine shed. No **52275**, seen in the background, came to Lees in August 1960. This picture was taken in May 1961. *A Brown*

(Right) Another early morning shot, this time taken on the footplate of an LYR 'A' class 0-6-0. I have my hand on the regulator while attempting to look awake and intelligent after an eight-hour shift that commenced at midnight. Home and bed was beckoning, but my colleague had just booked on and was brimming with enthusiasm! To help the reader understand the footplate of an engine, the first duty of a fireman on joining his engine is to check the water gauges (those two vertical rectangular glasses below the regulator) and notice the steam pressure (right hand gauge above my hand). He then levels the fire to create more heat and raise the steam pressure, to enable the injectors to be tested as early as possible. Injectors put water in the boiler. To do this, water is first turned on via a water-regulator handle before the steam valve (the wheel just below the LH gauge glass) is turned on, then the flow is controlled with the aforementioned water regulator handle until water ceases to spill out onto the track below the cab and a hollow sucking sound is heard instead. He should then look inside the firebox (the firebox door handle is on the quadrant below the steam injector wheel) to check that the fusible plugs, tubes, brick arch and the fire hole deflector plate are in good order. While building up the fire, the damper should be open and blower (handle immediately below the regulator) carefully applied to avoid smoke.

L Goddard collection

(Right-centre) I took this picture from one of the shed road pits at about 6.30 in the morning after checking the ash pan had been cleared out. I was going out on one of the Austerity 2-8-0s and had been drawing tools, detonators and flags from stores as well as busying myself preparing the fire and filling sandboxes. The goods shed and signalbox are barely visible in the early morning haze. *L Goddard*

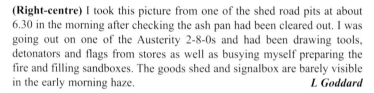

.................was heavy so new recruits soon built up a sturdy back and strong leg and arm muscles especially while assisting the disposal team. If a footplate crew had run out of hours when arriving on shed with their loco, it was left to the disposal men to clean out the fire grate, ash pan and smoke box. To clean out the grate, large tongues were used to ease three very hot 3ft long fire bars from their seating and haul them through the firehole door onto a metal part of the footplate. The clinker and poor parts of the fire were then raked through the resultant hole into the ash pan. That was the hot part of the job. The next part involved climbing down into the ash pit below the engine and removing blazing ash and dust with a long rake, all very messy especially in eddying winds. Finally, ash was shovelled out of the smokebox and the whole footplate was swept clean.

The LYR 'A class' 0-6-0s did mainly 'pilot' jobs shunting the goods yards at Oldham Mumps, Clegg Street, Glodwick Road, Royton Junction and Diggle. I enjoyed these jobs during day-light hours but less so at night. It was necessary to watch out for instructions from lamp-waving yardmen but in pouring rain such vigilance was guaranteed to lead to a partial soaking no matter what type of loco one was on, but more so on an 'A' class 0-6-0. If the tarpaulin stretched between engine and tender happened to crease during a shunting manoeuvre, several pints of rainwater could be dumped onto an unwary footplate crew. When this occurred, shunting was punctuated by periods of drying off, cursing, playing cards and drinking stewed tea in a yard cabin.

One Saturday dinnertime, we were about to take our LYR 0-6-0 back to Lees after several hours shunting at Clegg Street when we were approached by someone from the signal box to work overtime. Some urgently needed parcels vans had to be collected from sidings west of Manchester Exchange, so after some argument we set off via the Park Bridge line for the big city. A pilot man came aboard at Manchester Victoria and expressed some surprise at our elderly steed, which he considered was unsuitable for the task. Fortunately he jumped off as we returned through Victoria with the coaches and vans and we rushed Miles Platting bank for all we were worth. I ended up in the drivers place while he did what he could with the fire but we eventually reached Miles Platting and headed off towards Ashton while I looked for coal at the back of the tender! We were stopped at Ashton Charlestown so I acted on the driver's instruction to look inside the smoke box seeing as the whole front end was encased in a heat shimmer. The bottom of the smoke box door was glowing as I attempted to release the dog clips to open it. Accumulated ash was up to the blast pipe, which was my fault for not emptying the smoke box before we left for Manchester. The ash was shovelled out as quickly as possible before we got the 'peg' for Diggle. Job done, we left the engine on the ash pit, booked off and headed for home. The old engine looked forlorn and lifeless when I booked on at 8am the following Monday........

...........*continued on page 97*

(Above) A line-up of Lees Motive Power depot employees in front of a Class 3MT 2-6-2T 'breadvan' in the early 1950s. This picture allows us a clear view of the vacuum controlled regulator gear on the side of the smokebox, which was used while working of the 'Delph Donkey' push-pull trains. If memory serves me correctly, the gentleman on the left is the shed master or shed foreman, and is the person I spoke to when applying for a job at Lees. The other people appear to be fitters but I have been unable to discover any of their names.
J Davenport

(Left) Another Lees staff line-up taken after the construction of the new loco coaling facility and before renewal of the shed roof. From left to right: Steam raiser W.Lee, passed fireman P Clarke, Driver F Fisher, Passed Fireman H Smith and fireman C Ravey. *J Davenport*

(Right) It was not unusual for me to be assigned to assist the steam raiser on nights, a kindly but firm one-eyed man by the name of Mr Lee. It was our job to light fires in 'cold' engines, raise steam, and act as shed-turner. Being shed-turner meant driving engines off the ash pit road to the coaling stage, and when this was completed, stabling them on one of the shed roads in readiness for the next duty or whatever. I took this picture, a fireman's eye view if you like, during a pause whilst moving Austerity Class 8F No **90402**. Despite it being taken straight into the early morning sun, there is a clear view of the yard head shunt, the running lines under Oldham Road Bridge and the east end of goods yard in which container wagons can just be seen.
L Goddard

(Left) I am glad this picture was taken in late 1960 as, although I did not know it at the time, Austerity No **90708** would be the very last engine to leave Lees shed when it closed in 1964. I had been up on the tender taking water from the tank above and we were about to go off on one of those duties that kept me so busy it left me wondering where we were half the time. I also remember trying to avoid driving rain as we ran tender first from Castleton towards Manchester, and wishing I was somewhere else… like the Royal Oak, The Oldham Hotel, Grapes, Albion, Yates's Wine Lodge etc, etc.,
L Goddard collection

.........*continued from page 95*

On late turns, I was often assigned to assist the steam raiser, a kindly but firm one-eyed man who had been injured while a driver. We lit the fires and prepared engines for duty by raising steam and checking boiler water levels. Acting as 'shed-turner' gave me the opportunity to drive the engines from the disposal pit to the coaling plant. After coaling was completed, I moved the engine onto one of the shed roads and chalked its position on a large blackboard on the shed wall. One afternoon, I drove an Austerity 2-8-0 to the bottom of the yard, then wound the reverse gear just beyond the halfway point, and dropped off to change the points before the engine stopped and slowly lumbered back to me on its own. I thought it was such a smart move, but sheds have eyes and a senior driver asked me if I had considered what would have happened if I had failed to get back on board the passing engine. We discussed the destruction and injury a runaway engine could have caused then in a final deflationary note, he told me it was an old trick!

One night, I noticed the nearby sidings were filled with new Diesel Multiple units. They were in need of some remedial work and Newton Heath had decided the pits at Lees shed were the ideal place to carry it out. While the work was being done, our steam locos remained parked all over the yard, to the annoyance of fitters and the poor steam-raiser who had a natural animosity to Newton Heath. On the subject of shift work, night work does not come naturally to everyone. Fortunately, there was a relaxed attitude towards taking a bit of shut-eye in the warmth of the canteen, however, if the canteen stove was to go out while one was asleep, it was regarded as an act of treason.

In an era when most houses had coal fires, there was a tendency for coal to fall off engines at certain well-defined locations. One such location existed on the approach to a certain closed station occupied by a local engine driver. Timing was all-important when heaving a huge lump of coal off the footplate while travelling at speed, and my first attempt sent it scurrying across the station platform towards the buildings whereupon it demolished a door and entered the drivers' home quite un-announced!

.............*continued on page 99*

Here we have two views of Lees taken nine years apart. The upper picture was taken on 4th June 1950. On the left is the coaling shelter and water tower. The shed roof is clearly in need of attention. One LYR 0-6-0 is visible plus no less than six Fowler class 3MT 2-6-2 tanks, including the two non-push pull fitted examples, and three Fowler 7F 0-8-0s. Lees may have been a LNWR shed in LYR territory, but the presence of so many Derby designed locos at this period gave it the appearance of being in MR territory! Life on a running shed was often dirty, though no more so than many other jobs in heavy engineering, and so the old tin bathtub saw plenty of action mid-week in addition to traditional Sunday nights! This picture conjures up much that I remember of Lees, a Pennine village that smelled of damp plus the unique blend of hot oil, steam and smoke that only a steam railway shed could convey. The shed was a world apart that railwaymen understood, enthusiasts flocked to like a magnet, and women considered a pain in the neck especially on washday!

B Hilton

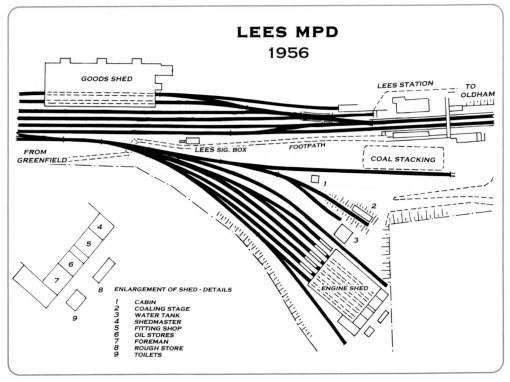

What a difference. Lees shed looks almost new in this June 1959 view. The hole in the water tower is boarded up following removal of track. A cement mixer is in use close by, perhaps putting a new floor in the ash pit. A wagon stands on the old No.1 road, while the locos on view from left to right are an 'Austerity' 2-8-0, an LYR 0-6-0, a withdrawn Fowler 0-8-0 behind it, another LYR 0-6-0 and two BR class 3 2-6-2 tanks Nos 84013 and 84014. An ex-Midland clerestory bogie coach has replaced the sheds old LYR tool van.

J Wells collection

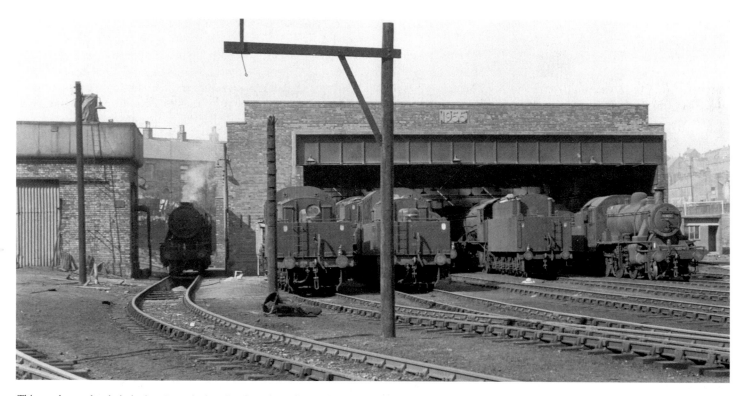

This one last melancholy look at Lees shed on Sunday 5th April 1964 just one week before closure and showing the changed order of things. The hangman's type post in the foreground (one of two) were put up sometime after 1961. I have been unable to establish their intended purpose. Most of the engines appear to be dead apart from an Austerity 8F 2-8-0 simmering by the water tower. Ivatt Class 2MT 2-6-0s dominate the scene, having taken over from the LYR 'A' Class 0-6-0s when the last of these old engines was withdrawn from Lees in October 1962 (52456 and 52275). The engines on shed are Fairburn 2-6-4Ts Nos 42079, 42115 and 42183, Ivatt 2-6-0s Nos.46419, 46449, 46452, 46484/5/6/7, and Austerity 2-8-0s Nos 90525, 90708 and 90718. After No 90708 departed on an Ashton Moss-Brindle Heath working on the Saturday night, the last moments of Lees as a working shed passed during the long night of 11th April 1964.   *P Hutchinson*

...........*continued from page 97*

A variety of firing turns came my way, including the evening Clegg Street to Mirfield parcels, which always drew one of the 2-6-4 Tanks. I recall the driver handing me a rag to tie around my mouth before we entered the 3-mile long Standedge tunnel while at the same time telling me to watch the injector did not knock off while in the tunnel. On another occasion we took a borrowed 'Black Five' 4-6-0 to Ashton Oldham Road goods yard, probably to hide it until required. It was a veritable Rolls Royce compared to one of our rough-riding Austerity 2-8-0s. When trip working materials to Park Bridge iron works, a quaint self-propelled crane belonging to the works occasionally met us to collect the wagons. Regrettably, my hopes of being assigned to the Delph pilot job and so a footplate trip down the Delph branch never materialized. With no hint of impending change, this way of life seemed as if it would go on forever.

Mary, my soon-to-be-wife, had expressed reservations about the railway and its unsocial working hours on several occasions so I eventually caved in and applied for a job with Oldham

Corporation as a bus conductor, or Guard as they were known in Oldham. Two weeks on 'probation' learning the ropes was followed by extreme good fortune, which to cut a long story short, meant me avoiding C-Group and W-Group, responsible for the busy Waterhead-Manchester route and Grotton-Lees-Hollinwood route. The following Monday I was given a 'Temporary track' in G-group with driver Cyril Caine. This group mainly worked the Limited Stop (express) services from Greenfield, Uppermill and Delph to Manchester, but as this provided insufficient work to fill a 31-week rota, G-group also worked miscellaneous turns on just about every other route in Oldham, which gave members very wide route knowledge. This temporary track became permanent and I remained on the 'expresses' until mid-1965. It was while working the 153 Uppermill Circular that we occasionally saw the 'Delph Goods' meandering down the branch to Delph. One morning, Cyril noticed the doors at Delph Station were open so we both took an inquisitive look inside the building while bemused passengers sat with their noses pressed against the windows! Waybills were

strewn around the place, but there was none of the reckless destruction of property that one has come to expect today. When Oldham's first brand-new Atlantean bus arrived, I was excused duty at the wishes of Manager Harry Taylor so I could take a canteen chair to the back of the garage to prepare a drawing of the new bus. The Oldham busmen, right up to Chief Inspector, were a good crowd to work with and I spent 4 1/2 enjoyable years on the Corporation. It would have been longer had not Mary and I took the decision to leave Oldham with our two children in 1965 to start a new life in North Wales.

Living at the seaside and spending ones summer holidays in Oldham became a regular, if eccentric, event on the 1970s. One reason for this was I owned a 1952-built double deck bus (SHMD No.61) which was stored along with other buses in a mill beside Greenfield Viaduct on the erstwhile Micklehurst Loop line. I had a licence to drive public service vehicles and the intention was to run enthusiast trips around Stalybridge, Hyde, Mossley and Dukinfield, areas in which the bus had once operated, but my enthusiasm for the venture waned and the bus was sold.

The Conservative government published its Beeching Report on 25 March 1963, which happened to be my 21st birthday, to map out a ruthless and inconsiderate future for British Railways. The Delph branch closed on 2nd November 1963 while the Oldham Branch to Greenfield, together with Lees shed, closed less than a year later on 11th April 1964. The last engine off Lees was Austerity No. 90708 on an Ashton Moss to Brindle Heath trip working. Officially, the shed closed on 13th April 1964 when the engine crews reported for duty at Newton Heath shed. The Conservatives were narrowly defeated in the general election of that year, but the Labour government continued with the Beeching proposals and was responsible for all closures that took place after October 1964.

Oldham Clegg Street station closed when passenger services over the OA&GB finished on 2 May 1959, but the line remained in use for freight and the parcels traffic. Locos from Lees Shed also used this route when working to and from the Manchester area. In 1960, the wooden station at Park Bridge burned down in spectacular fashion, to the accompaniment of exploding detonators that had been left in one of the rooms. Major repair work was even carried out on the nearby viaduct and the old iron works continued to be rail-served until it closed in 1964. Park Bridge village was the oldest surviving example in the county of Lancashire of an industrial community based on engineering with houses built solely for the workers and their families. The line between OA&GB Junction and Clegg Street closed completely in 1967. Park Bridge Viaduct, a major landmark in the district for so long, was pulled down in 1971. Thereafter, the LYR Manchester-Rochdale line served Clegg Street parcels depot until the latter closed in 1981.

LEES to OLDHAM AN ILLUSTRATED REVIEW

(Right - centre) 0-6-0 No 52427, one-time resident of Bolton shed but now based at its final home at Lees (26F), has just left the goods yard there and heads under St John Street bridge for Oldham Glodwick Road yard. The train left Diggle yard at 11am and is carrying Yorkshire coal for the boiler houses of Oldham. *J Davenport*

(Right - lower) Now looking in the opposite direction, Fowler class 3MT 2-6-2T No 40057 approaches Lees with a push pull train to Delph in the early 1950s. The first coach is a LNWR Diagram M11 and the driving trailer is an M49. This part of Lees was and still is relatively open land stretching across to Greenacres and Waterhead. Behind the signal can be seen fencing bordering allotments. The latter were encouraged during World War Two to help with food production, and from such places emanated the clucking of hens and the cockcrow as daylight dawned, sounds that were once familiar in urban areas. Allotments were a diversion from the toil of daily life and became the pastime of many a railwayman.

Jim Davenport

A light scattering of snow is on the ground as Fowler 2-6-2T No **40061** approaches Lees with a down 'Delph Donkey'. This less than perfect print shows quite a rare working. The leading vehicle is Period II open third No 3484, a coach familiar on these services for about twelve months or so, however, the driving trailer was a very rare bird indeed in the Oldham area. It started life as a Period I 2-window open third built to diagram 1692 in 1929. Four of these coaches gained driving compartments and centre entrances similar to those on the LNWR driving trailers during conversion to push pull circa 1938. Their running numbers following conversion were 3462-65. *J Davenport*

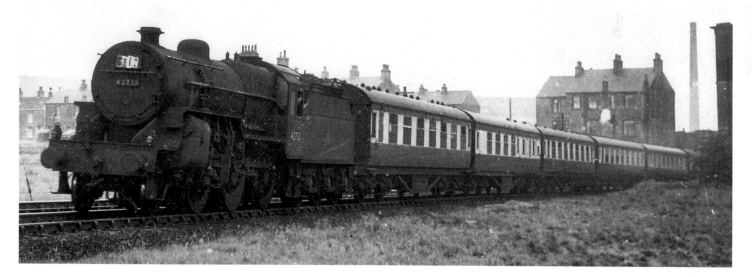

'Crab' 2-6-0 No **42713** heads a Greenfield to Llandudno 'relief' under St John's Street Bridge on a dull day in the 1950s. No doubt the passengers were hoping for better weather by the time they reached North Wales. BR had thoughtfully supplied corridor stock for this long working instead of the more usual non-lavatory stock, which inevitably led to long queues for amenities at such places as Blackpool, Rhyl and Llandudno during bank holidays. *J Davenport*

LEES

The driver of the Fairburn 2-6-4T No **42114** keeps a watchful eye on the road ahead as he prepares to bring his train to a halt at Lees signal box before setting back on to the Up road to gain access to the yard. Some wagons may possibly be dropped off here and any wagons for Delph would be attached. On this occasion, the 8.55am Oldham Glodwick Road Goods is a shipment of coal and coke. No 42114 was a regular performer on the 'Delph Pilot' particularly after the LYR 'A' class locos were withdrawn. *J Davenport*

(Above) When Fowler 2-6-2T No 12 was given the push pull equipment from sister engine No 58 in May 1947, it was re-allocated to Lees (26F) while No 58 departed for Patricroft (10C). No 12 became **40012** after Nationalization in 1948. On a warm June afternoon in 1952 we see 40012 well turned out and with a full head of steam approaching Lees with the 1.10pm Oldham Clegg Street-Delph. The push-pull corridor coaches are No's 3432 and 3407, which it is believed arrived on the line in the late 1940s. *J Davenport*

(Below) The 8.55am 'Delph Goods' is seen between Glodwick Road and Lees with Longsight-based LNWR class 7F 0-8-0 No **49428** assisting Ivatt Class 2MT 2-6-2T No **41281**. The 0-8-0 will probably detach at Greenfield and work light engine to Diggle to work a the 11am Goods back to Glodwick Road yard or perhaps take over the Micklehurst Pilot job. Greenacres Cemetery can be seen on the hill to the left of the 7F. Also prominent in the background is the Glen Mill. After being stationed abroad for several years, LG's father-in-law, William Wroe, ended up at this mill guarding German POW's. It was a well-located posting for a man from Waterhead! *J Davenport*

(Above) After passing under Lees Road at Clarkesfield, the line entered a stonewalled cutting as it approached the bottom of the moor at Mumps. This cutting was partially roofed over in the early days of the railway and must have offered a very depressing picture to the prospective rail traveller waiting on the platform at Glodwick Road station. These retaining walls are clearly seen looking east towards Lees on 21st May 1957, two years after passenger services ceased. The station canopies had been removed by this date and the overbridge had been replaced with a concrete and brick structure.

(Right) Oldham Glodwick Road Station merely reflected its drab surroundings in what was an unglamorous part of town. This street level view, taken in 1954 before Delph services ceased, shows the footbridge and the depressing street-level booking office. There was a passing loop for service 4 trams on this bridge until November 1937; on which date buses replaced the trams and took up service 'numbers' 4 and V. One of the tram poles can be seen on the left. Known as the 'Circular' route, it passed under LYR track at Mumps Bridge, over LYR track near King Street (railway in tunnel at this location) and over OA&GB tracks on Park Road. *British Transport Commission*

OLDHAM
GLODWICK ROAD

The station at Glodwick Road looked unprepossessing even in 1925 long before the run-down of the railways began. This interesting view looking towards Lees shows the station in all its glory complete with its original full-length platform canopies. A LNWR 50ft D375 full brake van is being unloaded in the bay platform normally used by trains on the OA&GB local service to Guide Bridge. If the infrastructure of a steam railway with traditional British trams running across the bridge were laid down today, it would be called a theme park though it is doubtful if the Oldhamer's of 1925 considered their town to be a theme park or trams to be anything other than a noisy nuisance!

Stations UK/Jim Peden

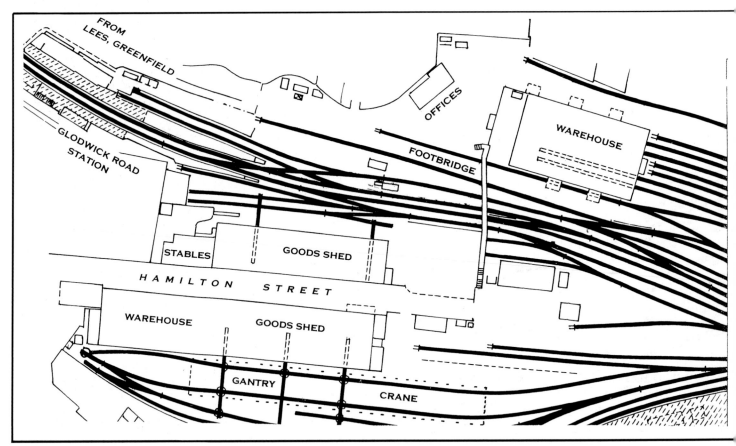

The station is seen on a beautifully sunny 5th July 1954, enjoying the penultimate year of passenger services, its canopies cut back to cover only the fronts of the buildings. The Oldham branch would have been busier if it had been linked to long distance trans-Pennine services instead of being treated as a branch run in close association with the Delph branch. Indeed, with a bit of foresight, it might still be open today. ***British Transport Commission***

OLDHAM
GLODWICK ROAD

TRAIN SERVICE

LMS

AND

CHEAP TICKETS

BETWEEN

TODMORDEN, ROCHDALE, OLDHAM, MIDDLETON, MIDDLETON JUNCTION AND MANCHESTER (Victoria).

BURY & MANCHESTER, via HEYWOOD (Victoria)

BOLTON, BURY AND ROCHDALE.

OLDHAM, DELPH & STOCKPORT,

JULY 18th to SEPTEMBER 11th inclusive, 1932.

Folder E 208 A (E.R.O. 53513/52)

(Left) The large double warehouse in Glodwick Road yard was still in use for parcels vans when this view was taken on 18th April 1978. Tracks of the LNWR Oldham - Greenfield branch have gone completely but Glodwick Road overbridge can be seen in the far distance behind the signal gantry. The lines in the foreground form part of the LYR Mumps complex. A 4-car train comprising Derby (Class 108) and Cravens (Class 105) sets departs Oldham Mumps with a Rochdale to Manchester Victoria train.

L Goddard

(Centre) BR Class 08 0-6-0 shunter No **08 475** puts in a mighty effort hauling a long train of vans from the goods warehouse at Glodwick Road to Clegg Street parcels depot on 18th April 1978. These locos bore a strong resemblance to the LMS/English Electric shunters that had first appeared on these duties in 1960 and had been withdrawn by 1971. Diesel shunters were used possibly because of the need to keep air pollution to a minimum when working around the then new Clegg Street parcels depot. An unidentified Class 40 ticks over outside the depot behind the new Oldham Mumps signal box. This box had replaced Waterloo Sidings box plus the signal boxes at Sheepwashers Lane, Werneth, and Mumps No's 1, 2 and 3 in 1967.

L Goddard

(Left) LYR 'A' class 0-6-0 No **52248** simmers between Pilot duties near Mumps station in May 1957. Lees men christened this loco the 'Port Vale Flyer' in 1953 after the engine was called upon to abandon its shunting duties at Mumps and stand in for a failed loco on an Oldham Athletic Football Club supporters special to Stoke-on-Trent. Following a crew change at Stockport, 52248 acquitted itself well until a tender hot box put paid to the fling just short of Longport (Port Vale). Sympathy for the loco and its unwilling crew was in short supply as angry Latics supporters arrived at the match just in time to catch the last 20 minutes of the game, but on a positive note, the loco lived on non-the worse for its outing until March 1962.

J Davenport

(Right) LM Ivatt Class 2MT 2-6-0's were no strangers to Lees shed, so when the last of the LYR 0-6-0s were officially withdrawn in September 1962, Lees crews no doubt welcomed these modern engines with open arms. Lees' allocation of 2-6-0's eventually totalled seven, No's 46419, 46449, 46452, 46484, 46485, 46486 and 46487, all staying until closure of the shed in 1964; No **46452**, by now reallocated to Newton Heath shed, is shunting vans into Oldham Mumps good yard in June 1965 and was the photographers parting view of Oldham as he left the town to live in North Wales.

L Goddard

(Above) Gas Street Footbridge spanned LYR and LNWR tracks as well as sidings and was a good place to watch trains heading eastwards but not westwards owing to one side being partially blanked off by a second bridge carrying electric cables from Greenhill electricity works. BR Class 4MT 2-6-4T No **80088** rolls downhill towards Oldham Central Station with a Rochdale to Manchester Victoria local in the mid 1950's. The leading carriage is a first class corridor coach, luxury indeed for an all-stations local train. The air duct along the roof gives away its origins but it is unlikely the passengers realized they were travelling in a carriage built for the pre-war 'Coronation Scot'! The prominent building in the background was the home of the Oldham Chronicle (better known as th' Owdam Rag). *J Davenport*

(Right) Some of tracks that passed beneath Gas Works footbridge can be in this 1950's view of Stanier Class 5MT 4-6-0 No **44735** working empty coaching stock to Manchester past Lees-based 2-6-4T No **42551** shunting carriage stock. All the carriages in view are of the non-corridor type, but of note is the LYR Lavatory-Third standing in front of the Corporation gas works. Incidentally, how many readers remember queuing up for coke at the gas works in the 1950s?

J Davenport

During the final days of steam operation on British Railways, Stanier 'Black Five' 4-6-0 No **45202** reverses away from Oldham Clegg Street Parcels Concentration Depot after doing a spot of shunting in June 1968. The depot partially obscures the presence of the unique LNWR curved goods warehouse at the bottom end of Clegg Street yard, although the curvature is not apparent from this viewpoint. Just visible is the third of the long-span public footbridges. This bridge spanned the goods yard and provided a convenient short cut to Clegg Street and Central stations from Woodstock Street and the Park Road area of Oldham.

J Davenport

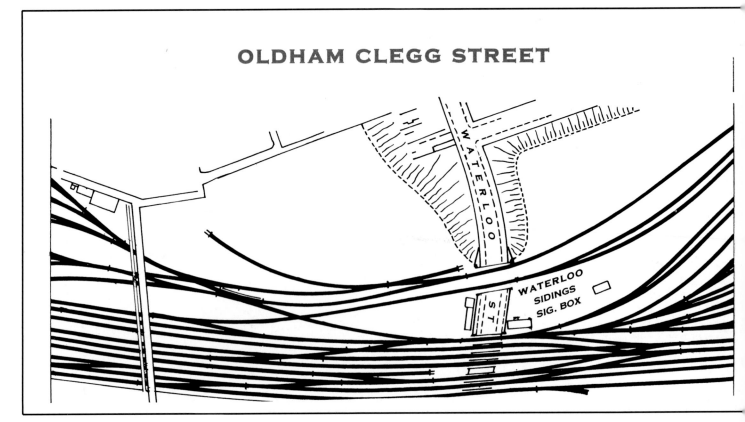

OLDHAM CLEGG STREET

WATERLOO

WATERLOO SIDINGS SIG. BOX

A diesel shunter stands outside Clegg Street Parcel Depot while packages are unloaded from a BR General Utility Van onto the trailer of a pre-war 3-wheel 'Mechanical Horse'. By this date, the 3-wheel Scammel's were for internal use only, hence the lack of registration plates, and their days of working through the streets carrying 'Goods' traffic as distinct from 'passenger' parcels were well and truly over. The parcels seen in this view would be forwarded to designate loading baskets for distribution by road to Greenfield, Middleton, Failsworth, Hollinwood, Chadderton, Coldhurst, Werneth etc. Places like HMSO at Chadderton and Ferranti at Hollinwood had their own 'baskets'. Waterloo Sidings signal box is visible in the distance behind the shunter.

British Railways (LMR)

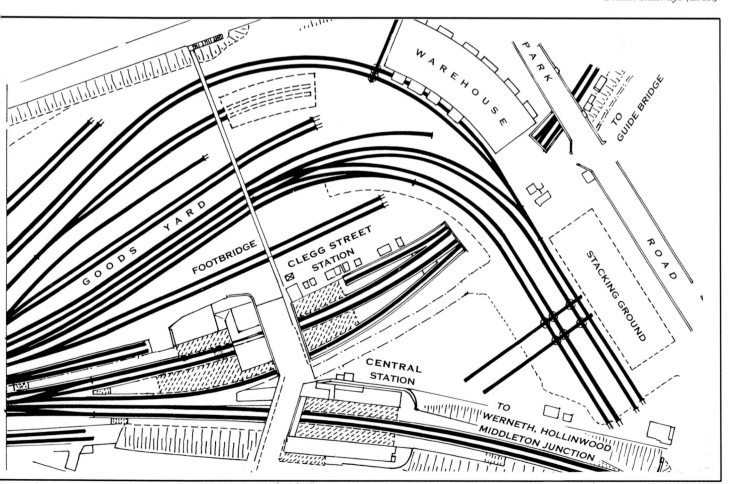

(Right) Clegg Street had been quite an imposing station in its day but this is what the frontage looked like on 25th June 1966, seven years after closure. The canopy over the entrance had deteriorated during the 1950s and was virtually glassless when Delph services ceased in 1955, so it was probably sheeted over during the time Guide Bridge trains terminated here between 1955-59. Central station booking hall is visible around the corner showing the close proximity of the two stations, while across the road from Central was the sleeper-built 'spotting' fence mentioned earlier in the text. *J B Hodgson*

CLEGG STREET

Lees based Stanier class 4MT 2-6-4T No **42551**, draws empty stock out of Waterloo sidings and into Oldham Clegg Street station for an Oldham-Stockport train in the early 1950s. The train is a non-corridor set, made up of a LNWR Brake Third to D333 built between 1916-22 and a LMS Lavatory Composite to D1686 built between 1926-29. Mill chimneys dominate the scene behind Mumps No.1 signal box and the gas works. *J Davenport*

(Left) The aforementioned sleeper-built fence was a boundary wall along a rough path and was low enough for small boys to look over yet high enough on the railway embankment side to deter people from climbing over. And this is the view! BR Standard class 4MT 2-6-4T No **80053** starts out from Central station with a Manchester-Rochdale train on 22nd September 1954. The train behind it is in Clegg Street Station waiting to leave for Delph behind a BR Class 2MT 2-6-2T. This is really the start of our journey on the Delph Donkey. *G Whitehead*

Fowler class 3MT 2-6-2T No **40056** stands in the Down island platform waiting to depart with a Delph train in June 1952. A train from Guide Bridge would arrive shortly to make a cross platform connection with the Delph train for passengers wishing to continue their journey via the Oldham branch. *J.Davenport*

A JOURNEY FROM OLDHAM TO DELPH BY LARRY GODDARD

In the warm glow of a July afternoon, a gentle breeze carries the soft hiss of escaping steam and the sweet aroma of smoke and oil up from the depths of Oldham Clegg Street station. A humming noise that I always associated with "motor fitted" locos, emanates from Fowler 2-6-2T No 40060 standing in the Down platform loop. The dusty gloom of Clegg Street's booking hall is the gateway to a fascinating world of trains and my friends and I can barely contain our excitement as we collect our tickets from the booking office and tumble down the broad flight of steps onto the platform below. There are First and Third Class waiting rooms, along with toilets, official rooms and porters room. The platforms are mostly covered by canopies and the station is quite gloomy at its western end. A Stanier 4MT 2-6-4T is drawing into the adjacent Central Station with a Rochdale-bound train so we dash to the eastern end of the

station to watch its departure. To our youthful minds, the Manchester-Rochdale trains are on the mainline and we stare spellbound as the train climbs vigorously through the maze of tracks towards its next stop at Oldham Mumps. Suddenly the safety valves lift on 40060 so we climb aboard the leading coach; its slightly recessed sliding doors having been left open by the guard. The smell of tobacco smoke and steam fills the air as we stand between two long inward-facing leather seats, seats that cry out to be slid along! The floor is quite wide at this point and straps are suspended from the ceiling to cater for standing passengers in a manner familiar to bus passengers. The centre portion of the coach consists of first class back-to-back seating on either the gangway, but these were downgraded to third class many years ago. The other end of the coach also has a standee area with inward facing seats. Ventilation is via pairs

of glass half-lights above each window that open like doors to draw in air. I discovered later in life that this 'Oerlikon' style coach was built to LNWR Diagram M12.

We walk through a flexible corridor connection into the adjacent coach and find ourselves in a spacious open saloon with low-backed tram-like seats that can be swung over to face the direction of travel. An identical saloon lies beyond a large central exit/entrance. Once again, ventilation is via opening glass half-lights above each window. The luggage compartment on this particular coach doubles as a driving compartment. When this coach is leading, as from Delph to Oldham, the driver controls the train from this compartment while the fireman remains on the locomotive at the back of the train. The atmosphere of these unusual carriages makes journeys far more appealing than riding in ordinary non-corridor stock, ...*continued on page 113*

The same inexorable march of progress that relegated the stage-coaches to side streets and museums eventually gave the the Delph Donkey its final marching orders, the dictator this time being he motor bus. The stationmasters at each end of the line, Messrs. W. J. Brown of Oldham Clegg Street station (top left), and A.Parkinson of Delph station (top right), were said to be the embodiment of courtesy. Holder of a gold medal for long service, there was 66 year old Martin Costello (lower left), the oldest employed official and the Donkey's last guard. J.Wrigley (lower right) was the District Relief signalman seen holding the single-line baton for the Delph Branch. The fatal last notice at the entrance to Clegg Street station says it all. State-of-the-art televisions from Pye were on sale for around ten weeks wages in the year ITV removed the BBC's monopoly of television in 1955. A Hillman Minx 1.3 car giving 30mpg at 50-60mph cost £480 plus £201 2s 6d purchase tax, small wonder most people continued to depend on public transport.

The Delph Donkey has just arrived in Clegg Street's main platform with a train from Delph on 22nd September 1954. When all the passengers have alighted, 2-6-2T No **84012** will propel its train along the OA&GB line under Clegg Street good yard and Park Road as far as Sheepwashers Lane signal box. There it will crossover onto the Down line and arrive back in Clegg Street station on the north face of the island platform. The two LNWR coaches are to Diagram M12 and M45, both described in this chapter and in which we travel on our imaginary journey to Delph.   *G Whitehead*

continued from page 111........although it has to be said the tram seats in the open saloon driving trailers were not designed for long journeys. This particular trailer was built to diagram M45. A few driving trailers have first class compartments but most were withdrawn from the Delph branch in 1953.

The 25-minute journey from to Delph will take us through the industrial suburbs of Oldham and out into the countryside that lies beyond the town boundary. In due course, the driver and fireman walk down the platform towards the engine while the guard strides purposely through the train banging shut all the doors behind him. As soon as he gives the right-away, our train pulls out of Clegg Street to the accompaniment of hollow ringing sounds from the coach wheels as they pass over the complex pattern of track work linking the LNW/G.C lines with those of the L&YR There are wagons of every description in the maze of sidings to the left and right of us as well as coaches and parcels vans. There is also the 93 yards long Anglo-American Co. siding, and the Oldham Corporation Siding, which serves

Greenhill electricity works. The railway dominates a large part of Oldham and the sound of shunting and whistling, which goes on day and night, is as much a part of the town as cotton mills and clogs. Much of this commotion dies down on Saturday afternoons and the yards slumber on Sundays ready for the week ahead. On passing Oldham Junction signal box the tracks fan out and we can see Oldham Mumps station on our left as we approach Oldham Glodwick Road station.

On departing this rather gloomy station, the sound of our loco reverberates off the stone-wall cutting that was once a tunnel, as it begins the half-mile climb at 1 in 94 towards Lees. The line descends a 1-in-100 grade for a short distance after passing under Lees Road before resuming the climb on an embankment across the valley of Lees Brook. Lees would be just another sleepy village if it weren't for the fact that it is the last place on earth one expects to find a Locomotive Depot. Opened in 1878, Lees shed is home to a number of Fowler 7F 0-8-0s. Big in size and sound, they are great favourites of mine. Also standing on shed are several

L.Y.R. Class 3F 0-6-0s, Fowler Class 3P 2-6-2Ts and a Fairburn Class 4MT 2-6-4T. Soon after passing the shed and a large cotton warehouse on our right, we duck under Lees Road once more before crossing open land. Springbank Mill siding and Clough mill Siding are shared sidings with access from the Up line. Springhead Mill sidings for Springhead Spinning Co. Grotton are sidings on the down side. Grotton & Springhead station is a mere 945 yards from Lees. At this point, we leave the last of the tall mill chimneys behind and enter a rural landscape.

From leaving Clegg Street the line has climbed 156 feet in just over two miles. Grotton is situated at the foot of Lydgate Hill and is a typical small country station with substantial brick buildings, small good shed and a level crossing. The Oldham Corporation letter T bus service (it was service 0 before the war), terminates a short distance from the station and has siphoned off passengers from the railway since it commenced running on 2 May 1928. From Grotton the line continues to climb at 1 in 117 to Lydgate Tunnel while the............ *continued on page 114*

continued on page 114

As other push pull services on BR's LM Region got more modern coaches, so more elderly LNWR push pull coaches arrived for stabling in Oldham's Waterloo Sidings. There were more coaches than were required to run the Oldham-Greenfield-Delph services and so they were often used to strengthen other trains, including those worked by Lees men to Stockport. The M12 and M45 coaches seen in the previous picture are seen leaving Clegg Street as empty stock behind LYR 0-6-0 No **52427** after working the 12.34 from Stockport to Oldham in 1954. The last two coaches are a LMS Period I lavatory brake third and a Period II non-corridor all third or composite.
J Davenport

..................main road climbs a further 206 feet to the summit of Lydgate Hill. Shortly after entering the 1331yds long tunnel the line begins a descent of 1-in-110. After a brief pause at Grasscroft Halt, we continue downgrade at 1-in-75 to Greenfield Junction.

The station and yard at Greenfield are built on a ledge and the platforms sit astride the busy Huddersfield & Manchester mainline. Greenfield Junction signalbox, dating from 1888, stands on the Up side of the mainline from where the signal man could observe the main junction as well as movements into sidings on the Oldham branch and the coal sidings beside the mainline. The coal depot with its coal-drops overlooks a cobbled yard sloping up from Shaw Hall Bank Road. The Down platform has an extension serving the Oldham branch, and is complete with its own set of waiting rooms and canopy. Access to this end of the platform can be had via a steep footpath from

Oldham Road, the entrance to which is beside some railway cottages. Oldham to Greenfield trains terminate in this bay platform whereas Delph-bound trains continue over the junction into the mainline platform and as often as not take water at the east end of the station. Trains terminating from Delph drop their passengers in the Up mainline platform before reversing over a crossover into the Down mainline platform in order to gain access to the Oldham bay. Sometimes, the carriages are stored on two carriage sidings, accessible from the Oldham branch.. A fan of sidings on the Up side of the mainline serve a tightly cramped coal yard and goods shed.

From Greenfield there follows a short sprint of 1319yds down the Huddersfield and Manchester line to Delph Junction where we stop at Moorgate Halt. The signal box is situated at the east end of the Down platform and Delph-bound trains collect a single-line token here before proceeding onto the

branch. The total length of the Delph branch is 1 mile 1077 yards between Delph Junction and Delph station and is operated as "one engine in steam" with a maximum permissible speed of 30mph. After observing the 15mph restriction through Delph Junction, we run parallel with the mainline for a distance of around 440 yards past the sight of Ladcastle Quarry before swinging away to the left away from the main line around a 15 mph speed restricted 7 chains curve. The mainline continues eastwards across Saddleworth Viaduct towards Saddleworth Station and Standedge. After crossing Ladcastle Lane there follows a brief stop at Dobcross Halt before proceeding over Tamewater Viaduct and on through the 26 yards long Streethouse Tunnel. Soon after passing Bankfield Mill siding, we pass under Wall Hill Road and proceed towards Measurements Halt, which is only used at peak periods to serve the needs of a nearby factory. The factory, erected in

1919, is built from reinforced concrete with large window spaces to permit a bright working environment. From here, we are on a gentle curve towards the terminus at Delph.

Delph station is a neat little branch line terminus with run-round facilities; goods warehouse and four sidings. A separate siding with its own lead from the running line serves coal drops and there is a private siding to Bailey Mill installed in 1877. Bailey Mill produced woollen shawls and blankets. The mill's height and proximity to the station makes the whole area a quite depressing place on damp days. A child's half-fare from Oldham Clegg Street to Delph at this time is 7d and to Greenfield it is only 4½d in old money. When our girlfriends were with us, it was essential to accompany them into the hills surrounding Greenfield Station lest they discovered our interest in trains! Even fifty years ago, it was necessary to maintain the equivalent of "street cred". Most other times, we used to hang around the station, staff permitting, to watch all but the largest locomotives pass through Greenfield on their way over the Pennines. 'Royal Scot' locomotives, in original and rebuilt form, appeared on the heavier passenger trains along with 'Jubilee', 'Patriot' and 'Black Five' 4-6-0s., and 'Crab' 2-6-0s. Many were double headed. Eastbound trains could be heard slogging upgrade past Mossley, and anticipation grew as the trains drew closer only to be dashed when they turned out to be on the Micklehurst loop line. Trains on the 'loop' crossed the centre of Greenfield on a viaduct some distance away from the line through Greenfield station. Boys being boys, we tended to last the day on a bottle of fizzy pop and crisps. One Saturday while travelling home in a M52 side corridor coach, we shared a compartment with two weary hikers who we recognised as having demolished the air raid shelters in our schoolyard. We in turn quickly demolished their remaining sandwiches when invited!

Passengers leaving Clegg Street for Delph would pass trains on the adjacent lines to Rochdale and Manchester. Stanier Class 4MT 2-6-4T No **42647** climbs towards Oldham Mumps with a Rochdale bound train formed on non-corridor stock. The coaches from the locomotive are: LMS lavatory composite, LMS brake third, BR Mk.I all third and LMS lavatory brake third. A Manchester-bound train headed by a BR Standard 2-6-4 is approaching Oldham Central with a LMS corridor third, LNWR non-corridor brake third, LNWR non-corridor composite and a LMS lavatory composite.   Both: *J Davenport*

(**Right**) Fowler 2-6-2T No **40061** arrives at Oldham Glodwick Road in the glare of early morning sunshine in June 1949. This is not the Delph Donkey though, but the 7.59am Stockport to Greenfield. The two LNWR corridor coaches are push pull fitted but it is possible this was a non-motor diagram. Glodwick Road goods shed and stables, which backed onto Hamilton Street, can be seen in the background.

115

(Above) The Delph Donkey leaves Lees station behind Fowler 2-6-2T No **40062** in April 1952. The leading diagram M47 non-driving trailer had recently received a repaint and BR style Gil Sans running numbers below the leading window. *J Davenport*

(Below) East of Lees the line climbs into open country and begins to leave the mill chimneys behind. BR Standard 2-6-2T No **84010**, working the 12.10 Oldham Clegg Street to Delph, makes a spirited run towards its next stop at Grotton in April 1955. The same two coaches as in the previous picture are in use and remained so right up to the last day of Delph Donkey services. *J Davenport*

(Right) The sun has already set on Oldham as a Corporation Leyland Titan PD1 tops Lydgate Hill following a steep climb from Grotton at sunset in the early 1950s. The bus will shortly pass Grasscroft, though at a much higher level than the railway, before reaching the bridge over Greenfield station. Service 10 will then take a dramatic plunge down a 1 in 8 incline past the station entrance and terminate a mile away at the end of Chew Valley road. DBU 256, fleet number 256, was delivered to Oldham Corporation in 1947 and was among the earliest examples nationally built to the newly permitted width of eight feet.

L Goddard

(Below) In this view of Grasscroft Halt, it can be seen just how much the rurality of the West Riding of Yorkshire contrasts sharply with industrial Lancashire at the other end of Lydgate Tunnel. Lydgate Hill dominates the landscape and a lone passenger walks towards the station exit as BR 2-6-2T No **84010** moves away with the Oldham-bound Delph Donkey in the spring of 1955. *J Davenport*

(Above) After arriving at Greenfield, the Delph Donkey made a short run down the Huddersfield & Manchester main line to Moorgate Halt before leaving at Delph Junction. The line to Delph is in the foreground while the main line continues across Saddleworth viaduct. Of note is the Down line catch-point and guide rail to derail runaways heading downgrade from Diggle and also prevent them fouling the Delph line. 'Jubilee' class 6P 4-6-0 No **45708** *Resolution* speeds past with the 2.02pm Hull-Liverpool Lime Street express. The substantial-looking leading coach is of Great Central origins, built at Dukinfield circa 1910, while the rest of the visible coaches are LNER wooden Gresley stock in teak brown livery and a LMS Period III coach in carmine & cream livery.   *J Davenport*

(Right) It seems strange to think that Saddleworth station, which lay on the opposite side of Saddleworth Viaduct, was originally considered as a possible terminus for trains from Delph. This would have entailed a reversal of direction in the vicinity of the 'Jubilee' seen in the previous picture, and as there was no provision for stabling trains at Saddleworth, one presumes they would have actually terminated at Diggle. Commonsense prevailed and Greenfield was chosen as the natural terminus. A Huddersfield-bound train, headed by an LNWR 'Benbow' 4-4-0, crosses the viaduct and climbs briskly through Saddleworth during the early years of the 20th Century. This rustic station survives in the 21st Century as a private residence.
Oldham MBC Local Studies Library

(Right) Some locomotives were re-branded very quickly after the formation of British Railways on 1st January 1948, while others continued to carry the old company insignia for several years to come. Fowler Tank No **57** of Lees shed passes Measurements Halt in plain black with interim number M57 on show in 1948. It would in due course be renumbered 40057 and the leading Diagram M11 open trailer would have its LMS insignia painted over. Cosmetic changes apart, it would be a case of *'business as usual'* on the Delph branch. ***J Cocker***

(Below) Some twelve months after passenger services ceased, the Stephenson Locomotive Society and the Manchester Locomotive Society ran a Railtour (reporting No.W599) over various lines and branches in the North West, including a trip to Delph. The 'Old Manchester Tour' started at Liverpool Road station double headed with LYR 2-4-2T No 50647 and LYR 3F 0-6-0 No 52438 (LYR No 123) and ran via Oxford Road station, London Road South Junction, Midland Junction, Ashton Branch Sidings, Brewery Sidings, Middleton Junction, the Werneth Incline, Royton Junction to Royton where the 2-4-2T pilot engine came off the train. The tour also took in Oldham Clegg Street station, Greenfield and Delph, finally visiting Facit on the Bacup Branch. This marathon tour ended at Oldham Road Goods station in Manchester. After collecting the single line token at Delph Junction, LYR 0-6-0 No **52438** draws its train of blood & custard coaches down the Delph branch towards Dobcross on 12th May 1956. ***J Davenport***

(Right) After arriving at Delph at 4.25pm, the 'Old Manchester Railtour' is seen at Delph terminus after No.52438 had run round its train. Passengers had until 4.43pm to record the occasion on their cameras before departing once more for Oldham Clegg Street, and a further reversal of direction for the run to Rochdale and Facit (arr. 6.25pm). The special train was composed of four LMS-built open saloon coaches, which allowed tour participants fine all round views during their extensive and varied journey.

F W Shuttleworth

(Right) On the final day of Delph Donkey services, BR Class 2MT 2-6-2T No **84015** stands at the buffers in Delph waiting to departs with yet another trainload of last-day well-wishers on 30th April 1955. The grey stone station buildings would continue to witness the arrival of the occasional train of coal for a further eight years.
R J Buckley/Initial Photographics

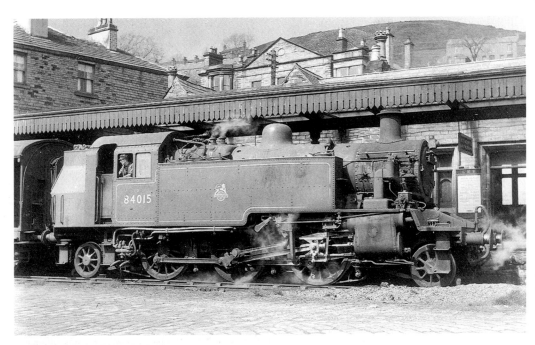

(Centre) The Delph branch closed completely at the end of 1963 and Delph station was eventually purchased as a private dwelling. The new owner, Mr Alf Hall, had planned a half-mile line at Delph and he acquired a small industrial loco and a BR Mk.I coach. The loco was No 2; an 0-4-0ST built by Robert Stephenson & Hawthorns Ltd., (Works No 7646) in 1950, pictured at Delph circa 1971. It worked at CEGB Percival Lane Power Station, Runcorn, before being transferred to Hartshead Power Station, between Mossley and Stalybridge, in April 1970. The loco went from there to Delph but was taken away for scrap in mid-1972. *Oldham Chronicle*

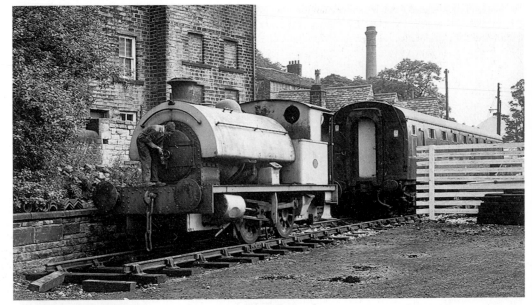

(Bottom) A second loco arrived at Delph on 19th September 1971, this being Brookes No **1** 0-6-0ST built by Hunslet Engine Co. Ltd, (Works No 2387) of 1941. It was used by Brookes Ltd., at their Lightcliffe Works until it closed in 1969; The works site was acquired for redevelopment by Philips Electronic & Associated Industries Ltd. who initially retained this loco on site for possible static display, but later decided to dispose of it to Alf Hall. This summer-time view of the engine in steam during a local steam rally captures something of the essence of old times at Delph station. Sadly, the venture never developed and the loco went to the Peak Rail at Buxton on 25th March 1983, the original operating base of Peak Rail. When Peak Rail operations moved to Matlock, the loco went to the Middleton Railway at Leeds in May 1991where it was rebuilt as a side tank loco and now operates as their "Thomas the Tank Engine". A loco not owned by Mr Hall was also stabled at Delph for a short time before being moved to the Yorkshire Dales Railway in 1975 and then to the Llangollen Railway in North Wales. This was Darfield No 1 built by Hunslet in 1953. *J Roberts*

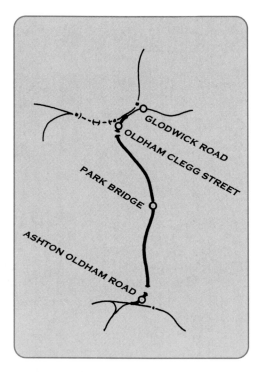

To ASHTON FROM CLEGG STREET

ALONG THE OLDHAM, ASHTON & GUIDE BRIDGE JUNCTION RAILWAY

The engines operating on the final day of OA&GB passenger services all carried headboards announcing the last day of service. The loco on the last train to Stockport did not carry a headboard, however, it was exceptionally clean. Fairburn 2-6-4T No **42114** of Lees shed is pictured in Clegg Street with its two-coach train of LMS Stanier stock waiting to depart for Stockport on 2nd May 1959. The coaches appear to be a non-corridor third and a corridor brake third. Clearly the station canopy had suffered a large loss of glass over the four years since Delph services finished. *A Moyes*

From 1862, the LNWR's Delph trains started and terminated at Oldham Clegg Street Station, while the opening of Glodwick Road Station allowed the OA&GB trains to extend their service to that station. The two companies' trains therefore overlapped between these two stations. MS&L Parker Class 3 2-4-2T No **576**, built at Gorton in August 1889, stands at Oldham Glodwick Road station with a train of six-wheel coaches in the brown and French grey livery in Great Central days. This engine was never push pull fitted and was withdrawn in May 1937. *Ray Webster/W A Brown collection*

To Ashton from Clegg Street

The Oldham, Ashton and Guide Bridge Junction Railway

Within weeks of the opening of the Oldham Branch, a group of representatives comprising the Mayors of Oldham and Ashton, John Platt and Nathaniel Buckley, asked the Manchester Sheffield & Lincolnshire Railway to build a line to Oldham. However, the MS&L was reluctant to do so without the cooperation of the London & North Western Railway and the Lancashire & Yorkshire Railway. Evidently, it did not want a major Parliamentary fight to get into Oldham. An agreement was reached between the three railway companies and the Oldham Ashton & Guide Bridge Junction Railway was incorporated on 10 August 1857, but then the LYR pulled out leaving the MS&L and LNWR to subscribe £50,000 each, the remainder to be found locally. The MS&L had a strong incentive to reach Oldham and to continue onwards to Rochdale. On 10 May 1857, the scheme received Royal Assent and the cumbersome name Oldham, Ashton-under-Lyne & Guide Bridge Junction Railway (OA&GB) was incorporated to form a company. J. G. Blackburne was appointed the Company engineer.

Work commenced on the Guide Bridge to Ashton section in early 1859. Board Minutes indicate that plans and sectional

drawings were ready by April of that year. Eleven contractors tendered for the work on the Ashton-Oldham section. That of James Taylor was accepted on 27 May 1859, his quotation of £50,000 to cover the coast of a double line of rails and to include the viaduct over the River Medlock at Park Bridge. To encourage the rate of progress Taylor was offered a bonus of £5,000 if the work was completed in eleven months instead of eighteen as originally planned. This was a tall order, however, especially in view of the then unknown weather conditions which were to impede progress, along with shortage of labour.

The major engineering features between Ashton and Oldham included the Turner Lane Tunnel (56 yards) at Smallshaw, Ashton; the Limehurst Embankment (80 feet high);and the Park Bridge Viaduct which crossed the Medlock Valley. The viaduct was the project's piece de resistance, forming a structure consisting of 12 arches (9 of 50ft. span and 3 of 23ft span). The length of the structure was 215 yards; its maximum height above the river 96ft 6 ins. The importance of the viaduct was acknowledged by the Oldham Chronicle, 8 October 1859, whem it reported an important occasion: " *A little after two o'clock on Saturday afternoon, the ceremony of laying the foundation stone of the viaduct as performed by Legh Richmond Esq., (Manager of the Earl of*

Following the demise of the F1 and F2 2-4-2Ts at the end of the Second World War, LNER Class C13's, with an occasional C14, took over OA&GB services. C13 4-4-2T No **67421** is at the head of one such working, having just arrived at Clegg Street where it will terminate. Both carriages are of GCR origin and are fitted for push-pull working; Mr J Leeson, writing in the Oldham Chronicle 5th June 1965, said some people were apt to call the service the 'Banana Boat', *"...the reason being because of the coaches peculiar colour. It is said to be yellow but was presumably the LNER teak finish that prompted the nickname"*. The LNER was some way off the beaten track in Oldham, and so this colour must have stood out in a locality dominated by the comparatively dull LMS crimson lake. The former 'Delph' side of the island platform became a siding after that service was withdrawn in April 1955, hence the train of stored corridor coaches.

J W Sutherland

Stamford's estates), in the presence of a number of ladies and gentlemen, the former obtaining a good view of the proceedings from a wooden structure erected for the occasion, tastefully decorated with evergreens".

The ceremony was accompanied by the band of the 96th Regiment of Foot and the Hartshead brass band. John Platt, the OA&GB chairman, presented Legh Richmond with a silver trowel appropriately inscribed to mark the event. On 30 December 1859 it was stated in Board Minutes that the work had been making satisfactory progress until late severe weather put a stop to all the principle portions. By now, the Guide Bridge to Ashton section was approaching completion and the need to complete the remainder was urgent. A month later plans had been drawn up to cover traffic arrangements on the line. It was suggested that the MS&L worked the local traffic between Oldham and Manchester (via Guide Bridge), and the LNWR the Oldham to Stockport services.

The Guide Bridge to Ashton section was to be opened first but owing to its incomplete state, Board of Trade inspection was postponed for four weeks. The weather again thwarted Taylor's attempts to finish the job and Board Minutes of 31 August 1860 indicate that unsettled weather was delaying the contractor and that opening would likely be delayed until the end of the year. Despite the unsatisfactory rate of progress, Taylor received his £5,000 bonus in the September, but his problems continued. By the end of the year the Company's patience had run out and Mr. Taylor was now working under inspection. The MS&L

Company finally arranged to take everything out of Mr. Taylor's hands and complete the work by direct labour.

It was not until 1 June 1861 that an inaugural trip was made along the almost completed line. The train consisted of an engine and two carriages, one of which carried OA&GB directors, and included Edward Watkin (Chairman of the MS&L) and John Platt (Chairman of the OA&GB). At midday the train left Guide Bridge and proceeded at a slow rate to Ashton station. Brief stoppages were made, including one at Park Bridge Viaduct here the directors descended the slippy embankment, passed beneath it, and then ascended the embankment at the Oldham end before crossing the viaduct to reach the awaiting train. The train continued to Clegg Street station where *"a goodly number of people were awaiting the arrival of the train"*. After viewing the station, the company proceeded on foot towards the LNWR station at Mumps *"which is about to be connected with Clegg Street Station by a single line of rails"*.

Three stations were constructed on inclines viz., Ashton on 1 in 70, Park Bridge on 1 in 90, and Clegg Street on 1 in 86. On 12 July 1861, Colonel William Yolland inspected the line from end to end: he considered Ashton station was too close to the junction with the L&YR line. He recommended Ashton station should be removed somewhat further to the north, and put on a gradient of 1 in 250 to 1 in 300, and the platform be discontinued *"near the piers of the wooden bridge carrying a tramroad and to install catch points "to catch any carriages..........continued on page 125*

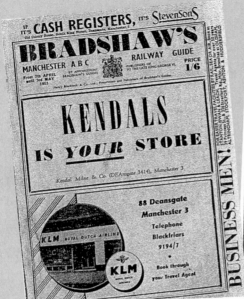

Reproduction of Bradshaw's Manchester Railway Guide cover for April 1953 together with the timetable for Oldham, Greenfield and Delph services.

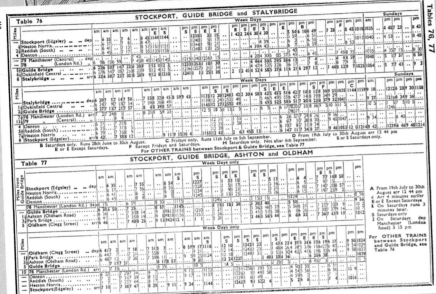

Reproduction of the British Railways Eastern Region (above) and LNER (below) Passenger Services Timetables for 1958 and 1941 respectively

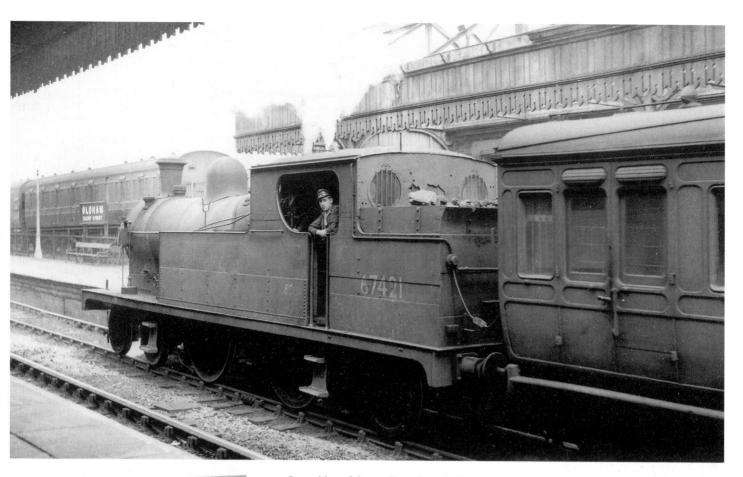

Some idea of the gradient through Clegg Street station can be gauged from the coaches stabled above platform level in Clegg Street yard. Class C13 No **67421** is seen again, this time in the Up platform after reversing near Waterloo Sidings Signal box. The leading GCR coach had something of a history in that it started life as an all first, but was then converted to a composite before final conversion to push pull. During the latter conversion in 1933, an end compartment was stripped and fitted with double doors to make a luggage compartment, as seen in this view, thus forming a luggage/composite push-pull trailer.

J W Sutherland

continued from page 123........... *or wagons that may break away in the act of starting...".* There were other problems too and Colonel Yolland could not recommend the opening of the line. This was not an auspicious start for the OA&GB, but it appears that remedial action was swift because Board minutes indicate that Colonel Yolland again inspected the line on 23 July and found nearly everything to his satisfaction.

On 26th August 1861 the Oldham Ashton & Guide Bridge Railway opened for passenger traffic (goods did not start until 1st February 1863) and this provided a more direct link between Oldham and Stockport. By an Act of Parliament, dated 30 June 1862, the MS&LR and the LNWR became joint owners of the OA&GB, and the stage was set for a long history of the only jointly owned railway in Oldham. On 1 July 1862 the LNWR's Delph to Oldham trains started and terminated at Clegg Street station. The opening of Glodwick Road station allowed OA&GB trains to extend their service to that station so that, in effect, the two company's trains overlapped between Clegg Street and Glodwick road stations. The timetable extract seen opposite on page 124 shows train movements between the LNWR Oldham Glodwick Road Station and the MS&L Clegg Street Station.

DESCRIPTION OF THE LINE
TO OA&GB JUNCTION, ASHTON-UNDER-LYNE.

The OA&GB line commenced from a double junction with the MS&L west of Guide Bridge through Ashton Moss to join the L.Y.R. Miles Platting-Stalybridge line at OA&GB Junction where it traversed the LYR for a few yards before branching off towards Oldham.. It served stations at Ashton Moss (closed February 1862), Ashton Oldham Road, Park Bridge, Oldham Clegg Street, and Oldham Glodwick Road. At this point it made an end-on junction with the LNWR. At Park Bridge were situated the extensive ironworks and bar rolling mills of Messrs. Hannah Lees & Sons, started around 1784. Park Bridge iron works started as a watermill and it became the nucleus of the rolling mill. When a purpose-built rolling mill was built, the old site became a cotton mill in 1886. The famous locomotive works of Isaac Watt Boulton were also situated on this line at Ashton. Between Oldham Central and Mumps (LYR) stations and Clegg Street and Glodwick Road (OA&GB) stations, the two lines ran side by side, and here a junction existed known as Oldham Junction, which allowed trains to cross from the OA&GB line to the LYR A large cotton warehouse was erected at Clegg Street, but was the property of the LNWR At

Obvious signs of dereliction such as existed at Clegg Street were not uncommon across the country in the 1950s, the origins of neglect having started during the 1939-45 war. Clegg Street was a sprawling station that was far too big for the sparse services that used it, yet how much worse it would have looked had it survived into the 'bus-shelter revival' period of the 1970s! On 27th December 1958, the driver and guard are in conversation at the "front" of the train, no doubt waiting for the photographer who was about to take a footplate trip down the line. Class C13 No **67417** would survive to work the final train to Stockport, leaving Oldham at 10.12pm on 2nd May 1959.

D L Chatfield

Waterloo sidings, between Glodwick Road and Clegg Street, connection was made with the Corporation Electric Works at Greenhill, and at Glodwick Road there was another large cotton warehouse belonging to the LNWR Initially the MS&L provided a local service between Guide Bridge and Oldham Glodwick Road as well as an express service from Manchester London Road. When the link from Crowthorne Junction to Denton Junction opened, The LNWR introduced an Oldham-Stockport service from 1 April 1876.

Oldham Clegg Street Station was rebuilt in 1899-1902. That this joint station was intended for major through services after it's rebuilding was evidenced by the provision of refreshment facilities, the only Station within the Oldham borough to do so. In 1910 there were 24 weekday trains between Guide Bridge and Oldham Glodwick Road with 11 on Sundays, while the LNWR offered 10 trains each weekday from Stockport to Oldham Clegg Street. Four of these trains terminated there, three continued to Glodwick Road, one went non-stop to Huddersfield and the other two crossed onto the LYR to reach Mumps and Rochdale. One

train conveyed through coaches from Euston to Rochdale. When the MS&L became the Great Central Railway (GCR) in 1897, it ran push pull services from Guide Bridge to Oldham Clegg Street, and these services continued under the LNER Some of these trains provided cross-platform connections to Greenfield and Delph. There were also connections to Rochdale trains from Central Station, although the only link between the two stations was via the street above.

OA&GB TRAINS

The earliest trains were composed of MS&L four and six-wheel coaches. Following the then prevailing fashion, the GCR built three self-contained steam railmotors numbered 1, 2 and 3 in 1904-5. The Great Central Railway also built a few steam railmotors but when these units went out of fashion, permission was given in 1922 for the carriage portions to be converted to driving trailers for push pull working. Most of the alterations were at the engine end and new 8ft wheelbase bogies were fitted in place of the original bogies with Dean type suspension. At least one of

The south end of Clegg Street was situated in a gloomy cutting surrounded on three sides by the goods yard. The station name board consisted of cast iron lettering screwed onto a wooden backing. Below it was a supplementary board proclaiming "Junction for Rochdale", which was a reference to the service through the adjacent Oldham Central station, although there was never a footbridge between the two stations to assist cross platform connections. The 3.30pm from Guide Bridge worked by C13 No **67421** can just be seen through the gloom on 14th April 1955. Being all of five miles from Guide Bridge, the fourteen minutes allowed for the journey to Clegg Street (arr 3.44) would normally prove to be more than adequate to enable the Rochdale connection at Central to be made. The 4.5pm ex-Manchester Victoria train to Rochdale (via Shaw) - which provided the connection - was not scheduled to reach Central until 4.23! Only six trains each weekday (SX) would ply the short distance between Guide Bridge and Clegg Street, the usefulness of the service being further eroded by the gap of 5¹/2 hours between nine 'o' clock in the morning and 3.30 in the afternoon. A number of other trains originating from Stockport traversed the route but omitted Guide Bridge by means of Denton and Crowthorne Junctions.   *H B Priestley*

these rebuilds entered the Manchester London Road motor-fitted pool and as such appeared regularly on Guide Bridge-Oldham services right up to the mid 1950s.

The GCR built three of 60ft 12-wheel open saloon composite driving trailers to accompany the steam railmotors in 1905. Numbered 4, 5 and 6, they had 6-wheel bogies and, like the LNWR open saloon driving trailers on the Delph branch, had recessed centre entrances. With the demise of steam railmotors, the trailer coaches were adapted for use in push-pull trains. Driving Trailers Nos.1-6 were renumbered 51902-51906 by the L.N.E.R. in 1923. In 1923/4, one of the twelve-wheel composites was converted to all third. Nos.51902-4 were each coupled to a six-wheel coach, of which two were of Lancashire Derbyshire and East Coast Railway origins. They were powered by GCR 2-4-2Ts with mechanically controlled push pull gear and worked in the Manchester area. In addition, an ex-GCR clerestory non-corridor composite was converted to work push pull to Diagram 147A in 1933. Numbered 5821, it ran with 51904 on Guide Bridge-Oldham services well into the 1950s. The two remaining 6-wheelers were replaced in 1933 by two non-clerestory all-firsts, which

had worked on London suburban services and had been converted to composites by having four compartments downgraded to third class. During the motor-train conversion an end compartment was stripped and fitted with double doors to make a luggage compartment, thus forming a luggage-composite push-pull trailer. Numbered 5974 and 5823, they initially ran with driving trailers Nos. 51903 and 51902 respectively. The ex-GCR driving trailers, including the ex steam railmotor conversions, retained LNER 'teak' brown livery after Nationalization, however, BR style Gil Sans running numbers were applied with an E prefix, for example 51904 became E 51904 (with no suffix). The brown carriages were a familiar sight on Guide Bridge-Oldham trains until replaced in the mid 1950s by wartime conversions of LNER Gresley non corridor brake thirds to push-pull driving trailers (wartime Diagram 317/320 Nos. 86983/4 and 86997).

In GCR days the motive power for these push pull trains were Class 12AM Sacre 2-4-0T's, which in 1922/3 were joined by Parker 2-4-2T's Nos. 575, 586 and 594, then recently fitted with GCR mechanical push pull gear. Ex GCR 2-4-2T No. 5729 was equipped with push pull gear in 1931. All the 2-4-2Ts had the......

(Above) This view looking south towards Park Bridge shows the name board has lost it reference to Rochdale. An unidentified LYR 'A' class 0-6-0 takes water in the Up platform while Class C13 4-4-2T No **67417** appears from under Clegg Street goods yard and enters the station with a solitary BR Mk.I coach on 11th April 1959. This working was the 11.45am Saturdays-only Guide Bridge to Oldham. Motor-train operation had ceased by this date and the various GCR and LNER push pull coaches had been replaced by ordinary non-corridor stock.   *P Hutchinson*

...... fittings removed 1936-7, but then 5594, allocated to Gorton, was re-equipped with LNER vacuum-control type. This loco worked Guide Bridge-Oldham services. C13 4-4-2Ts, Nos. 5009, 5190, 5191, 5193, 5359 and 5458, were initially fitted with mechanical push pull gear in 1933 for working Chester & Wirral services, but all were modified to vacuum-control type in 1937. In 1941, 5002 and 5115 were also fitted with vac-control gear.

Oldham Clegg Street station closed when passenger services over the OA&GB finished on 2 May 1959, but the line remained in use for freight and the parcels traffic. Locos from Lees Shed also used this route when working to and from the Manchester area. In 1960, the wooden station at Park Bridge burned down in spectacular fashion, to the accompaniment of exploding detonators left in one of the rooms. When collecting or dropping off wagons at H. Lees & Sons Park Bridge iron works sidings, moved the materials to and from the exchange sidings. Purchased new by Penmaenmawr Quarries in 1940, it arrived at Park Bridge in 1956. The iron works also used a self-propelled steam crane.

Major repair work was carried out on the nearby viaduct and the iron works continued to be rail-served until it closed in 1964. Park Bridge village was the oldest surviving example in the county of Lancashire of an industrial community based on engineering. The houses were built.......***continued in next column***

(Above) Services from Delph used to run empty stock to Sheepwashers Lane signal box where they crossed over to the Down line and returned to Clegg Street ready to work back to Delph. The bridge carrying Park Road and the tunnel under Clegg Street goods yard are visible beyond the signal box. The large LNWR cotton on the left was a curious building. The lie of the land forced the architect to lay it out on a curve, so much so that one end of the building is almost at right angles to the other.   *L Goddard*

.........solely for the workers and their .families. The line between OA&GB Junction and Clegg Street closed completely in 1967. Park Bridge Viaduct, a major landmark in the district for so long, was pulled down in 1971. Thereafter, the LYR Manchester-Rochdale line served Clegg Street parcels depot until the latter closed in 1981.

(Right) LYR 0-6-0 No **52410** is about to pass under Goddard Street Bridge, south of Sheepwashers Lane, with a train from Stockport in 1957. On this occasion, a pair of 1930s-built LMS non-corridor coaches had been found for the service. Residents of the well-to-do Honeywell Lane area requested a station be erected nearby in the 1880s but nothing came of the petition.

J Davenport

Although Lees had three 2-6-4Ts on its allocation that could have been used on Oldham-Stockport trains, the smaller 2-6-2Ts and even the LYR 0-6-0s appeared on these duties too. This early 1950s scene shows 0-6-0 No **52365** on a four-coach working from Stockport. The leading coach is a LNWR cove roof corridor third that had been converted to push pull to Diagram M75. It was in Oldham to work Delph services but I have been unable to find a photo of it on such duties after World War Two. It is running with a LNWR M52 Toplight push pull-dritrailer. Both coaches were being used as normal stock to strengthen the train of two LMS non-corridor coaches, that had worked through from Crewe.

J Davenport

(Above) Fowler Class 3MT 2-6-2T No **40061**, in early BR livery, runs down the 1 in 86 from Honeywell Lane bridge towards Park Bridge with a Greenfield to Stockport (via Oldham) train circa 1951. The leading LNWR non-corridor composite coach has been repainted in BR livery although the shade appears to be darker than the BR carmine red on the LMS non-corridor brake third. The LNWR coach has either received a coat of LMS maroon, which was commonly applied to LNWR stock in BR days, or it is a trick of the light. Oldham Alexander Park is behind the distant row of trees.

(Below) Sister engine No **40062** climbs past Snipe clough with the 12.34pm (Saturdays only) Stockport to Oldham Clegg Street on a chill March day in 1953. Once again, we see a 'Delph' push pull set in use as normal stock to strengthen a Stockport working. The coaches are a diagram M76, M52 and two LMS non-corridor coaches. After terminating in Oldham the loco would stable the coaches in Waterloo sidings before returning to Lees shed. Hartshead Pike can be seen on the distant hill.

Both: *J Davenport*

The OA&GB did not own any motive power or rolling stock whatsoever. The MS&L, later GCR, always provided locos and stock for the shuttle service between Oldham and Guide Bridge, and the LNWR provided its own on the Oldham-Stockport service. GCR coaches were a familiar sight on the Guide Bridge service well into the 1950s, many still in LNER unlined brown livery but carrying BR style running numbers. This interesting pair being propelled towards Park Bridge by C13 No **67417**, consisted of a clerestory composite converted to push pull in 1933 to Diagram 147A. Numbered 5821, it is seen with twelve-wheeled driving trailer No.51904 that had been built in 1905. The writing on the end of this coach proclaimed "MANCHESTER

LONDON RD. PUSH & PULL". Seating forward of the centre entrance consisted of reversible back rattan seats while the section between the entrance and the 7ft 9ins long luggage compartment had two 10ft 6ins long bench seats facing inwards. Nearest the camera is the driver's compartment. *J Davenport*

(Right) GCR 4-4-2T No **67421** is not unduly strained climbing away from Park Bridge with two coaches on the final leg from Guide Bridge to Oldham Glodwick Road in the early 1950s. It will be noticed the twelve-wheel driving trailer has a new companion following possible withdrawal of the clerestory coach seen on the previous page. The Up Distant signal would later have its arm removed, but for the moment it is off for a train travelling towards Park Bridge. *J Davenport*

Push Pull Coaches By Larry

(Right) The OA&GB line was a blessing to the Control Staff at Manchester, providing as it did a valuable relief route for getting trains out onto the ER and LMR main lines, and for this reason the viaduct at Park Bridge was kept in good repair. After local passenger ceased, the line continued to host goods, parcels and through excursion traffic. Class C13 Tank No **67417** was a regular engine on the two-coach push pull services, but on this occasion it had been landed with something more strenuous, assisting Black 5 4-6-0 No **44845** on a Skegness-Oldham relief train. *J Davenport*

(Centre) When engineering works were in progress on the mainline between Ashton and Greenfield on certain Sundays in the year, mainline expresses from Liverpool to Newcastle and Manchester to Leeds, and vice-versa, could be seen roaring their way along the OA&GB line on their way to regain the Huddersfield & Manchester mainline. On this occasion though, the line was playing host to another Skegness-Oldham Reilief train worked by Eastern Region Class K3 2-6-0 No **61865** piloting another K3 on the climb to Oldham. The 'Park Bridge' line, as it was known locally, was certainly full of surprises in terms of motive power. *J Davenport*

(Right-lower) Viewed from the bridge in the previous picture, Fowler Class 4MT 2-6-4T No **42379** leaves Park Bridge with a Stockport to Oldham Clegg Street train with LMS Period III and II non-corridor stock in tow. The Village of Park Bridge was in the middle of the country between Bardsley and Abbeyhills, yet it was not short of industry with mills and a large iron-works complex. The village people had reason to be worried when the line was up for closure and showed it in no uncertain form with protest meetings. Apart from private transport or going on foot, there was no form of transport other than travelling by train available to them. Ashton Corporation's bus, put on for them in 1947, only ran on Mondays and Fridays, leaving Park Bridge at 1.30pm for Ashton Market. Village representatives met BR with suggestions of a regular interval DMU service connecting Ashton (Charlestown) with Greenfield, then Greenfield to Oldham via Lees and Oldham to Ashton (Oldham Road) via Park Bridge, but it was a forlorn hope. *J Davenport*

PARK BRIDGE

Stanier Class 4MT 2-6-4T No **42551** crosses the lofty Park Bridge viaduct with the 12.27 (SO) Greenfield to Stockport train. The mill in the foreground had seen better days and looked to be out of use. Beside the mill ran the meandering River Medlock. Between Oldham Clegg Street and Guide Bridge there were no fewer than 29 bridges that the railway ran under or over. Notices along the OA&GB line were many and varied. At Honeywell Lane Bridge there was a small metal notice facing the road of OA&GB origin, while on the bridge itself there was a notice of the Great Central stating the manner in which the bridge should be used by road vehicles. Next to it was a larger notice of the LNER! Amongst the familiar trespass notices was only one stating the penalty for doing so. This was on the viaduct at Park Bridge as seen here.

J Davenport

(Right) Ashton Corporation Guy Arab IV waits for workers in Park Bridge in 1970. The photographer abandoned his car at Bardsley and rode on this bus into Ashton, then on route 30 to Hyde and back. XTC 854, Fleet No 67, with bodywork by Bond of Wythenshaw entered service in May 1956.

L Goddard

(Right) Standing above the village atop a hillside, the station at Park Bridge consisted of wooden buildings on a wooden platform with a booking office on both platforms. It has been suggested (Oldham Chronicle May 22nd 1965), that the buildings were made of timber from the large woods that abounded around Park Bridge at the time the railway was built. The nickname of the MS&L railway, probably given to it by some unfortunate shareholder, was *"Money Sunk & Lost"*, which may indicate that building stations from wood was the cheapest and best option so far as the MS&L was concerned! This picture was drawn on site by author LG over a period of weekends in 1959. It later appeared in the Oldham Chronicle.

(Left-centre) While compiling the pictures and writing captions for this book, this photo was handed to LG of a Class C13 4-4-2T photographed from almost the same spot from which I did the above sketch. No **67438** is calling at the station with the 11.51 (SO) Guide Bridge to Oldham Glodwick Road on 29th May 1948. Nationalization of the railways had only taken place five months previously yet the loco has already acquired British Railways lettering on its tank sides and a new number in the 60000 series in LNER numerals. *C A Appleton*

(Left-lower) Park Bridge signal box was situated at the south end of the down platform opposite the goods yard. Of note is the station name board, which displayed Parkbridge as one word whereas that on the box was split. The crew of Fowler Class 7F 0-8-0 No **49662** would no doubt be glad to get back to Lees shed having left there in the early hours to work the 4am Diggle to Ashton Oldham Road goods, and then spent most of the morning on pilot duty before working home with a lone BR goods brakevan. *J Davenport*

Class 7F No **49662** is seen on another occasion propelling an early LMS goods brake van across Park Bridge viaduct while working the 12.10pm Ashton Oldham Road to Glodwick Road goods. The OA&GB project was strongly supported by the MS&L as it gave them an entry into Oldham, and although the passenger traffic was not particularly remunerative, very heavy coal traffic from South Yorkshire coal pits had operated over the line at one time.
J Davenport

(Centre) Fowler 2-6-2T No **40062** is departing Park Bridge with a set of LMS Intermediate Cross Country Lavatory coaches forming the 4.31pm Huddersfield to Stockport train circa 1954. The goods yard curving away in the background also acted as an interchange point for materials in and out of Park Bridge iron works. The works sent its own crane and locomotives up a steep incline from the valley bottom to this yard.
J Davenport

(Below) It was in the 19th Century that Samual Lees founded the ironworks that provided the hub of prosperity for Park Bridge. Running horizontally across the top of the picture is Park Bridge viaduct. The OA&GB station and goods yard was situated at the Ashton end of the viaduct on the left of the scene. From the goods yard, a line ran down a steep incline and negotiated a horseshoe bend over a short river bridge before continuing down to the ironworks. The earthworks are clearly seen running vertically down the LH side and along the bottom of the picture, around the earth mound and down to the building with a clerestory roof. The line then crossed Alt Lane before going on to the old rolling mills, the roofs of which are clearly visible below the viaduct. Here, generations of people have looked down through the open barred windows above the rolling mill floor to watch the soft white hot steel squeezed back and forth through rollers until it was a long red hot snake of metal, always deftly handled by men who's skills had been finely honed over many years.
P G Hindley

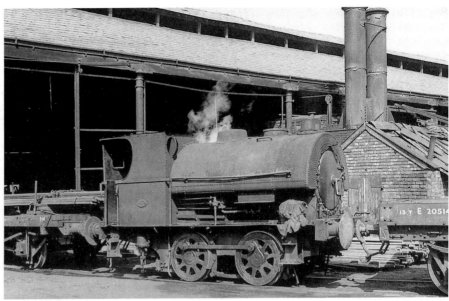

(Above-left) The self-propelled steam crane was standing in the goods yard behind Park Bridge station waiting to unload some BR wagons when photographed in 1960. It had worked up from the valley bottom accompanied by the works diesel shunter seen in the background. The latter was No **2069** *FOX*, built by Hunslet in 1940 for Penmaenmawr Quarry. It arrived at Hannah Lees & Sons ironworks in 1956. When the ironworks closed, *Fox* went to Thomas Storey (Engineers) Ltd of Stockport in February 1964. *L Goddard*

(Above-left) The ironworks rail system kept two Beyer Peacock 0-4-0 saddle tank locos employed for many years, which were rather unusual in having inside cylinders. *ORION* dated from 1889 while *PEGASUS* dated from 1901. *ORION* minus its nameplates is seen at the ironworks on 30th April 1955. This loco must have donated some of its parts to the other loco, as *PEGASUS* became *ORION* in 1956. *D L Chatfield*

(Below) One last look at Park Bridge ironworks as it was in April 1955. *ORION* stands outside the roofless loco shed having its saddle tank filled via a hosepipe from a trackside water-stand. Smoke is drifting up the line that descends steeply from the BR sidings to the works. A cobbled road that ran under the viaduct and out towards the main Oldham-Ashton thoroughfare also carried a railway track leading to other works in the village. *D L Chatfield*

(Right) The next station after Park Bridge was Ashton (Oldham Road). It stood close by the road it was named after and was some four bus stops out of Ashton town centre. The Oldham platform had a booking office, ladies waiting room, general waiting room, stationmaster's office and porter's room. Large ornate lamps suspended from the wooden walls provided lighting around the main building. A smaller booking office was also provided on the Guide Bridge platform.. While E.R push-pull coaches reigned supreme on Guide Bridge trains due to the specialised nature of the stock, E.R stock occasionally turned up on the L.M.R. trains to Stockport as seen here. BR Standard Class 2MT 2-6-2T No **84013** pauses at the station with a GCR matchboard non-corridor brake third and an LMS non-corridor composite while working an Oldham Clegg Street to Stockport train circa1955.
J Davenport

(Centre) Trains were down to a solitary BR Mk.I non-corridor coach during the final weeks of OA&GB passenger services. GCR Tank No **67417** enters Ashton station from under Oldham Road Bridge with a train for Oldham Clegg Street in 1959. The business of having a booking office on both platforms as at Park Bridge was unique to this area. The smaller office, which only held local-issue tickets, was built after a footbridge connecting the Up and Down platforms was declared unsafe and pulled down in 1914. This meant that the regular Booking Clerk had to sprint across the tracks when two trains were due in the station. However, a relief clerk, unacquainted with the stations peculiarities, could be taken unawares when the porter dashed in five minutes before a Stockport train was due to say that there were workers on the other platform waiting for tickets! *A Moyes*

(Right-lower) From Ashton Oldham Road, the line joined the Huddersfield & Manchester mainline and then turned off left to Guide Bridge at OA&GB Junction signal box, which is seen towering above the distant bridge. This line eventually divided with the LNWR line to Stockport and the GCR line to Guide Bridge parting company. Fairburn 2-6-4T No **42696** negotiates the junction and takes the Oldham line with a Manchester Victoria – Oldham Clegg Street parcels train circa 1960.
J Davenport

(Right) Eastern Region trains from Oldham terminated at Guide Bridge. Class C13 4-4-2T No **67416** propels a push pull train towards the station in the early 1950s. The driving trailer was originally built as a steam railmotor by the GCR. It was converted to a push pull driving trailer by the LNER as was the GCR luggage composite behind the engine. *J Davenport*

(Below) The 5.14pm Stockport-Greenfield train (arr 6.01pm) was a London Midland Region working and is seen passing Heaton Norris Junction behind Lees-based Fowler 2-6-2T No **40062** in September 1954. This picture could come under the heading, *'A prototype for everything Department'*, showing as it does a pair of 'Delph Donkey' push pull coaches bowling along the busy London Euston mainline! The leading pair (Diagram M47 and M49) started out from Oldham Glodwick Road at 4.32pm and returned from Stockport attached to through coaches from Crewe. Not for the Oldham passenger the tiresome journey across Manchester, but a stroll across to the "little train" in the bay on No.5 at Stockport, then a journey taking in stations at Denton, Ashton, Park Bridge, Oldham Clegg Street and Lees, and familiar landmarks such as Hartshead Pike and Alexander Park before finally reaching Greenfield. *J Davenport*

(Above) LNWR 57ft Third Class push-pull open saloondriving trailer to diagram M49. This 4mm scale model carries LMS 1923-34 fully lined livery and was the first model I produced in photo-etched brass. *L Goddard*

PUSH - PULL COACHES BY LARRY GODDARD

This chapter could almost be the story of the push-pull coaches that saw service on the Delph Branch, for it is doubtful if any other Branch in Britain saw so much variety particularly in the 1950s. LNWR push pull coaches came in a complexity of types and styles, some being converted from former loco-hauled stock and some purpose built. No less than 68 separate diagrams of motor-fitted coaches were issued covering driving and non-driving trailers of all types, and it may come as a surprise that the normally 'standardized' LNWR went to so much trouble (and expense?) to create so many separate one-off diagrams for much of its motor-fitted stock. It surely cannot really have been necessary. However, since the conversion or design of stock did not take place all at one time, but was generally undertaken only when specific need arose for push pull coaches, it can be appreciated why so many were built as one-off vehicles or in very small batches. In addition to coaches converted from ordinary stock, variety was added by new stock.

The LNWR introduced a whole series of saloons during the years 1910-16, with recessed end or centre entrances, and all bore more than a passing likeness to the preceding Steam Railmotors. The Composites were to Diagrams M11-MI8, and the Thirds were to M44-M50. In addition, non-driving trailers to Diagrams M11-13 had low-elliptical roofs and so when attached to a driving trailer; the difference in roof profile was noticeable. I will describe the open saloons in order of appearance. All the running numbers quoted here are the second LMS numbers, which continued to be carried in BR days.

When the **Diagram M44** driving trailer No.15851 was built in 1910 to run with the last–built M6 LNWR steam rail motor, it also set the body style for all the open push pull driving trailers built over the following two years, although its 60' length was not repeated. Large windows and half-size windows, the latter with droplights, and all crowned with typical LNWR 3-element louvers, were used in various combinations on all the driving trailers built in 1911/12.

Diagram M15 No.15846, was the first of the composite driving trailers to appear in 1911. With eleven small windows and only two large windows per side, its appearance was not as tidy as the M44. It had two first class coupes that were situated at opposite ends of the coach, and the proliferation of small windows was necessary to accommodate interior partitions between first and third class compartments. Henceforth all driving trailers had first class accommodation concentrated at the luggage end. I have found no pictures of **Diagram M16** No.15847, but the **Diagram M17** composite No.3421 had a tidier window arrangement of alternating large and small droplight windows. **Diagram M46** No.15844 and **Diagram M49** third class driving trailers Nos.3413-6 and 3411-2 followed suit. The following year a composite and an all third, in the form of **Diagram M14** No.3422 and **Diagram M48** No.15845 appeared. In 1912/13 the LNWR built three observation cars to **Diagram M50**, one of which is now preserved on the bluebell Railway, and they introduced a new window arrangement. Instead of windows with louvers above them, they had large fixed windows, each with pairs of opening half-lights above them. This arrangement was to be standard from now on. The fact that the Observation Saloon's were listed as push pull coaches might seem strange when they were usually attached to non-motor fitted trains.

PUSH - PULL COACHES CONTINUED........

As far as I can ascertain the Diagram M50 Observation Saloons could be used as push pull coaches, however, this requires some amplification. While one saloon worked the Conwy Valley branch and another worked to Llanberis, it was possible to convert the spare saloon into a form of driving trailer for use as a propelled route-learning vehicle when required. The 'driving gear' as such was portable and consisted of a simple lever for destroying the vacuum in case brakes needed to be applied in an emergency.

There was no regulator control, and messages were relayed to the fireman, who remained on the footplate, via bell pushes. This portable gear could be plugged into either end of the Saloon and was removed before the coach returned to normal duties. An auto-fitted loco was used for short distances, but tender locos were used for longer distances. Besides covering the North Wales mainline and branch lines, the saloons travelled wherever the need arose and ventured as far a field as Blackpool.

This model of the LNWR Diagram M47 Trailer Open Third was built as a companion for the M49 Driving Trailer, again finished in LMS full livery. Coaches like this made travel on the Oldham - Delph services so interesting.   *L Goddard*

In 1913, the first of the non-driving trailers, No.3423, was built to Diagram M47. It was a third class open saloon with slightly bowed ends, deeply inset hinged doors at the ends, and nine fixed windows per side. Above the main windows were half-lights hinged along their top edge to push outwards. In the same year Diagram M18 composite driving trailer No.3424 appeared with the new toplight window arrangement, there being four (per side) in the third class saloon behind the driver's compartment, and two in the first class section next to the luggage space. Four Toplight third class driving trailers to Diagram M45 appeared in 1913 and these coaches later carried numbers 3417-20. Interestingly, driving trailers built to Diagrams M17, M18 and M45 ran with corridor connections at

both ends until their removal from the driving end the driving end during the Second World War.

Another non-driving trailer also appeared in 1913, this time an open composite to Diagram M13 No.3426. It appears to have been somewhat experimental with deeply inset hinged doors at one end, as on the M47, and slightly recessed sliding doors at the other. It also introduced a new low elliptical roof profile. Experiments continued with another open composite non-driving trailer, built to Diagram M11 1914. It had eight windows per side with 'push-out' opening half-lights and deeply recessed hinged doors; however, on this occasion the doors were angled the opposite way to those on Diagrams M47 and M13. This coach became No.3427 in 1933.

This is what the classic LNWR push-pull coaches looked when first introduced on the 'Delph Donkey'. A 4mm scale model built in 2002 of the Diagram M15 Composite Driving Trailer. *L Goddard*

The final open composite non-driving trailer was built to Diagram M12 in 1916, again with a low elliptical roof. This time, all hinges were dispensed with and slightly recessed sliding doors were fitted instead. In fact, this coach was all-but identical in outline to Oerlikon electric stock the LNWR built for its London suburban electrification programme in 1914. The opening half-lights were similar to those on later driving trailers, and instead of being hinged along the top; they were hinged to open like a door. This coach became No.3425.

LNWR Diagram M75 was one of three side corridor thirds with cove roofs converted by the LNWR from D264 vehicles, while Diagram M76A consisted of thirteen side corridor coaches converted by the LMS from LNWR D265 corridor 3rds. A luggage space was created at one end by utilizing one lavatory and one compartment. The latter were only 8' 6" wide.

Side-corridor driving trailers also worked Delph services. LNWR Diagram M52 consisted of four Toplight driving trailer thirds built new as push pull coaches in 1913. Numbers 3407 and 3410 were known to have worked around Delph.

LNWR diagram diagram M52 was one of a batch of driving trailers built in 1913 to normal 'toplight' coach design with side corridors, but with a driver's compartment and end windows at one end. One of these coaches had the corridor connection removed at the drivers end. This 4mm scale model was built to order for Mr David Holt. *L Goddard*

In 1938, the LMS converted four Period I open thirds into driving trailers by fitting a driving compartment into the space once occupied by an entrance and lavatory. A small luggage compartment with double doors was fitted at the other end in place of the entrance and lavatory. A separate recessed double-doors entrance was provided for passengers as per the LNWR open saloons. The LMS numbered the conversions 3462-65, and one of these coaches worked Delph services for a short spell in the 1950s. Finally, three LMS D1807 Period II open thirds were converted by BR to push pull operation in 1951 and No. M3484M appeared on Delph services attached to the diagram M15 driving trailer.

From a technical viewpoint, the LNWR Driving trailers were unusual in that vacuum brake cylinders were situated on the same side of the under frame instead of being diagonally opposed as on most railway coaches. When built the push-pull apparatus was mechanical and, while one can never be absolutely certain in these matters, it is possible the brake cylinders were positioned on one side in order to clear the necessary push pull linkage. Of the six Diagram M49s, all except 3415 were fitted by the LMS with Vacuum Regulator Control in 1927, this odd one out simply retaining rodding, according to the diagram book.

It is known some of these coaches worked around Bedford, Bletchley, Delph, Oxford, and St. Helens, Warrington and on some branchlines in North Wales. As mentioned earlier, the last-built 60' steam railmotor was transferred to North Wales after working the Delph line. When it was withdrawn in 1928, its companion M44 driving trailer continued in use as a push pull vehicle. It is not known if it ever returned to Delph, but it definitely worked around the Warrington area during the Second World War.

Prior to arriving at Delph, the coach - to Diagram 15 (Page 146) - had worked at Rhyl for a number of years. The stock left Rhyl every weekday as the 6.20am Rhyl-Holywell Junction empty-stock before one of the driving trailers took up Holywell branch services while the other worked the 7.50am or the 8.33am Holywell Junction-Chester turn, which occasionally worked Motor. The driving trailers returned each evening as the 9.50pm Holywell Junction-Rhyl empty Motor (11.30pm Saturdays only). Diagram M49 driving trailers also worked the Holywell branch from 1935 until 1951. When Holywell services ceased on 6th September 1954, the M15 driving trailer was transferred to Delph.

In the early 1950s the sidings between Oldham Clegg Street and Glodwick Road became a gathering point for LNWR push pull coaches displaced from other parts of the country, and they weren't just put to work on Oldham-Greenfield--Delph services either. This surfeit of motor-fitted stock was used as normal coaching stock at peak-hour and weekends for strengthening Stockport-Stalybridge-Oldham - Greenfield trains as well as football specials.

With no further need for push pull coaches in the area after passenger services ceased in 1955, the stock languished in sidings around Oldham to await its fate, but there was life after Delph for the chosen few. For instance, the Diagram M15 driving trailer travelled south to St. Albans and found work for another four years. Whilst a number of driving trailers went on to work until late 1958, the open saloon trailers had all gone by 1956.

All LNWR-built push pull coaches carried full plum and flake white livery from new until the formation of the LMS in 1923 after which they gradually exchanged it for full panelled crimson lake. Unfortunately, there is a dearth of photographic evidence showing these coaches in the 1930s so one can only guess what happened when the LMS adopted a simpler form of lining in 1935. Due to their comparatively low mileage and sphere of operation, some push pull coaches probably carried full panelled livery into the war years and went straight to unlined maroon during the war years. At least one of the LNWR Observation Saloons returned to normal duties in North Wales after the war in LMS simple livery with lining at the waist.

Many wooden bodied coaches began to have their raised beading removed when panels were repaired during the war, and push-pull coaches were no exception. On Nationalization the 4 inch yellow shaded red LMS running numbers were prefixed with a 3 inch letter 'M' that had obviously been clipped from an LMS transfer. The ex-LNWR push pull coaches I saw in Oldham looked dull and I'm pretty sure I would have remembered if any were in such a bright colour as carmine red. I think BR must have reckoned the elderly push pull vehicles were not worth spending money on in view of their work and low daily mileage.

The colour slides I saw in the 1990s led one to believe some coaches were lighter than others, the assumption being they were carmine red. New technology has removed the colour casts and shown that the coaches were in fact maroon, but the revarnished ones looked lighter. It made sense for BR to patch paint replacement panels or apply a fresh coat of varnish instead of a full repaint. Perhaps the most unusual variation was M15 driving trailer No.M15846. Between leaving Rhyl and reaching the Delph branch in 1954, it was given an overhaul and was either varnished or repainted in LMS maroon. However, the running number was also applied in LMS yellow/red transfers instead of BR Gill sans transfers, thus, the coach arrived at Delph in immaculate LMS livery 6 years after that company had ceased to exist! Coaches with corridor connections were in theory eligible for BR blood & custard livery but only the push pull converted D1807 open third push pull vehicle carried this livery on the Delph line.

WORKING THE PUSH PULL/MOTOR TRAINS

Special instructions were laid down for the operation of rail motors and motor trains additional to all the general and special Rules and Regulations that applied to normal workings. Under the section dealing with attaching to "Rail Motor" (a vehicle with a self-contained non-detachable engine), one "Motor Train" means a train consisting of detachable engine with specially fitted coaches capable of being driven from either end of the train. Not more than four specially fitted coaches may be attached at the leading end of the engine except by the authority of the Chief operating Manager. Additional vehicles may be attached in rear of motor trains as laid down for passenger trains…. but no additional passenger carrying vehicles may be attached on sections on the line where there are halts, without the authority of the Chief Operating Manager.

In the event of there not being time to arrange for a similar class of vehicle and the service is one which serves halts, the train most be replaced by a corridor brake third or corridor composite brake, and (if necessary) a corridor third, and ladder provided. The compartment doors must be kept locked and arrangements made for passengers to leave and enter through the brake compartment.

When there are coaches on both ends of the engine, the driver will be responsible for switching the electric lights on and off from the driving compartment in which he is riding when passing into or out of tunnels. passenger-carrying vehicle or horsebox, cattle wagon or other 4-wheeled vehicle may be attached to L.N.W. type rail motor No. 29988 and all L.Y. type of rail motors.

Guards must ride in the vestibule of the "open" cars, except when they may require to go into the passenger compartments to deal with tickets or into luggage compartments for the suppose of dealing with traffic. In trains of the compartment type, guards must ride in the rear driving compartment where there is more than one, or in the rear brake compartment if there is one on the train. Guards must use every care in getting passengers into and out of vehicles safely and quickly. They will be responsible for seeing that doors are closed and fastened before moving. Passengers must be requested not to ride in vestibules.

Motor sets fitted with vacuum controlled regulator gear cannot be worked with any motor coaches other than those fitted with the vacuum control regulator gear.

The fares to be charged are announced on the public bills. A list of such fares must always be exhibited in the vehicles running on sections of the line where there are halts, and guards are responsible for seeing that lists are properly exhibited.

PUSH PULL SYSTEM

H.C.H. Burgess, one time fitter at Swansea had the following to say on push pull trains: -

The system involved fitting locomotives with an entirely separate regulator valve in the main steam pipe between the smoke box header and cylinders, plus a vacuum cylinder mounted outside on the foot-framing to operate it. The intended method of regulator control from a coach driving compartment was that whilst working in push and pull mode the main regulator should remain open and control of the steam admitted to the cylinders was vested in the drivers vacuum control regulator valve, to which was connected a vacuum gauge, in theory registering and infinite choice of regulator positions between closed, 0", and fully opened, 21". But it did not work like this on the Webb Coal Tanks, whose VCR cylinders had pistons with leather sealing washers, which needed regular dosage of caster oil if they were to work at all.

Footplate men had learned from bitter experience that this cylinder gave but two positions; open and shut, with nothing in between. They had devised a simple method to deal with this. When at a station the fireman kept his eye on the VCR vacuum gauge and as soon as he saw the finger move away from the zero position he would open the main regulator and, as speed increased, alter the opening to suit demand and adjust valve travel as necessary.

Of course, even with a vacuum control regulator that operated satisfactorily he would still have to adjust valve travel and look after the regulator if wheel slip occurred, as it would be doubtful if the driver would be aware of wheel slip from two coaches distant. There was an electric bell code system between coach and footplate and a mechanical linkage to the loco. It was a case of, whistle if all else failed.

The bell code in ERO 46483 October 1935 instructions for working Motor Trains was as follows:
Emergency stop: 1 long
Tank hand brake off: 2 short
Open regulator on engine: 3 long
Shut regulator on engine: 2 short 2 long
Driver leaving driving compartment to carry out Rule 55: 6 short
Set back: 2 long.

LNWR Push Pull Composite Saloon to Diagram M11

The Diagram M11 composite open saloon built in 1914 marked a return to the low eliptical roof even though thre slightly older Dagram M47 had a full eliptical roof.

The deeply recessed end doors were angled in towards the coach ends, the opposite way to those on the M47. The drawing shows the coach with its original panelling, some of which was removed from 1940 onwards during works repairs. Fowler Class 3MT No.40056 passes Measurements with the M11 and a M49 in tow. The different roof profiles are evident. **Photo by Jim Davenport, courtesy Brian Green.**

PROTOTYPE DETAILS

Built 1914
LNWR number 1726
1sr LMS number 9522
2nd LMS number 3427
Withdrawn August 1955

Ran on the Delph branch in later years downgraded to third class, and was usualy coupled to Diagram M49 driving trailer No.3416.

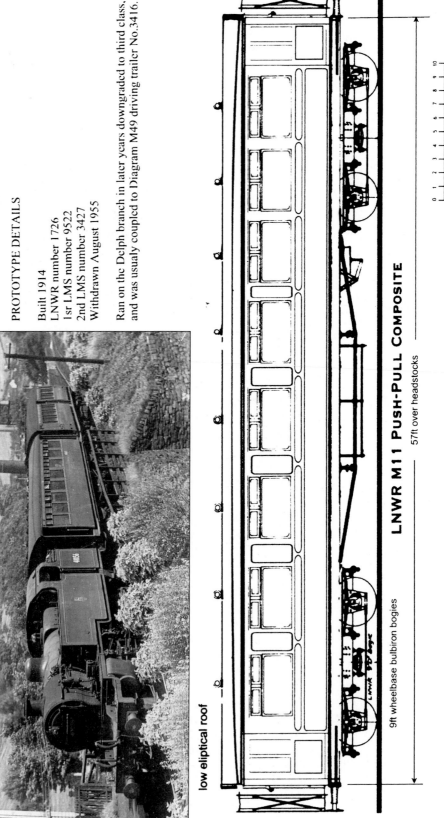

low eliptical roof

LNWR M11 PUSH-PULL COMPOSITE

57ft over headstocks

9ft wheelbase bulbiron bogies

0 1 2 3 4 5 6 7 8 9 10

LNWR PUSH PULL COMPOSITE SALOON TO DIAGRAM M12

This carriage was the last of the push pull open saloons to be built in 1916. The roof profile was low eliptical, which was visibly lower than a normal hieght roof (see picture below). Apart from raised wooden beading, this coach was identical to Oerlikon electric stock which had been introduced on local lines around Watford in 1914.

All the LNWR push pull open saloon coaches built during the years 1910-1916 were somewhat experimental, and it appears the company couldn't decide whether to angle the hinged doors inwards towards the saloon or the ends. The M12 was built with sliding doors! Similar doors had been adopted two years earlier on the 'Oerlikon' stock. The doors slid between the coach side and a glazed panel inside the passenger saloon. Originally built as a composite, it was downgraded to third class in 1930. Skinley drawing No.5307 is recommended for details of ends and interior.

Jim Davenport

PROTOTYPE DETAILS

Built 1916
LNWR number 3727
1st LMS number 9523
2nd LMS number 3425
Withdrawn September 1956

Ran coupled to Dia. M18 No. 3424 on Delph branch until circa 1953, then ran with Dia. M45 No. 3419 until 1955.

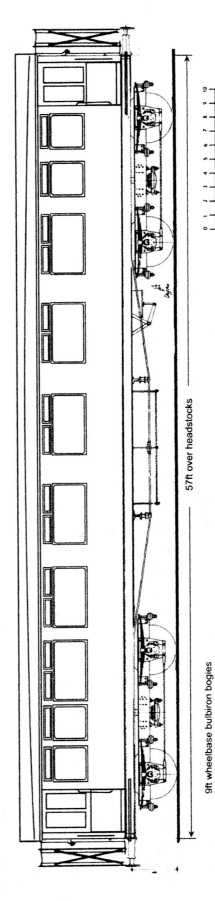

57ft over headstocks

9ft wheelbase bulbiron bogies

LNWR PUSH PULL COMPOSITE DRIVING TRAILER SALOON TO DIAGRAM M15

The Diagram M15 composite driving trailer was the very first to be built for running with push pull fitted locomotives, and bore a strong resemblance to the final LNWR steam railmotor. This coach had quite a charmed life and was amongst the last withdrawals in 1958. It operated in North Wales in the 1930s working over the Rhyl to Denbigh line and the Holywell Branch before transfer to Oldham in 1954. It had an overhaul in 1953 and was fully repainted in LMS maroon with its running number in LMS yellow/red transfers. As with many push pull coaches, it was downgraded to an all-third around 1930. A first class compartments was at each end, hence the small windows between compartment partitions. It is pictured coupled to Diagram M58 No.M3404, an arc roof driving trailer at Rhyl in September 1952. **Authors collection**

PROTOTYPE DETAILS

Built 1911
LNWR number 3723
1st LMS number 9518
2nd LMS number 15846
Withdrawn June 1958

Arrived on Delph branch in 1954 from North Wales. To St.Alabans in 1956.. Ran with LMS open third No.M3484M on Delph branch, then from 1954 with M52 driving trailer M3407M
No. 3421 until the latter was withdrawn in 1953. Then ran with M49 No. 3414.

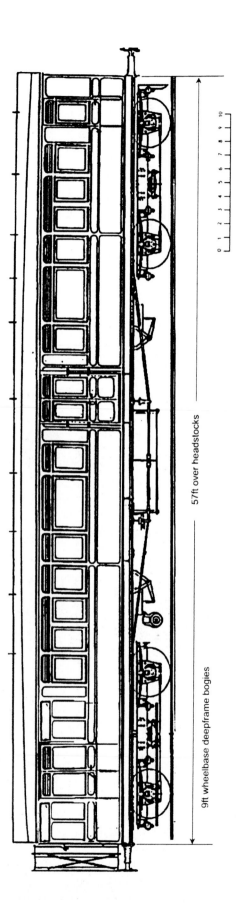

57ft over headstocks

9ft wheelbase deepframe bogies

LNWR PUSH PULL COMPOSITE DRIVING TRAILER SALOON TO DIAGRAM M17

The Diagram M17 composite driving trailer followed the M15 driving trailer, but differed in having the first class compartments at one end next to the luggage compartment. This coach arrived on the Delph Branch in 1951 but was withdrawn two years later. While at Delph, it worked with the Diagram M47 non-driving trailer. It was downgraded to an all-third in 1930. LMS livery was carried into BR days with a small LMS style "M" prefix. The yellow/red insignia is visible in the photo of the drvier handing the Delph branch single line token to signalman W. Hobson at Delph Junction circa 1952. Moorgate Halt platform is also visible.   **Jim Davenport. J. Wells collection**

PROTOTYPE DETAILS

Built 1911
LNWR number 3724
1st LMS number 9520
2nd LMS number 3421
Withdrawn July 1953

Arrived on Delph branch in 1951 and ran with Diagram M47 non driving trailer No. 3423.

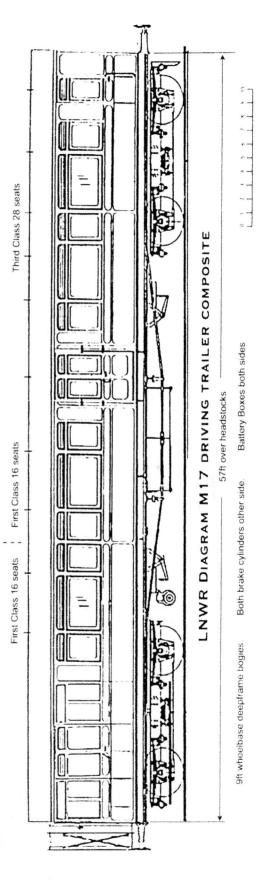

First Class 16 seats | First Class 16 seats

Third Class 28 seats

LNWR DIAGRAM M17 DRIVING TRAILER COMPOSITE

9ft wheelbase deepframe bogies.   Both brake cylinders other side.   57ft over headstocks   Battery Boxes both sides

LNWR Push Pull Composite Driving Trailer Saloon to Diagram M18

The Diagram M18 is basically a toplight version of M17. The earlier external body design of windows surmounted with louvered vents was superseded by this design with small opening windows above the main windows, producing a very attractive vehicle. This coach worked on the Delph-Oldham services in the 1930s and possibly earlier. After the Second World War, it was attached to M12 non-driving trailer No. 3425 before being transferred away in 1953. The picture shows the pair at Moorgate Halt in the early 1950s. At this period, both coaches were still in LMS livery with yellow/red running numbers and an 'M' prefix. **Jim Davenport.**

PROTOTYPE DETAILS

Built 1913
LNWR number 3725
1st LMS number 9521
2nd LMS number 3424
Withdrawn May 1958

Left Delph Branch in 1953.

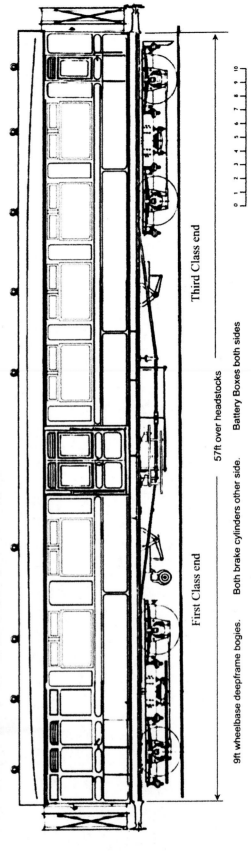

First Class end

Third Class end

57ft over headstocks

9ft wheelbase deepframe bogies.　　Both brake cylinders other side.　　Battery Boxes both sides

LNWR PUSH PULL 3RD CLASS DRIVING TRAILER SALOON TO DIAGRAM M45

Diagram M45 all-third was to the same Toplight style as the M18 composite, however, the luggage compartment doubled as a driving compartment. Four vehicles were built to this Diagram. No. 3419 went to Delph in 1954 to replace M18 No.3424. Although the exterior of the coach was attractive, the interior was rather spartan with low-back tram style seats, which could be flipped over to face the direction of travel. This coach made ocassional forays to Stockport on peak hour workings, making for an interesting journey! Built with corridor connections at both ends, the end elevation drawing depicts a typical postwar driving end following corridor connection removal (during World War Two) and lower panel repairs

H. C. Casserley

PROTOTYPE DETAILS

Built 1913
LNWR numbers 132 - 135
1st LMS numbers 5198 - 5201
2nd LMS numbers 3417 - 3420
3417 withdrawn in June 1956
3418 withdrawn in 1957
3419 withdrawn in October 1958
3420 withdrawn in January 1951

3419 to Delph Branch in 1954.

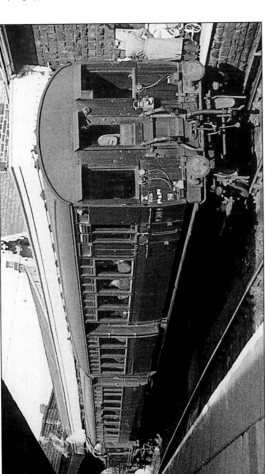

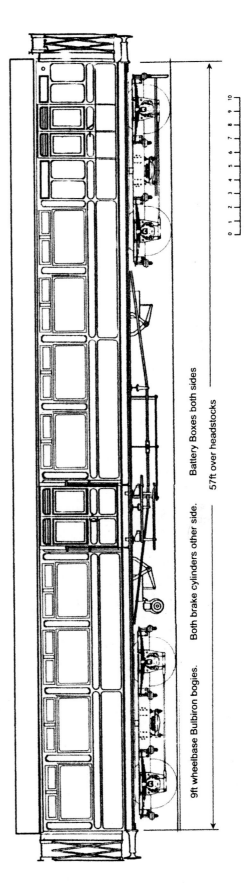

9ft wheelbase Bulbiron bogies.   Both brake cylinders other side.   Battery Boxes both sides

57ft over headstocks

0 1 2 3 4 5 6 7 8 9 10

LNWR Push Pull Third Class Saloon to Diagram M47

The Diagram M47 third class saloon had a full eliptical roof, although the roof looked like no other on the LNWR with its steeply curved sides that were almost verticle where they met the coach body. The experimental nature of this vehicle was also evident in the ends, whch were bowed and not flat. This coach was easily recognisable because of its deep caves panel above the windows. The M47 is seen near Grott0n. It has come to light the seats were of the back-to-back type and not of the flip-over type as fitted in the third class driving trailers. The recessed doors were angled in towards the coach body with the door and grab handles at the outer ends.

J.Davenport

PROTOTYPE DETAILS

Built 1913
LNWR number 500
1st LMS number 5203
2nd LMS number 3423
Withdrawn July 1955

Arrived on Delph branch in 1951. Ran with M17 driving trailer No. 3421 until the latter was withdrawn in 1953. Then ran with M49 No. 3414.

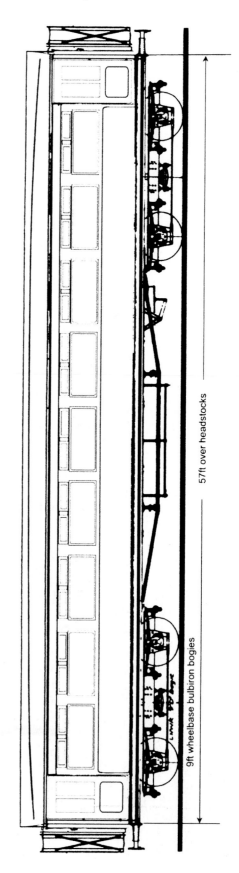

57ft over headstocks

9ft wheelbase bulbiron bogies

0 1 2 3 4 5 6 7 8 9 10

LNWR Push Pull 3rd class Driving trailer Saloon to Diagram M49

Diagram M49 all-third was built to the traditional 'Steam Railmotor' design with louvers above every window. Six vehicles were built between 1911 and 1912. It is possible these coaches worked on the Delph Branch from the outset in 1912. No. 3416 was a familiar sight on Oldham-Greenfield-Delph services after World War Two. No. 3414 arrived at Delph in 1951

and both languished in the sidings outside Clegg Street after passenger services ceased. 3416was given a revarnish or repaint in LMS maroon and recieved a BR Gil Sans running number. The picture below shows 3416 at Delph on 4th August 1953 (with M11 No.3427). Of note are the cast rectangular vents on the luggage doors instead of wooden louvers.

F. W. Shuttleworth

PROTOTYPE DETAILS

Built 1911 - 1912
LNWR numbers 1540-3 & 2490-4
1st LMS numbers 5205-8 & 5209-10
2nd LMS numbers 3413-6 & 3411-2
3411 withdrawn June 1958
3412 withdrawn June 1955
3413 withdrawn December 1958
3414 withdrawn July 1955
3415 withdrawn November 1951
3416 withdrawn December 1955

3415 & 3416 withdrawn from Delph.

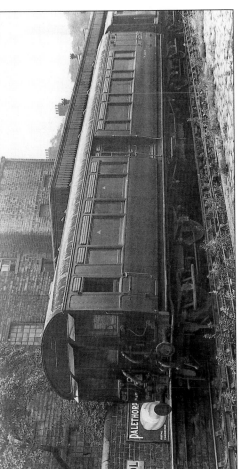

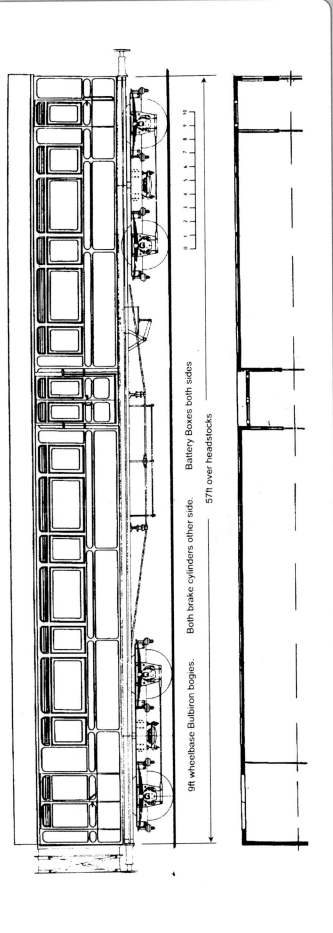

9ft wheelbase Bulbiron bogies.　Both brake cylinders other side.　Battery Boxes both sides

57ft over headstocks

LNWR PUSH PULL CORRIDOR 3RD CLASS DRIVING TRAILER TO DIAGRAM M52

These 50ft corridor third push pull driving trailers originated in 1913 to Diagram M52, and were the only LNWR side corridor coaches equipped with driving compartments. They had gangway connectors at both ends except for 3410 (passenger end only). 3407 and 3410 ran on the Delph Branch from 1951. 3407 was coupled to LMS D1807 open third conversion, the latter carrying in BR carmine & cream livery. Latterly it ran with M15 driving trailer M15946M. This pair worked the final pasenger services on the branch and are seen at Delph

during the final week in April 1955. 3407 and 3410 were never repainted in BR days, although they acquired BR Gill sans insignia, and looked rather tatty towards the end.   **L.Goddard collection**

PROTOTYPE DETAILS

Built 1913
LNWR numbers 492, 506, 514, 533
1st LMS numbers 5211-5214
2nd LMS numbers 3407-3410
Withdrawn between February 1952 and October 1958.

These coaches usualy ran with a LNWR M76 corridor third (ex-D265) or a cove roof M75 (ex-D264). Both types worked on the Delph branch

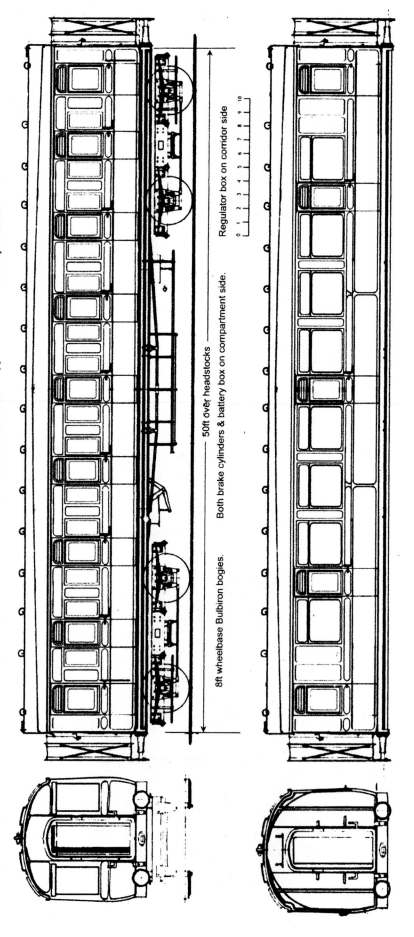

50ft over headstocks

8ft wheelbase Bulbiron bogies.

Both brake cylinders & battery box on compartment side.

Regulator box on corridor side

0 1 2 3 4 5 6 7 8 9 10

LNWR PUSH PULL CORRIDOR THIRD TO DIAGRAM M76A

These 57ft corridor third non-driving trailers were post-1923 LMS conversions from D265, the standard 8ft 6ins wide corridor third of 1908-10 period. A luggage space was created at one end utilising part of the lavatory and one compartment, but retaining the lavatory at the other end. The ends had the lower steps moved inwards to leave room for push pull jumper cables. Note latterday board repairs to lower body panels and doors. M76A No.3432 and M52 No.3407 are seen near Delph Junction in 1950 in LMS unlined maroon livery.

Jim Davenport

PROTOTYPE DETAILS

Built 1908 - 10
LNWR numbers : Various 392 - 2171
1st LMS numbers : 4435/37/47/50/88/89, 4502/15/31/33/56/85.
2nd LMS numbers : 3431 to 3443.
Withdrawn between January 1951 and June 1956.

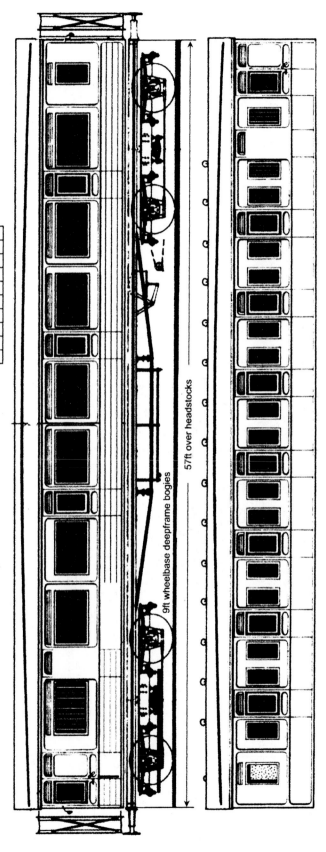

0 1 2 3 4 5 6 7 8 9 10

9ft wheelbase deepframe bogies

57ft over headstocks

APPENDICES

APPENDIX 1 : Motor-fitted carriages known to have worked Oldham-Delph services.

DIAG	QTY	DATE BUILT	NUMBERING Pre-group	1st LMS	2nd LMS	REMARKS
M6	1	1910	5507	10700		Steam railmotor. Wdn 1928
M11	1	1914	3726	9522	3427	Wdn. 8/1955
M12	1	1916	3727	9523	3425	Wdn. 9/1956
M13	1	1913	3751	9526	3426	Wdn. 7/53
M15	1	1911	3722	9518	15846	To Delph 1954. Wdn. 6/58
M17	1	1911	3724	9521	3421	To Delph 1951. Wdn. 7/53
M18	1	1913	3725	9521	3424	To Delph 1951. Wdn. 5/58
M44	1	1910	1777	5197	15851	Ran with steam railmotor M6
M45	4	1913	132-5	5198-201	3417-20	*See Appendix III*
M47	1	1913	500	5203	3423	To Delph 1951. Wdn.7/55
M49	6	1911-2	1540-3 2490-1	5205-8 5209-10	3413-6 3411-12	*See Appendix II*
M52	4	1913	492, 506, 514, 533	5211-4	3407-10	Driving trailers. Toplight 50' side corridor thirds.
M76A	6	1908-1910	Various: 392-2171	Sample: 4488,	3431-43	57'corridor thirds. LMS conversions from D264.
D1692	4	1929	LMS	Sample: 8477	3462-5	Period 1 two-window stock. LMS Conversion c.1938
D1807	3	1951	LMS		Sample: 8723	3484-6. BR conversions from Period II open thirds in1951.

APPENDIX 2 : Diagram M49 third class Driving Trailers

I am grateful to David Jenkinson for the following information				
LNWR 1540	LMS 5205	Later 3413	Built 1912	Withdrawn 12/58
LNWR 1541	LMS 5206	Later 3414	Built 1912	Withdrawn 7/55 (Delph 1951-5)
LNWR 1542	LMS 5207	Later 3415	Built 1912	Withdrawn 11/51
LNWR 1543	LMS 5208	Later 3416	Built 1912	Withdrawn 12/55 (Delph)
LNWR 2490	LMS 5209	Later 3411	Built 1911	Withdrawn 6/58
LNWR 2491	LMS 5210	Later 3412	Built 1911	Withdrawn 6/55

APPENDIX 3 : Diagram M45 third class Driving Trailer

LNWR 132	LMS 5198	Later 3417	Built 1913	Bletchley-Bedford when Scrapped in 6/56
LNWR 133	LMS 5199	Later 3418	Built 1913	St.Helens in 1951. Scrap 3/57
LNWR 134	LMS 5200	Later 3419	Built 1913	Delph in 1954. Scrap 10/58
LNWR 135	LMS 5201	Later 3420	Built 1913	Scrap 1/51. No other details.

APPENDIX 4 : The Great Escape by Jim Roberts

Jim Roberts, long-time resident of Delph, recalls a local farm in the Delph area bred white mice. *"Every week night, boxes of mice arrived at Delph station to be despatched to various laboratories for medical experiments. It was quite common for the odd mouse to escape and be found running around the station. One night I visited the station with a friend to have a chat with the porter Albert Lawton. To our surprise, Albert was sat on the top of the booking table with about a dozen white mice running around the Booking Office. Apparently, a box had been dropped and all the mice escaped. It was quite fun to see the mice running into one end of the fender around the fireplace and out at the other end"*. Jim and his friend managed to catch most of them, much to Albert's relief, and get them back in the box.

"The first twenty years of my life I lived on Oldham Road, New Delph. The back of the house overlooked the railway line. My friend next door David and I used to spend hours on the railway embankment putting coins on the line or blackberry picking. David's father had an allotment with a large greenhouse. During school holidays, we would raid the greenhouse to collect tomatoes. When the 'A' class came up with the morning goods train, we would offer the tomatoes to the driver for a ride on the footplate. We got to know most of the drivers and spent many mornings on the engine during shunting. Later we would ride on the engine or sometimes in the guards van as far as Dobcross Halt, or sometimes Saddleworth viaduct when we would drop off and walk home along Ladcastle and through Stonesfield".

Jim confirmed something LG had heard from a friend some years before: *"It was not unknown for one of the engine crew (fireman) to drop off at Greenfield and go for a pint in the Railway Hotel while the other crew member took the train up to Delph and back on his own. On one occasion, the loco came off the line at Delph and the guard borrowed a bike to ride back to Greenfield with the single-line staff. He gave it to the fireman just in time as the Lees breakdown train arrived in Greenfield station. The fireman boarded the breakdown train, gave the driver the staff to show at Moorgate signal box, and no questions were asked!"*

"Albert Lawton was quite a character and he did not get on very well with the signalman at Moorgate box. When the train left Delph on its return journey, the station porter had to ring Moorgate to let the signalman know it had left. When Albert was doing the duty, he would bellow down the phone "Just left you TUP". This brought a suitable reply from the signal man and there followed a few cross words. I don't know where the word 'TUP' came from but this went on for years".

Jim also recalls a derailment at Delph. *"The original track plan had no entry from the main line into Mallalieu's Bailey Mill coal siding. Trains had to use a shunting spur then reverse over the main line on a crossover. I well remember an 'A' class 0-6-0 over-running the buffers on the shunting spur and it was hanging precariously over Delph New Road. A Midland 3F arrived with the Lees Tool Van to re-rail the arrant loco, the only time I can remember a 3F at Delph".*

Some quite lengthy excursions worked out of Delph: *"In the late 1940s, Mallalieu's took their employees on a day trip to Blackpool. The train arrived at Delph pulled tender first by a Newton Heath based Black 5 4-6-0. The engine ran round its train of around eight or nine coaches"*. Jim continued: *"Just after the war, Lumb Mill was used as a Royal Mail Sores. Every weeknight a 2-6-4T would arrive, possibly from Stockport, and would leave hauling one or two parcels vans, which I was told went to Portsmouth."* Norman Wisenden of Greenfield also referred to this working: *"One night, a rough-shunt sent a van through the goods shed doors!"*

Jim concluded: *"I had many friends on the footplate and would often ride on the engine to Oldham on my way to work. I was often allowed to drive by the fireman, the driver having gone to sit in the 'motor coach', as we called it, for the push pull working. Happy days!"*

APPENDIX 5 : Aspects of the Oldham Branch by Jeffrey Wells

Grasscroft

Two and a quarter miles of the Oldham Branch were situated in Saddleworth, in the West riding of Yorkshire, until 1974. This stretch embraced Grasscroft Halt, Lydgate Tunnel, and Grotton station.

During the short existence of Grasscroft halt, it consisted of two timber platforms, the up side boasting a crude timber shelter from which projected a modest canopy. Access to the halt coud be made via a set of stone steps and a sloping footpath, one for each platform. The Halt was "temporarily" closed on 16 July 1917, much to the chagrin of the local inhabitants, many of whom were contract ticket holders derived of their mains of travelling by rail to Oldham. Their protest was taken up by Saddleworth Council whose meeting on the subject was debated on 25 July 1917. Replying to a letter from the clerk of the Council, the LNWR justified itself by saying that the halt had been closed *as a war measure in order that the railway coppany could provide two engines for use by the Government abroad".*

Reporting the protest, the Mossley & Saddleworth Reporter, 28 July, commented that *"There was, however, a second reason which was that someone had written to the Board of trade regarding overcrowding, and the railway company did not like it"*. Was the Halt closed in a fit of pique? Perhaps not, but the Council too was much displeased, pointing out to Mr Lindley, the LNWR's General Manager, *"that the company agreed to open the halt on condition that Saddleworth would lend support to them in their opposition to the Oldham tramways Bill, and now the company had broken faith…….".* Despite appeals, the die had been cast for the time being. The halt eventually re-opened as promised by the LNWR (as soon as hostilities were over) on 1 January 1919.

Barely any features associated with the Oldham Branch stll exists, save for the remnants of Grotton and Springhead station. Nevertheless, a short stroll from the latter in the direction of Grasscroft brings the walker to the horseshoe shaped portal of Lydgate Tunnel. It is hard to believe that over forty years have passed since the last regular train service steamed through the 1,332 yards long tunnel.

A tunnel between Grotton and Grasscroft was necessary due to the physical eminence known as Lydgate hill, which rises to a height of 860 feet above sea level. The tunnel was the Branch's piece-de-resistance as far as construction was concerned, and was engineered between 1854 and 1856 under the superintendence of John Hawkshaw, with messrs Locke and Errington his engineers in chief. The tunnel had to be driven through coal Measures, these being a series of sedimentary rocks containing coal seams. The miners who were employed to explode and hack their way through found that the rock much faulted, a feature giving rise to mining difficulties.

Five shafts were required to be sunk before tunnelling could commence. Shafts provided access to the workface below its surface, a means of hoisting and lowering men, materials and debris, and ventilation when work was completed. During construction, it was necessary to use fans to extract foul air charged with a highly dangerous gas known as Choke Damp. There were five shafts separated at a distance of 230 yards. The one nearest to Grotton was a temporary shaft, making use of a disused colliery shaft. The other four permanent shafts were left in place, their position marked by a top, which projected 12 feet above the ground. Each shaft was circular in section, about nine feet in diameter, and unfortunate size since it was slightly too narrow to allow the platform hoists to pass up and down at the same time without hitting each other… a cause of many delays. Two locomotive engines on temporary rails were used to provide the hoisting power. Some notion of the progress of the mining is given by the following details: -

From Shaft	Total Length	Time occupied
1	283 yards	Decr 1854– March 1856
2	196 yards	March 1855 – March 1856
3	203 yards	March 1955 – March 1956
4	264 yards	Feb 1855 – March 1856

The method of excavating the tunnel varied according to the material to be removed. Rock and strong shale were blasted with powder whilst the softer material such as clay and loose shale was removed with pickaxes. The roof of the tunnel was supposted with larch beams and uprights, larch being the most suitable on account of 'its strength and elasticity'. The earth was removed in iron skips, each of 0.5 cubic yards capacity, these being placed on light trolleys, which were pushed along a temporary tramway between the work faces and the shafts. The contract price for this work was 4s 6d per cubic yard, a price that included the timbering for supports.

The wages earned by the miners ranged from £8 to £18 per yard, depending on the nature of the rock.As soon as the miners had done their work it was the turn of the bricklay-

the miners had done their work it was the turn of the bricklayers and masons whose job it was to line the tunnel floor, walls and roof with either brickwork or stone. Much depended on, whether the surrounding rock was strong or weak, for example, about 632 yards of sidewall were lined with stone rubble, whilst 700 yards of roof had to be bricked. The shafts were also lined with brickwork 9 niches thick or 12 inches of masonry. The total cost of the work done by the masons and labourers came to £14 16 7½ per foot of tunnel, or about 4s 9d per cubic yard. Mortar used to make firm the brickwork was composed of crushed limestone mixed with coal ashes, in the proportion of 2 to 1, ground into a powder by heavy rollers. It was used fresh when required. Ground water seeping into the workings and the finished tunnel was a constant problem.

Covered rubble formed the side walls, the beds of the stones being hammer-punched. The footings were about 18 inches below the formation level, and the walls were carried 7ft 3ins above rail level.

The tunnel was straight for 47½ chains, and on a curve of 74 chains radius for 13 chains at the Grotton end. Tunnel width was 25 ft. Height of tunnel roof above rails was 20 ft. The rail sleepers were set in a ballast of broken stone to a depth of 12 inches and covered with ashes to the level of the rails. Lydgate Tunnel is now a disused monument to the work and skill of the contractors, miners, navvies and the LNWR engineers.

Source material: Proceedings of the Institute of Civil Engineers, 1862/63, volume 22, pages 372 – 377.

Grotton

Grotton station opened on 5 July 1856 and retained this name until 1 April 1900 when it assumed the name Grotton & Springhead. The station could be approached by vehicle or on foot along a gently inclined Station Road (a railway road, maintained by the railway company), which led from Oldham Road, Grotton Hollow. The station buildings were situated at the west end of the Up platform, and consisted of a Station Masters residence, added to which was a Booking Hall. Tucked away round the back was the outside Gents. Passengers crossed the line by a long wrought iron lattice footbridge in order to reach the Booking Office.

Grotton goods yard and a stone-built goods shed lay on the Oldham side of the footbridge. A timber-built signal box of 1901 vintage stood opposite the goods shed. The box, which housed 22 levers, had replaced an early Saxby box of 1875.

Lees

The next station along the line was Lees. The location was unusual in that the county boundary between Lancahsire and Yorkshire struck across the area so that the passenger station and engine shed were located in the red rose county, whilst the massive goods warehouse and the signal box lay in the white rose county. All the elements of railway infrastructure at Lees lay between Hey Lane, which crossed the railway west of the station, and Oldham Road. Leeds goods yard occupied ground on the up side and reached back from Oldham Road Bridge. It had the merit of tasking up land in both counties, with the stop blocks firmly in Lancashire!

Until the 1870s, the LNWR's locomotive shed at Mumps had sufficed, but by the middle of that decade it was decided (in the LNWR boardroom) that a new loco shed was urgently required. Nothing materialized immediately, but the LNWR Locomotive committee minutes, dated 23 April 1879, inform us *"That the land for the engine shed at Lees has now been arranged for and Mr. Wells (the LNWR Chief Mechanical Engineer) suggests that Mr. Worthington be authorised to level the ground so that he can get a shed to hold 12 engines erected there as soon as possible".*

Mumps shed was bursting at the seams; it was capable of accommodating 3 locomotives but was having to house 7. the estimated cost of the shed and associated features had by now risen from an estimated coast of £4,620 in 1977 to £5,500. The proposal was approved of and the coat spread over two years. By the summer of 1879 work was in progress. The Oldham Chronicle, 26 July, reported, "During the week the excavation in connection with the erection of a new engine shed at Lees railway station has been commenced, The shed will be situated on the Hey side of the line and will be used instead of the small and inconvenient one at Glodwick Road (sic)". Concern was expressed that a footpath leading to the passenger station from Springhead district would be obliterated. The footpath linked the station with Hall's Terrace on Station Road, and was effaced.

Work on the structure continued throughout the rest of 1879. not until the spring of 1880 was the Oldham Chronicle able to state in its 17 April edition that *"The new engine shed… has been completed and yesterday morning several locomotives made their appearance the first time in the vicinity, with trucks of coal, etc. we hear that several houses have been taken in Lees by those connected with the locomotive department…".* In those days of early morning starts and very late turns, it was convenient, if not essential, for railwaymen to live close to their place of work.

The six-road straight shed was built of brick and had a timber north-light roof. Being only 125 feet in length it was on the small side. During the years following erection of the new shed, little attention was paid to it by the local press. Day in, day out, month-by-month, year on year, the shed fulfilled its purpose quietly and without fuss. Lees always remained a backwater, the only improvements over the years appear to have been a new canteen, and finally a new loco shed roof in 1955.

One of the first references to the station at Lees, twenty years after te opening of the Oldham Branch, if found in Worrall's Oldham & district directory of 1975 in which it stated under the *"Lees, Hey, Springhead and neighbourhood"* that John Turnock was the station master. He lived at Taylor Green, Hey. If his term of office continued for another five years, he would have been aware of the frequency of trains that stopped at the station. There were as below in January 1880:

Weekday down

6.53am; 8.18am; 9.29am;10.22am; 11.15am; 12.10pm; 1.11pm; 3.13pm; 4.43pm; 5.29pm; 6.24pm; 8.21pm; 9.45pm.

Weekdays Up

7.55am; 8.54am; 10.25am;11.20am;11.47am;1.08pm;1.50pm 4.13pm; 5.34pm; 6.25pm; 8.06pm; 9.27pm; 10.13pm.

Sunday trains amounted to five in each direction; two in the morning, and three in the afternoon/evening. In the previous April, John Turnock would also have been aware of the express train which passed his station without stopping. The Mossley and Saddleworth Reporter, 5 april 1879, felt it worth informing its readers that *"For the first time since the line was opened a through service from Leeds via Greenfield and Oldham to Stockport commenced running on Tuesday last, the express train leaving Leeds at 1.40, departing from Greenfield at 2.40, passes Grotton and Lees stations without stopping, arriving at Oldham at 2.45, the distance from Leeds to Oldham being done in just over one hour"*.

By the early summer of 1880, the Lees Local Board had a major concern about the station. It had been frequently observed by the Clerk of the Board that a potentially dangerous situation existed when people crossed the line to reach one platform or another, or simply reach their destination on the south side of the railway. About four times a day people were crossing the lines at a time when two trains were approaching from either direction. The Local Board remonstrated with the LNWR pointing out that *"the railway company had land on both sides of the station to erect a bridge"*. In turn, the LNWR replied that one of its representatives had visited Lees, *"looking at the question of providing an underground passage, or an overbridge for crossing*

the station". Neither of these solutions could be recommended to the directors, especially in view of the fact that the general public were crossing the lines *"as a highway"*, an action bordering on trespass.

Undaunted, the Local Board threatened to report the matter to the Board of Works, on the basis that *"The village had been cut in two entirely by the railway" a solution which prevented ordinary communication with one district and another"*. The local Boards persistence paid off. By the beginning of December 1880 it was generally known that the LNWR proposed to spend £30,000 on alterations and extension at the station, inclusive of a footbridge. Exactly what the company proposed and carried out in unclear. Certainly a LNWR Minute, dated 18 May 1881, refers to W.A.Peters & Sons tender of £12,200, which was accepted for the erection of a goods shed. On 9 April, the Oldham Standard announced the completion of *"a handsome bock of stables"*, and the purchase of horses, lorries and carts, and the railway company had begun carting under their own name to the district mills. By late August 1881, the much-needed footbridge had nearly been completed.

As found elsewhere, Lees Station was the starting point for many a jaunt at Ester, Whitsun and Wakes time. A few examples suffice to illustrate the intrepid nature of Lees trippers:-

16 July 1881: Leesfield Band of hope and Temperance Society annual picnic at Greenfield. 76 foks left Lees station at 3.30pm alighting at Greenfield station for Mr.Marsdens farm at Boarshurst, and trekking back when rain set in.

23 July 1881: St.Agnes School church choir held its first annual picnic. Departing glodwick Road at 1.40pm the party arrived at Buxton at 4pm. Poole's Cavern and its museum were visited.

3 September 1881: One hundered and tenn operatives of the Livingstone Spinning Company took an excursion to Belle View, Manchester, and enjoyed *"a first class sandwich tea"*, whilst there. The party arrived back at Lees at 11pm the same night *"highly delighted with their outing"*.

2 September 1882: A special excursion left Lees for Barmouth on the coast of Wales. Many people went but the consensus was *"that it was too far for a day trip, as something like 16 hours was spent in the railway carriage"*. The return train arrived at Lees at 4am the following day!

On Saturday 2 September, large numbers of people left Lees for London, Blackpool, Isle of Man, and other places. This was the Wakes holiday, when all the mills in Lees and neighbourhood had been shut down on the previous Thursday. The Oldham Standard, 1 October 1881, reported an incident involving a drunken worker ravelling from Lees to Greenfield on the 6.30pm train. Having climbed into a crowded compartment he took up a position near the door, informing his fellow passengers that he would rather sand than sit. During the journey, whilst the train *"was proceeding at a good speed"*, the inebriate *"fastened the door to his own satisfaction and then leaning against it began to deliver a somewhat amusing address... however, the oration was very abruptly cut short, the carriage door flying open"*. Luckily, the mans departure from the compartment was arrested and he was pulled back in by startled passengers.

A five storey goods shed was located on the up side of the line served by two through roads and six 30cwt hand operated cranes built on an end to end stage. The nerve centre of the shed comprised a small office and weigh office attached to the west end. The massively built shed was erected at a time when already there were numerous cotton mills in the Lees and Springhead districts, and it was envisaged more were to follow. The cotton bales, baskets of yarn, machinery, food stuffs and other commodities to keep Lees at work and adequately fed had to be accommodated under cover somewhere!

Across the cobbled yard were two pairs of coal sidings into which lines of wagons could be held, buffer to buffer, for unloading, the coals carted off to be burned in mill furnaces and in domestic grates. By the Great War, Lees and Springhead combined possessed 14 cotton mills, six of which were giants with over 90,00 spindles. The number of home fires is unknown but the insatiable demand for coal must have been enormous.

Appendix 6 : Siding Details

The presence of a railway stimulated local industry to obtain a private siding for the reception of raw materials and the despatch of finished goods. One of the earliest in Oldham, for example, was that of Platt Bros., the textile machinery manufactory, which had a siding and platform at Werneth for exclusive use. This was formed out of an agreement between Platt's and the Manchester 7 Leeds Railway company in 1839.

Private sidings were owned by, or leased to, customers for their use only. Except where such sidings were shunted entirely by the railway company, the hand over of wagons between the railway company and the customer took place in what was known as transfer sidings, which linked the two concerns. Often the boundary between the two was marked by a gate beyond which neither was permitted to stray. Private siding agreements defined ownership of land, length of sidings, track and wall maintenance, the upkeep of subsidiary buildings such as weigh bridge offices, mess huts, turntables, loading platforms etc., as well as defined arrangements for safe working. Details of private and industrial sidings (these being owned by railway companies) are outlined as far as available information if known:

Bailey Mill Siding, Delph. Messrs D & H Mallatieu's siding was insdtalled on 4 March 1877 with an extension laid on 18 October 1890.

Dobcross Siding, Delph branch. Served a set of coal shoots lying adjacent to Bridge Mill. These were shown to be disused and disconnected from the Branch, January 1915. Railway owned.

Bankfield Mill Siding, Delph Branch. Originally owned by Messrs Sykes & Compinot. A facing point connection on the Down side of the Branch was situated 59_ chains from Delph station. No agreement.

Chatterton Quarries Ltd Siding, Ladcastle Quarry, Delph Branch. These consisted of a loading wharf served by a single road, 110 yards long. Retaining wall and boundary walls were maintained at Chatterton's own cost. Agreement dated 13 May 1904 and 24 July 1907. Sidings removed in 1918.

Charlotte Mill Siding, Greenfield. R R Whithead & Bros. Ltd. Siding connection on the down main line 908 yards from Greenfield station, leading back to a private siding. Agreement dated 27 February 1905.

Springhead Mill Sidings for Springhead Spinning company Co., Grotton. These were LNWR sidings on the down side from trailing connection 11 chains from Grotton station. A private siding 89 yards long crossed Bridge 7A over an access road to Radcliffe Mill. The siding terminated at a wagon turntable from which a 37-yard extension approached Springhead Mill. Agreement with David & John cooper and William Halliwell, dated 30 November 1854.

Springbank Mill Siding and Clough Mill Siding, Grotton. These were shared sidings with access from the up line, 26 chains from Lees station. Agreement with David & John Cooper and William Halliwell, dated 30 November 1854.

Oldham Corporation Siding, Oldham. This served Greenhill electricity works. Agreement with Oldham corporation, dated 19 March 1903.

Anglo-American Oil Co. Siding, Oldham. 93 yards of LNWR siding were maintained at the trader's cost. The first agreement date was 9 July 1891, with subsequent renewals up to 20 December 1822.

SCALE MODELS by LARRY GODDARD

This story has its beginning in 1963 in the Handyman/Model Shop which was situated on the corner of Huddersfield Road, Oldham. Frank Roscoe (the owner) and I were browsing through some Skinley blueprints when we came across an LNWR Oerlikon electric coach. We both agreed it looked remarkably like one of the push-pull saloons that had once worked on the *'Delph Donkey'*. I left Frank's shop armed with blueprint No.5307 and several sheets of Slaters 'Plastikard' of varying thicknesses, a material that was quite new to the hobby at the time.

Working split turns on the buses still left plenty of time to do other things, so within a few days the styrene sheet developed into a 4mm scale model carriage built as per the blueprint. The model had to make do with a roof from a Triang BR Mk.1 coach but it looked the part for all that. I was so impressed with 'Plastikard' that I used this material to construct a Fowler Class 3 2-6-2T loco body to fit on a modified Triang 2-6-2 chassis. Very little information about railway carriages existed in those far off days, and although members of the LMS Society had begun publishing scale drawings in the model press, infor mation on LNWR carriages was still hard to come by. There was no choice but to build an LMS standard driving trailer as a companion for the M12. I count myself fortunate in having known some very knowledgeable people, and it was due to them that the project moved forward. Jim Davenport gave me photographs of trains he had taken on the Oldham-Delph line in the 1950s and these kept the flame burning until another valued friend, David Jenkinson, published *'An Illustrated History of LNWR Coaches'* in 1978. A study of Jim's photos alongside information in David's book made it possible to match pictures with diagrams and identify the various purpose-built LNWR pus-pull vehicles. Official railway drawings of LNWR push-pull carriages probably no longer exist but with David's assistance, I finally embarked on preparing scale drawings in the year 2000.

I had already determined the model coaches would be photo-etched on brass following experience with drawing artwork for etching model bus radiators. However, the thought of drawing coaches several times larger than the finished product was a bit daunting. Fortunately, another good friend, Adrian Rowland of Northstar Design, offered his services and prepared the necessary artwork on CAD, a computer programme, for presentation to the etcher. After soldering the first carriage together, I went on to build over one hundred more for other people, but that is another story. My aim in 1963 of building a model of the *Delph Donkey* was finally completed some forty years after the project started.

The ***Delph Donkey*** waiting to return to Oldham Clegg street from Delph in 1954. The LNWR Diagram M15 driving trailer No 15846 has retained LMS maroon while the LMS trailer open third No 3484, converted in 1951 to push-pull, carries BR carmine and cream livery.

J Davenport